Frommer's®

Vienna
day BY day™

2nd Edition

by Teresa Fisher

WILEY

John Wiley & Sons, Inc.

Contents

Published by:

Wiley Publishing, Inc.

111 River St.
Hoboken, NJ 07030-5774

ISBN: 978-0-470-49768-5

Editor: Alexia Travaglini
Production Editor: M. Faunette Johnston
Photo Editor: Richard Fox
Cartographer: Guy Ruggiero
Production by Wiley Indianapolis Composition Services

For information on our other products and services or to obtain technical support, please contact our Customer Care Department within the U.S. at 877/762-2974, outside the U.S. at 317/572-3993 or fax 317/572-4002.

Wiley also publishes its books in a variety of electronic formats. Some content that appears in print may not be available in electronic formats.

Manufactured in China

5   4   3   2   1

A Note from the Editorial Director

Organizing your time. That's what this guide is all about.

Other guides give you long lists of things to see and do and then expect you to fit the pieces together. The Day by Day guides are different. These guides tell you the best of everything, and then they show you how to see it *in the smartest, most time-efficient way*. Our authors have designed detailed itineraries organized by time, neighborhood, or special interest. And each tour comes with a bulleted map that takes you from stop to stop.

Hoping to retreat from civilization? Lose your cares on a pristine white Caribbean beach, or under aquamarine waters on a coral reef teeming with Technicolor fish? Maybe you'd rather pamper yourself in a coconut paste and banana leaf wrap at a seaside spa? Or trace the footsteps of the ancient Maya among the Yucatán's many pre-Columbian ruins? Whatever your interest or schedule, the Day by Days give you the smartest routes to follow. We take you to the top attractions, hotels, and restaurants. And what's more, we help you access those special moments that locals get to experience—those "finds" that turn tourists into travelers.

The Day by Days are also your top choice if you're looking for one complete guide for all your travel needs. The best hotels and restaurants for every budget, the greatest shopping values, the wildest nightlife—it's all here.

Why should you trust our judgment? Because our authors personally visit each place they write about. They're an independent lot who say what they think and would never include places they wouldn't recommend to their best friends. They're also open to suggestions from readers. If you'd like to contact them, please send your comments our way at feedback@frommers.com, and we'll pass them on.

Enjoy your Day by Day guide—the most helpful travel companion you can buy. And have the trip of a lifetime.

Warm regards,

Kelly Regan

Kelly Regan, Editorial Director
Frommer's Travel Guides

About the Author

Joy Hepp is a travel writer and blogger who divides her time between Mexico and Los Angeles. She prefers flour tortillas over corn, black beans over pinto and tequila over mezcal.

Acknowledgments

This book is dedicated to all of the strong women—*guerreras, amas, luchadoras, escritoras, y adventureras*—who have accompanied me throughout my journeys in Mexico. Thanks for the inspiration, *mujeres*.

An Additional Note

Please be advised that travel information is subject to change at any time—and this is especially true of prices. We therefore suggest that you write or call ahead for confirmation when making your travel plans. The authors, editors, and publisher cannot be held responsible for the experiences of readers while traveling. Your safety is important to us, however, so we encourage you to stay alert and be aware of your surroundings.

Star Ratings, Icons & Abbreviations

Every hotel, restaurant, and attraction listing in this guide has been ranked for quality, value, service, amenities, and special features using a **star-rating system.** Hotels, restaurants, attractions, shopping, and nightlife are rated on a scale of zero stars (recommended) to three stars (exceptional). In addition to the star-rating system, we also use a **kids icon** to point out the best bets for families. Within each tour, we recommend cafes, bars, or restaurants where you can take a break. Each of these stops appears in a shaded box marked with a coffee-cup-shaped bullet ☕.

The following **abbreviations** are used for credit cards:

AE American Express	DISC Discover	V Visa
DC Diners Club	MC MasterCard	

Frommers.com

Now that you have this guidebook to help you plan a great trip, visit our website at **www.frommers.com** for additional travel information on more than 4,000 destinations. We update features regularly to give you instant access to the most current trip-planning information available. At Frommers.com, you'll find scoops on the best airfares, lodging rates, and car rental bargains. You can even book your travel online through our reliable travel booking partners. Other popular features include:

- Online updates of our most popular guidebooks
- Vacation sweepstakes and contest giveaways
- Newsletters highlighting the hottest travel trends
- Podcasts, interactive maps, and up-to-the-minute events listings
- Opinionated blog entries by Arthur Frommer himself
- Online travel message boards with featured travel discussions

A Note on Prices

In the "Take a Break" and "Best Bets" sections of this book, we have used a system of dollar signs to show a range of costs for 1 night in a hotel (the price of a double-occupancy room) or the cost of an entree at a restaurant. Use the following table to decipher the dollar signs:

Cost	Hotels	Restaurants
$	under $100	under $10
$$	$100–$200	$10–$20
$$$	$200–$300	$20–$30
$$$$	$300–$400	$30–$40
$$$$$	over $400	over $40

An Invitation to the Reader

In researching this book, we discovered many wonderful places—hotels, restaurants, shops, and more. We're sure you'll find others. Please tell us about them, so we can share the information with your fellow travelers in upcoming editions. If you were disappointed with a recommendation, we'd love to know that, too. Please write to:

Frommer's Cancún & the Yucatán Day by Day, 2nd Edition
Wiley Publishing, Inc. • 111 River St. • Hoboken, NJ 07030-5774

16 Favorite
Moments

16 Favorite **Moments**

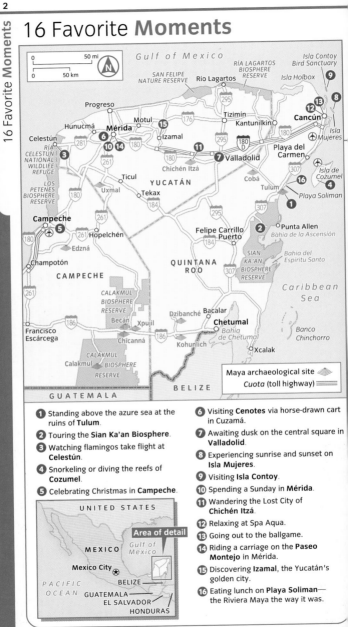

1. Standing above the azure sea at the ruins of **Tulum**.
2. Touring the **Sian Ka'an Biosphere**.
3. Watching flamingos take flight at **Celestún**.
4. Snorkeling or diving the reefs of **Cozumel**.
5. Celebrating Christmas in **Campeche**.
6. Visiting **Cenotes** via horse-drawn cart in Cuzamá.
7. Awaiting dusk on the central square in **Valladolid**.
8. Experiencing sunrise and sunset on **Isla Mujeres**.
9. Visiting **Isla Contoy**.
10. Spending a Sunday in **Mérida**.
11. Wandering the Lost City of **Chichén Itzá**.
12. Relaxing at Spa Aqua.
13. Going out to the ballgame.
14. Riding a carriage on the **Paseo Montejo** in Mérida.
15. Discovering **Izamal**, the Yucatán's golden city.
16. Eating lunch on **Playa Soliman**—the Riviera Maya the way it was.

Previous page: The ruins of Tulum.

Asking a guide writer to compile her list of favorite moments in Cancún and the Yucatán is like asking Imelda Marcos to choose a dozen favorite pairs of shoes. From Campeche's wild Calakmul biosphere reserve, to Mérida's colonial carriage rides, to Cancún's world-class resorts, every step you take is magical, and every breath is full of life. Each state—Campeche, Yucatán, and Quintana Roo—has its own unique charm, and each small city is full of surprises. Alas, here is my interpretation of the region's most shining moments.

① Standing above the azure sea at the ruins of Tulum. The first time I stood among the ruins of this walled city, high on a cliff overlooking the Caribbean's turquoise waters, it took my breath away. Facing east, Tulum is especially spectacular at sunrise, which inspired the Maya to call it Zamá, city of the dawn. If it's hot, have a swim in the warm sea below. *See p 20.*

② Touring the Sian Ka'an Biosphere. The ancient Maya called this place "Birth of the Sky." Now it's federally protected, and naturalist guides offer hiking, cycling, and boat tours into its 526,110 hectares (1.3 million acres) of salt marshes, beaches, and lagoons. Birds, iguanas, jungle cats, crocodiles, manatees, turtles, and some dolphins make their home here. You can float down the warm, swift channel current past an ancient Maya customs house, half-hidden in the reeds and mangroves. *See p 45.*

③ Watching flamingos take flight at Celestún. Rent a launch to see thousands of pink flamingos feeding and nesting in the lagoons at Celestún on the Gulf coast. Afterwards, choose one of the many beachside restaurants and lunch on *pescado frito* (whole fried fish) while you watch the frigate birds float overhead. Celestún makes a great day trip from Mérida—and don't forget your swimsuit. *See p 86.*

④ Snorkeling or diving the reefs of Cozumel. The myriad colors of the fish are stunning, and the shapes of the giant coral just below your flippers are clearly visible in

Tulum, along the Riviera Maya.

the crystal-clear waters. Divers and snorkelers go by boat offshore to drift along in the current, right over the spectacular reefs made famous on film by oceanographer Jacques Cousteau. *See p 34.*

5 **Celebrating Christmas in Campeche.** If there's magic in the air anywhere in the tropics at Christmastime, it's in the old walled city of Campeche. Twinkly lights, strung from 300-year-old, pastel-colored houses, reflect on its narrow cobblestone streets, while revelers stroll the plaza in front of the Cathedral of the Conception, built in 1639. A gem, Campeche was named a UNESCO World Heritage Site in 2000. *See p 91.*

6 **Exploring the cenotes in Cuzamá, a world underground.** Climb down the steps into the underworld where the ancient Maya thought the spirits dwelled, at Chelentún, Chacsinic-Che, and Bolonchojol. *Cenote* is the name for a lake that forms from underground when the water table breaks through fragile limestone. The Cuzamá *cenotes* are accessible only via antique-style wooden, horse-drawn carriages. *See p 111.*

7 **Awaiting dusk on the central square in Valladolid.** As dusk descends on the colonial town of Valladolid, hundreds of squawking birds fill the trees around the central square. The cacophony of their calls signals that it's dinnertime for tourists and locals. Grab a table in the street-side restaurant of Maria de la Luz or in the center courtyard of the Meson del Marqués hotels and enjoy the transformation from day to night in a 500-year-old town. *See p 124.*

8 **Experiencing sunrise and sunset on Isla Mujeres.** Wake up with the birds to watch the sunrise from the edge of a cliff on Isla Mujeres, the "Island of Women," just off Cancún. The rocky promontory boasts what's left of a Maya watchtower at the easternmost point in Mexico. After a day of island fun, settle down at the Sunset Bar on the north beach to watch the red sun drop below the horizon. Another day in paradise. *See p 102.*

A pelican takes flight at the Sian Ka'an Biosphere Reserve.

Doublebar bream fish off the coast of Cozumel.

9 Visiting Isla Contoy. From Isla Mujeres, speed across the waves in a fishing launch—or take the old wooden-hulled sailboat, *Estrella del Norte*—toward Isla Contoy. This bird sanctuary was established in 1961 to protect the 100-plus avian species that visit the island park. On the way, your boat will stop above a colorful reef for a snorkeling break, and the boat crew will cook you a fresh fish lunch after you explore the uninhabited island. *See p 41.*

10 Spending a Sunday in Mérida. The largest city in the Yucatán brims with cultural happenings. Every day there is something to see or do in the historical center, where modern mixes with ancient. Our favorite time is Sunday, when folkloric dancers balance beer bottles on their heads as they perform in the Plaza Mayor, a brass band accompanies, and artisans ply their wares to tourists and locals strolling the shady square. *See p 108.*

11 Wandering the Lost City of Chichén Itzá. Even the most jaded visitor will find the magnificent remains of the northern Yucatán's best-preserved ruins breathtaking. In 2007 the archaeological zone was voted one of the New 7 Wonders of the World, so arrive early to avoid the crowds of visitors who wish to check it off their list. The dominant architectural feature is "El Castillo," a huge pyramid in the center of the

The platform of Eagles & Jaguars at Chichén Itzá.

Izamal, the Golden City.

expansive, ancient ceremonial grounds. Stay for the nighttime light show to get the full experience. *See p 55.*

12 Relaxing at Spa Aqua. Whether you've been spending all your time haggling with souvenir vendors or swimming with dolphins, you may need a vacation from your vacation. One of my favorite places to get away from it all is actually right in the middle of Cancún's Hotel Zone—Spa Aqua at the Aqua Cancún hotel. With a focus on the four senses, treatments include underwater chakra alignment and shiatsu massage. *See p 62.*

13 Going out to the ballgame. While *futbol,* or soccer, reigns king in the rest of Mexico, baseball is the sport of choice in the Yucatán, and competition is fierce among the major cities. One of the best places to see a game

is at Parque Nelson Barrera right next to the coast in Campeche: The Campeche Pirates will give you a reason to cheer. *See p 91.*

14 Riding a carriage on the Paseo Montejo. Designed to resemble the Champs-Elysées, the Paseo Montejo lies just north of the historical center of Mérida. An evening horse-drawn carriage ride on the wide boulevard—past the soft lights of trendy restaurants, museums, and hotels scattered amid the stately mansions built during the boom times of the henequén trade—is a memorable highlight of this charming city. *See p 115.*

15 Discovering Izamal, the Yucatán's golden city. Long before the Spanish Conquistadors built the huge Franciscan Convento de San Antoñio de Padua on the top of a gigantic pyramid, the sleepy town of Izamal was of great religious importance to the pre-Columbian Maya people. No one knows why, but all the buildings in town are painted gold. Peruse the narrow cobblestone streets in a horse-drawn buggy known as a Victoria, and then enjoy a typical Yucatecan lunch at Kinich Kakmó restaurant. *See p 85.*

16 Eating lunch on the Riviera Maya, the way it was. You won't stumble upon many deserted places these days, now that tourists and mega-hotels have discovered the beautiful beaches along the Riviera Maya. But you can still capture that Jimmy Buffett feeling at Oscar y Lalo's restaurant on its own horseshoe-shaped beach at Playa Soliman. Have a refreshing lunch at a beachside table, snooze in a hammock under palm trees, snorkel the reef offshore, or take a dip in the deep *cenote.* Great food, primitive bathrooms. *See p 31.* ●

1 Strategies for Seeing the Yucatán

Strategies for Seeing the Yucatán

The Yucatán is home to pearl-white beaches and deep green jungle, as well as pre-Colombian ruins and breakneck modern development. It encompasses three states—Yucatán, Campeche, and Quintana Roo—spread over 134,400 sq. km (52,400 sq. miles) and has 3,500 years of civic history since the Olmec developed the region's first large-scale human settlements in 1500 B.C. It's also the setting of five UNESCO World Heritage sites. The Riviera Maya's paradisiacal seashore, luxury hotels, fine dining, and exciting nightlife have become the most popular reasons to visit, but the region offers so much more to see and do: Explore ancient Maya ruins, watch the world go by at a corner cafe, explore *cenotes* and other unique natural wonders, or just relax on the beach and think about all the things you're going to do—*mañana*.

Rule # 1: Remember, you probably came here to relax— so keep your options open. Travelers who enjoy their south-of-the-border vacations most are those who understand and accept that things don't always go according to plan. Use this book as a reference, but don't try to do everything. Roll with the punches, and you won't be disappointed when plan A bites the dust; just move on to plan B (or, if necessary, plan C).

Previous page: An old form of travel on a beach lost to time.

Rule #2: Choose, you can't lose.

The Yucatán's attractions are diverse enough to keep you coming back again and again, but the region still offers two basic vacation profiles—sand and sun or history and culture. The coast from Cancún south to Tulum is known as the Riviera Maya. With its blue water and perfect white sand, it's graced with some of the best beaches in the world. Inland, travelers encounter impressive Maya ruins and native villages, charming colonial towns, lots of natural beauty—and last but not least, lower prices. Choose one region if your time is limited or combine them for the broadest experience.

Rule #3: Decide whether to hotel-hop or just flop.

Decide whether to book accommodations in one place and take day trips, or change hotels frequently and venture farther afield. For shorter stays, it's better to hole up in Cancún, the Riviera Maya, or Mérida and explore from there. Lodging in one place gives you the greatest stability but limits the distances you can traverse. Wandering allows you to cover more ground and follow your whims, but you may end up feeling that you need another vacation to recover from all the packing and traveling around. Decide which approach suits you best or combine them for the best of both.

Rule #4: Pick the key activity of the day and then plan other activities in the surrounding area.

Regardless of whether you're a sightseeing fool or a beach bum, plan your fun around the key activity you've chosen for the day. For example, a visit to the ruins of Tulum in the heat of the day could

be accompanied by an afternoon of snorkeling at Xel-Ha. Or a boat trip to see the flamingos at Rio Lagartos could include a stop at the Ek Balam ruins, on the way, just north of Valladolid. Better yet, schedule your day around lunch. Planning to check out the Aktun Chen caverns? Arrive early enough to go to Oscar y Lalo's restaurant (p 31) at nearby Playa Soliman. In Mexico, lunch is often a big meal, and dinner can be a lighter, late-evening affair.

Rule #5: Expect the unexpected.

Cancún and the Yucatán is a safe destination to travel around as long as you observe the same precautions you would in any major North American city. While Mexico has faced newsworthy problems with recent drug violence, most of the incidents have taken place along the northern border within the United States. Nonetheless, don't even think about purchasing any illegal substances during your stay. Also, be sure to make photocopies of your passport and other important documents in case the originals should be lost or stolen.

The Mayan Ball Court and Pyramid at Uxmal.

Rule #6: Don't drink the water.

That's a bit of an old folk axiom about Mexico. The water is actually safe in Cancún and all the major hotels up and down the Riviera Maya, and in large cities such as Mérida as well. Ice everywhere is undoubtedly made from purified water, so you don't need to ask. We do recommend that you use bottled water for drinking, but don't have a panic attack if you realize you accidentally just brushed your teeth using tap water. You should wash your hands frequently (which will also help you avoid the dreaded H1N1 virus), and, if you do get sick, have your hotel contact a local doctor. Most speak English, and many have trained in the United States.

Rule #7: You can get there from here.

Street addresses in Latin America are often determined by the

A palapa on the beach at Sian Ka'an.

The Estrella del Norte sails from Isla Mujeres to Isla Contoy.

distance from someplace else. The Cancún Hotel Zone, for instance, has just one road (Kukulcán), and the street numbers are determined by the number of kilometers from downtown. In more rural areas, you don't need exact addresses; often there's only one road with lots of signs.

Rule #8: Don't become a victim of "La Mordida."

While most law enforcement officers have tourists' and citizens' best interests in mind, a few less reputable ones are after la mordida: This "little bite" is a small bribe of generally about $20 to $100. Avoid any possible confrontation by following all traffic laws, particularly in heavily touristed areas. You might also consider traveling to major destinations by bus; first class is fast, inexpensive, and comfortable. ●

The Best **Full-Day Tours**

The Best of the Yucatán in **Three Days**

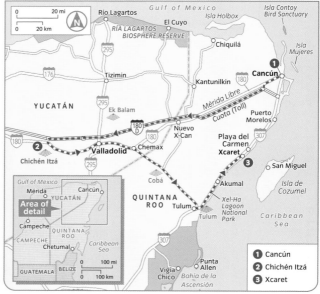

1 Cancún
2 Chichén Itzá
3 Xcaret

A 3-day trip to the Yucatán is best spent primarily along the Riviera Maya—the cool, pearl-white Caribbean shoreline that runs from Cancún south to Tulum. If you're like most travelers, you'll devote those 72 precious hours to doing nothing on the beach. While I'm just as big a fan of tan lines and paperback beach reads as anyone, I've organized this itinerary to demonstrate the variety of short excursions you can work into even a quick Yucatán getaway. If you want a break from the beach but more rest and relaxation than this itinerary affords, see the "The Best of the Yucatán in One Week" tour, on p 16, and follow the recommendations for days 1, 2, and 3. START: **Cancún Hotel Zone.** The Hotel Zone begins just 10km (6.25 miles) from the airport on Kukulcán Boulevard. Total trip length: 520km (322 miles).

A Note on Hotels & Restaurants

For additional information on sights, shops, and recommended hotels and restaurants in Cancún, see chapter 7.

1 **Cancún.** Cancún is almost like two cities in one—a downtown shopping and residential area, and a tourist-specific Hotel Zone that runs along a 27km (16.75-mile) island, shaped like the number 7—thus its

Previous page: A performer at Xcaret Ecopark.

name, meaning golden snake in Maya. Cancún's beaches are spectacular, but those on the long side of the 7 (the Caribbean side) sometimes have strong surf. Taxis or inexpensive buses marked Ruta 1 and Ruta 2 run the length of Kukulcán Boulevard, the zone's only road, where addresses are simply kilometer numbers (lower numbers are closer to downtown).

Check into the **Westin Resort & Spa Cancun** *(p 145)*, a luxurious resort hotel on a magnificent piece of beach near the southern end of the Hotel Zone, on Kukulcán, Km 20. **Beach and pool time** there will help you acclimate to Mexico, and the hotel can be your home base for the next few days of touring.

Next stop is the **Coral Negro** market, Km 9.5, where you'll encounter a traditional Mexican *mercado* plying traditional Yucatecan gifts and handicrafts—silver jewelry, T-shirts, sombreros, blankets, and the like. Comparison shopping and negotiating are expected,

One of the region's many outdoor produce vendors.

so it pays to haggle in this warren of indoor and outdoor stalls. Across the street is **La Fiesta**, a two-story, air-conditioned store brimming with fixed-price, kitschy souvenirs.

Follow the locals to **Rio Nizuc Restaurant.** This joint is all about cheap fish and beer on a plastic table under a *palapa.* It's a bit hard to find, up a sandy path along the estuary at the Punta Nizuc bridge. Ask the bus driver to let you off nearby; taxi drivers know where it is. The best part: *Gringos* will be in short supply.

Take a *siesta* or another swim before venturing to Cancún's **Archaeology Museum** (☎ 983/837-2411) at Km 9.5. If you're pressed for time but want to get a glimpse of the region's cultural riches, this museum is a must. Built in 1982, it houses hundreds of pre-Hispanic objects from the Maya culture that were found at nearby archaeological sites Tulum, El Rey, and Cobá.

Make advance reservations for your next 2 days of adventure, then dine at **Casa Rolandi,** an inviting Italian bistro in Plaza Caracol, at Km 8.5 (p 137). A mixed seafood platter is the signature dish, but live lobsters are also popular. If you have any energy left, don your dancing shoes and party away the evening at **Azucar,** at Km 9 *(p 132),* an exciting live-music Latin-dance club and bar at Punta Cancún. Many of the groups come from Cuba, and the music is top-notch. ⏱ *1 day.*

Take Highway 301 for 72km (45 miles) south of Cancún.

❷ **Chichén Itzá.** You won't be able to avoid the crowds or fully appreciate this expansive Maya city in just 1 day, but Chichén Itzá is still a must-see stop on any Yucatán vacation, however brief. Explore this lost civilization's magnificent ruins, which the Maya abandoned in 1220 after a war with a rival city. Make reservations the day before for the earliest possible tour. It costs about $85, including lunch, for a 3-hour bus ride through the northern Yucatán's flat topography and scrub jungle.

The guided tour of Chichén Itzá runs about 1½ hours, highlighting the most impressive and important structures from the Classic and Post-Classic periods.

The **Temple of Kukulcán** dominates the sprawling, open grounds around it—which inspired the Spanish Conquistadors to call it **El Castillo (the castle).** Although visitors can no longer make the rigorous climb to the top of the 25m (82-ft.) pyramid, I challenge you to have your picture taken in front of El Castillo without any other tourists in the background. It's rare, but I've seen it done.

Other worthy stops on a 1-day tour are the **Cenote of Sacrifice,** a large, deep open well with sides steep enough to throw victims over;

Chac Mool in the Templo de los Guerreros at Chichén Itzá.

Temple of the Skulls (compare your cranium to the ones decorating the temple); **Temple of the Warriors;** and the **Group of a Thousand Columns.**

It can get very hot, so bring a hat, drink lots of water, and apply copious amounts of sunscreen. If you still need to cool down, make a pit stop in the excellent visitor center's snack bar and gift shop.

For detailed information on Chichén Itzá, see the "The Pre-Columbian Yucatán" tour in chapter 4.

Back in Cancún, complete your Yucatán experience with a fine meal in an authentic Mexican setting at ★★ **Hacienda El Mortero** (Km 9; ☎ 998/883-1133). ⏱ *1 day.*

Take Highway 180 for 190km (118 miles) west of Cancún.

③ ★★ kids **Xcaret/Playa del Carmen.** One of the Riviera Maya's most popular attractions is **Xcaret** (*Ish*-car-ret; ☎ **998/883-0470;** save 10% at www.xcaret.com), an eco-themed recreational park an hour south of Cancún. On the site of the pre-Columbian trading port of Polé, it offers tourists myriad tropical vacation diversions—most centered on the fabulous turquoise waters of the Caribbean, its lagoons, and the jungle's natural beauty. A series of walking paths meander past its attractions, including bathing coves, a snorkeling lagoon, and the remnants of small Maya temples.

The best-known Xcaret rides are Underground River and Mayan River—life-jacket floats down either of two underground rivers opened and widened to allow snorkeling. Other water-based attractions include SNUBA diving, a way to "walk" on the bottom attached to a breathing hose; swimming with dolphins; and enjoying gorgeous beaches on the ocean and lagoon. A personal favorite is the round rock

Mayan Indian dancer at Xcaret theme park.

pool, with ocean waves that make it a bit like swimming in a natural Jacuzzi.

Besides some minor archaeological sites, there's a spa service, butterfly garden, coral-reef aquarium, and a *Charreria* horse show with cowboys and riders from the state of Jalisco. There's also a replica of a Mexican cemetery, where the **Day of the Dead** is celebrated every day, and where Totonac Indians from Veracruz perform the death-defying pre-Columbian aerial ceremony **Voladores de Papantla.**

After freshening up in the locker rooms, catch a taxi to Playa del Carmen for a sand-in-your-toes meal at ★ **La Tarraya Restaurant** (p 123). Afterward, take an evening stroll down the charming Fifth Avenue (p 121).

Funky buses provide transportation from Cancún's Xcaret terminal on Kukulcán at Km 9; reservations are recommended but not required. The cost for a day, including transportation and buffet lunch, is about $110 per adult. ***Note:*** Visit on weekends, when fewer cruise ships and tourists are around. *For more details on Xcaret see "The Yucatán for Families" in chapter 4.* ⏱ *1 day.*

Plumed serpent head at the base of the Temple of Kulkucán.

The Best of the Yucatán in **One Week**

1 Cancún		**5** Xcaret	
2 Isla Mujeres		**6** Tulum	
3 Chichén Itzá		**7** Aktun Chen/ Playa Soliman	
4 Playa del Carmen			

If you have a full week in the Yucatán, I suggest unwinding in Cancún for the first few days. Then, take a side trip to the Maya ruins at Chichén Itzá and spend a few days along the Riviera Maya. After 7 days, you'll boast a tan and a spectrum of fond memories. We've arranged this itinerary so you need to rent a car only on your fifth day, in Playa. START: **Take a taxi or shuttle from the airport to your accommodation in Cancún's Hotel Zone, just 10km (6.25 miles) away on Boulevard Kukulcán. Total trip length: 675km (419 miles).**

A Note on Hotels & Restaurants

For additional information on sights, shops, and recommended hotels and restaurants in Cancún, see chapter 7; Isla Mujeres (p 102); and Playa del Carmen (p 120).

1 Cancún. Cancún's Hotel Zone is a 27km (17-mile) -long beach in the shape of a figure 7. Cancún boasts some of the most beautiful beaches in the world, so unpack your bags and jump in the warm blue water— you're in Mexico now.

Travel Tip

Boulevard Kukulcán is the 27km (17-mile) road that runs the length of Cancún's Caribbean shoreline. Addresses on Kukulcán are given by kilometer number; the lower the number, the closer the address is to downtown.

Unwind, relax, and when you're hungry, hail a cab, or a public bus marked number #1 or #2 (75¢) to the city center. Get off the #1 bus when it turns on to Tulum Avenue, the major thoroughfare; or get off the #2 at the Chedraui department store on the corner of Tulum. Each side of the street has eateries, stores, and lots of shops, including flea market *mercados* for souvenir shopping.

Make your way to the west side of Tulum Avenue and walk down one of its side streets through Palapa Park, a central location for Cancún's many afternoon and nighttime festivals. It's a safe place to return to after nightfall if you find something of interest. The road parallel to Tulum Avenue is the busy Avenida Yaxchilan. The north end of this street is wall-to-wall bars, nightclubs, and

restaurants. Go there to enjoy a late lunch at **La Parilla,** on Avenida Yaxchilan near Rosas *(p 138)*. Mariachi musicians perform in the late afternoons, and in the evenings the place is packed.

If you didn't get side-tracked shopping on Tulum, walk about 3 blocks up Avenida Sunyaxchen to the post office. Behind it on avenidas Tankah and Sunyaxchen is a classic, **Mercado 28** *(vain-tee oh-choe; p 131)*. This market sells every type of Mexican handicraft and souvenir imaginable. Know the exchange rate before you begin bargaining, and start negotiations by knocking off at least 60%.

Return to the hotel for a *siesta* or a languid swim until evening. If you're up for dressing smart, dine on delicious Italian food at **La Dolce Vita,** on the lagoon at Km 14.6. For a more casual evening, try ★ **Pizza Rolandi** downtown. See p 139. 🕐 *1 day.*

Take either the ferry from the Hotel Zone (Km 9 or Km 4; $15) or the "people ferry" ($4) from either dock at Puerto Juárez, a few kilometers north of downtown Cancún.

A palapa-topped pier in Cancún.

Playa del Carmen.

② Isla Mujeres. This skinny "Island of Women" is just a few kilometers off Cancún's coastline, but a world apart in style. Less developed and commercial than Cancún, Isla Mujeres offers a taste of the Mexican beach-village experience, which is becoming increasingly rare. Originally, the Maya came here to worship Ixchel, the goddess of fertility; a small ruin of her temple remains at the island's easternmost point, high on a cliff overlooking the sea. It's the first point of land in Mexico touched by the morning sun. Isla was a fishing village, and in the 1960s and '70s, it became a favorite stop for sailboats and yachts. It's now a popular day trip from Cancun for shopping, swimming, snorkeling, or exploring.

The island's sandy, cobbled downtown is only a few blocks, but some wonderful little shops, hotels, and restaurants are squeezed into its narrow streets. Once you've had your fill of town, rent a golf cart or motorbike and head to **Playa Lancheros,** on Carretera Garrafón, for a leisurely afternoon of sunbathing,

snorkeling, swimming, and a *Tikin-Xik* lunch: fish filets grilled over a charcoal fire and flavored with traditional *achiote* spice (not hot).

Back in town, watch the sun set from the ★ **Palapa Bar** at the Na Balam Hotel, and then dine at the hotel restaurant ★★ **Zazil Ha,** notable for its Caribbean and international cuisine, on Avenida Zazil Ha at the northern end of town. *See p 107.*

If you fancy a drink, head to ★★ **Bar Om** (☎ 998/820-4876), on Avenida Matamoros, for a cup of tea or a beer served from a tap at your table.

Before the day is up, don't forget to make tour or rental-car reservations for tomorrow. The last ferry back to Cancún's Hotel Zone is at 9pm; 12am to Puerto Juárez. ⏱ *1 day.*

Take Highway 180 or the *Cuota* toll road for 190km (118 miles) west of Cancún.

③ Chichén Itzá. Chichén Itzá is an unforgettable ruined Maya holy city that's sure to impress even the most jaded visitor. It's an all-day excursion, and you can arrange a day tour in advance from Cancún through any hotel travel agent. Rent a car the night before and drive yourself to the ruins in the early morning. Driving conditions are quite good in the Yucatán; the terrain is flat, and major roads are well marked.

Check into ★★★ **Hacienda Chichén Resort** (Carretera Puerto Juárez–Mérida Km 120; ☎ 999/920-8407; www.haciendachichen.com; doubles $120–$165), just a short walk from the ruins' back entrance. This is the smallest and most private of the three hotels near the site. In the early 1900s, American consul Edward Thompson owned the property. He put Chichén Itzá on the archaeological map after sending local artifacts to the U.S.

Spend a day at the ruins. Hire a guide or tag along with a docent-led group for explanations of the many interesting facets of each ruin. You'll learn fascinating details, such as the fact that the long stone steps of the pyramid cast the shadow of a slithering serpent on the Spring and Fall equinoxes.

An overnight stay makes it easier to attend the fascinating nighttime light show at the ruins.

If you're in the mood for a hot lunch and a cool swim, drive back on the highway to the ★ **Dolores Alba** (p 56). This hotel has a very good *palapa* restaurant with a pool just a few feet away. Better yet, ask to swim in their second pool, built like a *cenote* with a swim-through cave.

The next morning, take the *Cuota* back toward Cancún and follow the signs for Playa del Carmen, south on Highway 307. If you return to Cancún that night, dine at a Hotel Zone landmark, ★★★ **Lorenzillo's,** Km 10.5 (p 138), serving fresh lobsters on the lagoon. 🕐 *1 day.*

From Cancún, take Highway 307 for 68km (42 miles) south of Cancún. Express buses run frequently from Cancún's terminal on Avenida Tulum to Playa del Carmen.

④ **Playa del Carmen.** Once a sleepy port town at the other end of the ferry to Cozumel, Playa is now huge; at press time, it was the fastest-growing city in the Americas. It's still the "in" place to vacation on the Riviera Maya, but its cachet is fading as more of the *hoi polloi* find out about it. Check into your hotel when you arrive and make reservations for Xcaret tomorrow.

From the ferry dock north, crowds of tourists throng the long, pedestrian-only Fifth Avenue, a street lined with an enticing mélange of chic stores, hip bars, cool cafes, boutique hotels, and classy restaurants. This seaside city's Cannes-meets-Coney Island atmosphere is especially appealing to the many Europeans who visit.

Exterior of a home, Playa del Carmen.

Chac Mool.

Needless to say, shopping, looking, drinking, and eating are professional sports on the people-friendly main drag. But Playa isn't all about commercialism; its alabaster-white beach, strewn with sun worshippers, is fabulous. And the turquoise Caribbean makes for great swimming and snorkeling on the reef just offshore.

See p 122 for recommended dinner and nightlife choices. ⏱ *1 day.*

It may not be Tuscany, but many Italians who come to Playa go to **Ciao Gelato,** on Fifth Ave (between calles 2 and 4), to cool off with some lower-fat ice cream.

Take Route 307 4km (2.5 miles) south of Playa del Carmen.

5 **kids** **Xcaret.** Spend the entire day a few kilometers south of Playa at **Xcaret** (*Ish*-car-ret; ☎ 998/883-0470; www.xcaret.com), an eco-themed recreational water park suitable for the entire family.

Once a thriving port for pre-Columbian trade in the Maya world,

Xcaret now thrives on the thousands of tourists who visit daily. The highlight here is the snorkel trip down an underground river. Other attractions include an inviting snorkel lagoon, beatific beaches, dolphin swims, an aviary, an orchid garden, a Mexican graveyard, horse shows, and four big restaurants. But Xcaret's *pièce de résistance* is its evening spectacular—which is just that. Through music and dance, more than 300 performers tell Mexico's colorful history. *See p 14.*

Return to Playa for the night.
⏱ *1 day.*

Take Route 307 63km (39 miles) south of Playa del Carmen.

6 **Tulum.** Either take the bus from 5th Avenue's station or rent a car in Playa and drive south to the Maya ruins of **Tulum,** on a breathtaking bluff above the azure Caribbean. Arrive before the crowds and heat of the day, or visit late in the afternoon.

Enter the small, walled site and walk past the various ruined temples to its largest pyramid, El Castillo. The

Playa Soliman.

Young girls in traditional dress.

view of the sea below is breathtaking. Tulum is not the most significant archaeological site in the Yucatán, but to close your eyes and feel the warm sun and sea breeze wash over you is magical.

You can no longer climb to the top of the pyramid, but there's plenty to "ooh" and "aah" about inside the post-Classic holy site or right below it on the sandy beach. *For detailed coverage of the Tulum ruins, see p 60, "The Pre-Colombian Yucatán."*

South of the ruins, a series of *hotelitos*—small hotels that run the gamut from sand-floor *palapas* to four-star suites—lines the shore down the Boca Paila Road. If you can, check into one of the cabanas at the charming ★★★ **La Zebra,** Boca Paila Road (☎ 984/115-4276; www.lazebratulum.com; from $155), and take a dip away from the crowds on Tulum.

Seaside dinner at ★★ **Qué Fresco** (Boca Paila Rd. at Zamas Hotel) is a real treat. Lights go out at 11pm; after that it's candles and starlight. *See p 75.* ◷ *1 day.*

Take Route 307 north, toward Cancún, 47km (29 miles) to Aktun Chen.

❼ Aktun Chen/Playa Soliman. On your last morning, sneak in your next-to-last ocean swim before breakfast and then drive west from Tulum toward the Cobá ruins. Take a quick look at the **Gran Cenote,** an underground river in an open cavern. Swimming is allowed, but don't wear sunscreen. Admission is 80 pesos.

Return to the highway north; drive 47km (29 miles) toward Cancún for the **Aktun Chen Caves,** a stunning series of well-lit caverns full of spectacular stalactites and stalagmites. Discovered by *chicle* workers who took shelter in them from a hurricane, the caves culminate at an incredible crystal-clear green *cenote.* They're up a sandy, 3km (2-mile) road on the left. *See p 47.*

Lunch on fresh fish or Yucatecan/Mexican food on a nearby private beach at **Oscar y Lalo's Playa Soliman** *(p 31).* At Lalo's you can swim on the half-moon beach, sea kayak on the bay, or snorkel the reef. The beachfront hut is clean, and the food is excellent (but the bathrooms are a bit rough). Hang out in their shaded hammocks, and maybe enjoy a *siesta* until it's time to return to Cancún and home. ◷ *1 day.*

A window onto the Caribbean at the Maya ruins of Tulum.

The Best of the Yucatán in **Two Weeks**

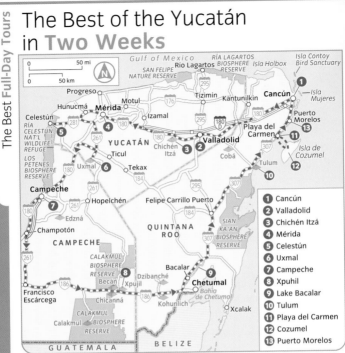

1. Cancún
2. Valladolid
3. Chichén Itzá
4. Mérida
5. Celestún
6. Uxmal
7. Campeche
8. Xpuhil
9. Lake Bacalar
10. Tulum
11. Playa del Carmen
12. Cozumel
13. Puerto Morelos

The Yucatán's good roads and fairly contained shape—a broad, relatively symmetrical limestone plateau—allow for a complete circuit of the peninsula within a 2-week time frame. I recommend moving counterclockwise, so you'll save the best beach time for the end of your trip. You can take this tour by first-class bus (with a few side trips) or rent a car for maximum flexibility. START: **Cancún Hotel Zone, 10km (6.25 miles) from the airport on Boulevard Kukulcán. Total trip length: about 1,200km (744 miles).**

A Note on Hotels & Restaurants

For additional information on sights, shops, and recommended hotels and restaurants in Cancún, see chapter 7; on Valladolid, see p 124; on Mérida, see p 108; on Campeche, see p 90; on Playa del Carmen, see p 120; and on Cozumel, see p 96.

① **Cancún.** The Hotel Zone is where you will spend your first day. Unwind with a swim before heading downtown to ★ **Ty-Coz** for lunch, on Avenida Tulum across from the bus station. Comparison shop at **Mercado 28** before grabbing a table for dinner at ★★ **La Habi-chuela.** Rent a car or buy your bus ticket to Valladolid for tomorrow. ⏲ *1 day.*

Take the Cuota for 152km (94 miles) west of Cancún or follow signs from Cancún city for the Mérida Libre.

② **Valladolid.** This small colonial-era city played a major role in the 1800s rebellion known as the Caste War. Before the Conquest, it was a sacred Maya city. Compact and walkable, its highlights include **La Parroquia San Servacio Church, Main Plaza, Municipal Palace, San Roque Museum, Ex-Convento,** and *cenotes* **Zaci, Xkeken,** and **Samula.** Lunch and people-watch at **★★ Maria de la Luz** on the square. Dine and spend the night at **★ El Meson del Marquéz.** *For more details, see "Valladolid" on p 124.* 🕑 *1 day.*

For a hot cup of distinctive Chiapas coffee or a cold ice cream, grab an upstairs window table at **Café Kabah,** on the corner opposite the Municipal Palace.

Take Route 180 an hour west of Valladolid, near the town of Pisté.

③ **Chichén Itzá.** These magnificent ruins are one of the wonders of

Street vendors in Valladolid.

the world. **Hacienda Chichén Itzá** is a good hotel right outside the back entrance of the ruins. Re-enter for the evening light-show spectacular. *For more details, see "The Pre-Columbian Yucatán" on p 54.* 🕑 *1 day.*

Take the Cuota 2 hours west of Chichén Itzá.

④ **Mérida.** The capital of Yucatán state, Mérida is the region's center of culture and history and well worth a few nights' stay. It also makes a good base for excursions into the countryside or to the beach.

A carriage in Izamal.

Folkloric dancers in Mérida.

A good introduction to the city is a horse *calasa* (carriage) ride along the **Paseo Montejo,** with its *Bella Epoca* mansions, or catch a lift around the main plaza. Stroll the latter, which is surrounded by 500-year-old buildings built from the stone of Maya pyramids torn down by the Spanish Conquistadors.

Mérida deftly balances the old with the new and has something for everyone. Each evening, free cultural events take place, often in the many small parks that grace the historic district. Sunday is a big day for festivities.

Some of the many highlights clustered near the **Plaza Mejor** include **San Ildefonso Cathedral, Casa de Montejo, Municipal Palace, Governor's Palace, City Museum,** and the impressive Italianate gem, the **Teatro Peón Contreras.**

When Mérida gets hot and humid, cool off with some ice cream at **Dulceria y Sorbeteria Colón,** underneath the arches on Calle 61, across from the Main Plaza. *See p 112.*

Mérida is an ideal place to buy Maya **handicrafts,** Yucatecan **hammocks,** *huipiles* (traditional embroidered dresses or blouses), or *guayaberas* (men's tropical dress shirts). 🕐 *2 days.*

Izamal, the Golden City

If you are driving to Mérida from Chichén, consider a detour through Izamal. For details on this doubly sacred town, see p 85, "The Western Yucatán," in chapter 5.

Directions: Take Route 281 92km (57 miles) west of Mérida through Hunucmá.

⑤ Celestún. From Mérida, Celestún is a fun day trip that combines a day on the beach with a boat trip to see flocks of pink flamingos in the ecological biosphere. This Gulf-side little fishing village is very laid-back, if not rustic. It's a good place to collect shells. Book a day tour or drive. Return to Mérida for your last night. *See p 44.* 🕐 *1 day.*

Take Route 261 80km (50 miles) south of Mérida through Uman, a 90-minute drive.

6 Uxmal. As you head south, you'll see the amazing Maya ruins of Uxmal. Some contend they're as good as Chichén Itzá's, but they're definitely less crowded, more compact, and—at press time—still climbable. Clearly marked roads lead you to this ancient city, which features the Pyramid of the Magician, Nunnery Quadrangle, Governor's Palace, and the Great Pyramid. Like Chichén, they offer an evening light show. Stay overnight at the Lodge at Uxmal, just outside the entrance. *See p 57.* 🕐 *1 day.*

Take Route 180 251km (156 miles) south of Mérida through Uman, a 90-minute drive.

7 Campeche. This walled city is the best preserved in the Americas. The United Nations declared it a World Heritage Site in 2000, which secures protection for its narrow cobblestone streets and pastel colonial-era buildings. In Campeche city, see the Parque Principal, Cathedral of the Conception, the Baluartes on the surviving walls, the Malecón, City Museum, and, near sunset, Fort San Miguel, which dominates the harbor. Lunch at Marganzo, dinner at Casa Vieja, and an overnight at Hotel America come highly recommended (p 94). The next 2 days involve long-distance driving. 🕐 *1 day.*

Take Route 261 about 150km (93 miles) southeast of Campeche to Escarcega. Then head east on Route 186 for 172km (107 miles) to Xpuhil.

8 Xpuhil. Leave Campeche early to reach **Edzná's** incredible Maya ruins, about 50km (31 miles) southeast. *For further details, see p 58.*
Then it's a long drive through Escarcega to **Xpuhil** (also spelled Xpuhil), where the ★★ **Chicanna EcoVillage** (☎ 981/811-9192; www.chicannaecovillageresort.com) is a welcome terminus. Easy-to-access local ruins are **Xpujil, Chicanna,** and **Becán.** *See p 60 for archaeological details.* 🕐 *1 day.*

Take Route 186 about 110km (68 miles) east of Xpujil. Then head north on Route 307 for about 37km (23 miles) to Bacalar.

9 Lake Bacalar. You're on your way home now from Xpujil. Stop to see the stone masks in the **Kohunlich** ruins, and then have a late lunch in **Chetumal,** Quintana Roo's capital, at ★ **Los Cocos Hotel** (☎ 072/969-6999; www.hotelloscocos.com). Spend the night 37km (23 miles) north of the city at **Rancho Encantado** (☎ 998/884-1181; www.encantado.com), a lovely hotel on the edge of ★★★ **Lake Bacalar,** known as the Lagoon of Seven Colors. *For more details, see p 82.* 🕐 *1 day.*

Take Route 307 about 211km (131 miles) north of Lake Bacalar to Tulum.

Local men hunt for snakes and small animals near the House of the Magician at Uxmal.

Hotel Bacalar in Chetumal, capital of Quintana Roo.

🔟 **Tulum.** After an hour-and-a-half's drive north to Tulum, you'll reach the crystalline blue waters of the Caribbean. For some rest and relaxation, plan to spend 2 nights on the beach at **Zamas** (info@zamas.com for reservations; www.zamas.com), a well-known hotel. Dine there and at **Il Giardino di Toni y Simone** or **Don Cafeto's,** in Tulum town. You'll have 2 days to swim, relax, beachcomb, or indulge in a spa treatment. Be sure to visit the Tulum ruins early in the day, before the crowds arrive. Consider a nature tour of the **Sian Ka'an Biosphere,** just south of Zamas; the **Aktun Chen** caves; and **Playa Soliman.** *For detailed information on Tulum, see p 60.* 🕐 *2 days.*

Take Route 307 63km (39 miles) north of Tulum to Playa del Carmen.

🔟 **Playa del Carmen.** Playa del Carmen is the kind of place you either love or hate. Millions of tourists adore it each year, but it's very different from what you've experienced so far. Everything centers around **Fifth Avenue,** the pedestrian-only shopping, dining, drinking, and partying mecca that unwinds parallel to Playa's alabaster-white *playa.* Swim,

relax, and have dinner at **John Gray's Place.** *See p 123.* 🕐 *1 day.*

Before the sun climbs too high in the sky, plop down outdoors at **Coffee Press,** Calle 2 and Fifth Avenue, for java as good as it smells.

⑫ **Cozumel.** The next morning, take the ferry to **Cozumel,** where you can **dive** the reefs, **golf,** or **rent a motorbike** to explore the wild, windward side of the island. Eat a fried-fish lunch at **Chen Rio** facing the Caribbean, **snorkel** or **swim with the dolphins** at **Chankanaab Park,** see the **Cozumel Museum,** visit the small **San Gervasio** ruins, have dinner at ★★ **La Veranda,** and return to Playa on the ferry. *See p 96.* 🕐 *2 days.*

On an airy upstairs veranda, **Cozumel Museum Cafe** is the perfect place for a relaxing lunch, snack, or bottomless cup of coffee overlooking the waterfront. *Avenida Rafael Melgar (between calles 4 and 6).* ☎ 987/872-1475.

Take 307 north to Puerto Morelos, halfway between Playa del Carmen and Cancún.

⑬ **Puerto Morelos.** This little fishing village is one of the best-kept secrets of the Riviera Maya. Development has mostly passed it by, although the new mega-resort El Cid opened south of town. The reef just offshore is a **National Marine Park** and rivals Cozumel's for its beauty and abundance of fish. This is an idyllic spot for your last hours in Mexico. **Snorkel,** swim, and enjoy a fresh-fish lunch at ★★ **Pelicano's,** on the beach. If you're still here at dinnertime, try **Hola Asia,** on the square. *See additional details on p 72.* ●

3 Best of the Yucatán Outdoors

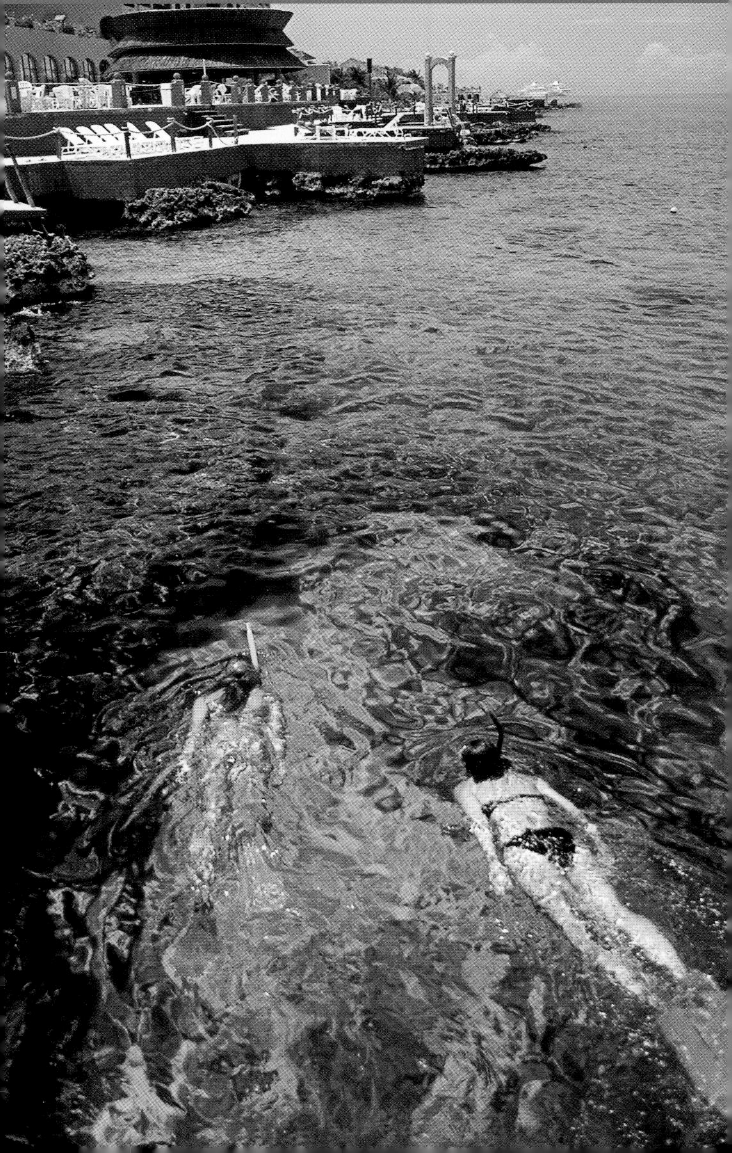

The Best Yucatán **Beaches**

1 Isla Mujeres
2 Cancún
3 Puerto Morelos
4 Punta Bete/ Xcalacoco
5 Akumal
6 Playa Soliman
7 Tankah
8 Tulum

Airport
Ferry route
Reef
Ruins

Isla Mujeres

Punta Sam
Puerto Juárez
Cancún

Isla Cancún

Gulf of Mexico
Mérida
YUCATÁN
Cancún
Area of detail
Campeche
QUINTANA ROO
Isla de Cozumel
Caribbean Sea
Chetumal
GUATEMALA BELIZE
0   100 mi
0   100 km

Mérida Libre
Cuota (Toll)
To Mérida

Croco-Cun

Puerto Morelos
Jardín Botánico
Tres Ríos Nature Park

QUINTANA ROO

Punta Maroma

Playa del Carmen
Xcaret
Puerto Calica Cruise Port
Paamul
Puerto Aventuras
Xpu-Ha

Punta Bete

San Miguel de Cozumel

ISLA DE COZUMEL

Cobá

Akumal
Xcacel
Xel-Ha Lagoon National Park
Tankah
Tulum
Tulum

CARIBBEAN SEA

0   10 mi
0   10 km

The Yucatán shoreline stretches nearly 1,600km (1,000 miles), and its eastern, Caribbean-side beaches are among the world's finest, famed for their dazzling turquoise waters and bright-white sands. Composed of shell fragments broken and tumbled smooth by heavy wave action, the picture-perfect shore remains cool underfoot in even the hottest temperatures. Some stretches are full of sunbathers, *palapas,* and hotels. Others—hard as it is to believe—are lined with nothing but palm trees. So visit now, before developers gobble up these last deserted stretches.

For specialized outdoor adventures, see "Extreme Yucatán" and "The Yucatán for Ecotourists," in chapter 4, "The Best Special-Interest Tours."

A Note on Hotels & Restaurants

For additional information on sights, shops, and recommended hotels and restaurants on Isla Mujeres, see p 102; in Cancún, see chapter 7.

1 **Isla Mujeres.** My favorite laid-back beach time is just a ferry ride away from Cancún, on Isla Mujeres. The windward side of this tiny island is great for beachcombers and shell collectors, though most locations

Previous page: Snorkelers offshore in Cozumel.

are too rough for swimming; the **North Beach** is shallow, warm, and ideal for young children and families (despite an occasional, discreet topless sunbather). The leeward side, facing Cancún, has the best swimming and snorkeling in the bay's protected waters. Most notable of these beaches are **Garrafón Park,** near the southern tip; **Playa Lancheros** and **Sac Bajo,** about halfway down the island; and the big beach near the ferries and working lighthouse downtown.

2 Cancún. Its gorgeous, bright-white beaches and stunning aquamarine water put Cancún on the map. The Hotel Zone, a 27km (17-mile) sliver of land in the shape of a figure 7, affords two types of beach getaway. The long side, with spectacularly good-looking beaches, widened after Hurricane Wilma, faces the Caribbean and can have strong waves when it's windy. The top of the 7 is on the Bay of Mujeres, where the water is not nearly so blue but is rarely as rough. Playa Delfines, a public beach off Kukulcán, Km 18.5, is often considered the most dramatic.

All beaches are public in Mexico, but generally guests use ones associated with their hotels. The Hotel Zone's public beaches are usually crowded on Sundays when local families come to play.

3 Puerto Morelos. This quiet fishing and residential village is a favorite of North American snowbirds, who often stay long-term in winter months. Its snow-white beaches are inside an offshore reef, so they don't get big waves, but they do get big raves for crowd-free snorkeling and swimming. Catch a 1½-hour-long snorkel trip from the pier for $25. Ask to see the *ojo de agua* (eye of water), where fresh water enters the sea from an underground river.

The town of Puerto Morelos has just a few modest hotels; most of its accommodations take the form of guesthouses, small condominium complexes, or small hotels. A local dining favorite is ★★ **Pelícano's,** a seafood restaurant on the corner of the square and the beach. Puerto Morelos is about halfway between Cancún and Playa del Carmen.

4 Punta Bete/Xcalacoco. Just north of Playa del Carmen is **Punta Bete,** a superb, isolated, pure-white beach with swaying palm trees and

The beach and ruins of Tulum.

The beach at Puerto Morelos.

rustic, beachfront accommodations. Get here before it's sullied; these 5km (3 miles) of gorgeous beach are bound to be developed.

Stay in comfortable, charming, rustic cabins at ★★★ **Coco's Cabañas** (☎ 998/874-7056; $50–$75). Surrounded by tropical gardens, these intimate cabañas are just steps from the beach. Eat fresh seafood

Some like it hot, and some prefer the shade on Playa Soliman.

next door at **Los Piños,** a rustic *palapa* beach bungalow where the hut specialty is *Tikin-Xic*, grilled filet of fish flavored with *achiote*.

⑤ **Akumal.** Akumal's offshore reefs and wonderful half-moon-shaped bay have attracted divers and inveterate beach lovers since 1958, long before other coastal resort areas developed. These days, condominiums, private villas, and boutique hotels line the beach, which remains uncrowded.

Akumal is suitable for North Americans who appreciate familiarity, given that *gringos* own most of the homes here. And you can't ask for a better beach.

Inland, super snorkeling and swimming opportunities abound at the **Yal-ku Lagoon,** a similar but smaller version of nearby Xel-Ha. At the northern end of the town road, **Yal-ku** (admission $7) also affords a safe snorkeling experience among its clear water and rocky inlets.

Look out over Akumal Bay from a suite at ★ **Hacienda de la Tortuga** (☎ 984/875-9068; www.haciendatortuga.com), a pleasant, small hotel on the beach. *Tortuga* is

Spanish for turtle, which is what Akumal means in Maya.

Dine *al fresco* at the appealing, ★ **Lol-Ha Restaurant & Bar,** in Hotel Akumal.

6 Playa Soliman. ★★ Oscar y Lalo's put pretty Playa Soliman on the map. Fresh fish and Yucatecan/Mexican food in an unhurried atmosphere make repeat visitors out of anyone who stumbles across this modest rustic restaurant on the beach.

The open-air bungalow restaurant offers free hammocks for *siestas*, ocean kayaks for exploring the bay and reef, a hidden *cenote* for swimming, and good food in the shade of its *palapa*. Except for Lalo's, no hotels or buildings are visible from the beach in either direction. Playa Soliman is a very special, singular place.

7 Tankah. The beaches of Tankah feature exclusive guesthouses and small boutique hotels in a setting that is, as yet, unspoiled. Heavenly pure white sand and blue waters are the staples. Eat American-style Tex-Mex at the ★ **Casa Cenote**

Restaurant on a rocky beach. Opposite this restaurant, along the beach road, is **Tankah Cenote.** This natural underground river is one of the deepest and clearest around.

Stay overnight in the heavenly ★★★ **Blue Sky Inn** (☎ 984/801-4004; www.blueskymexico.com), a short way down the sand street from Casa Cenote.

8 Tulum. Tulum's plethora of facilities and its reputation as a remote escape from the demands of civilization make it the hippest place to stay on the Riviera Maya. It was inevitable that the demand for lodgings on the gorgeous beach along the **Boca Paila Road** would mean more small hotels on the coastline between the ruins at **Tulum** and the protected nature preserve, **Sian Ka'an Biosphere.** The beaches are beyond beautiful; even the sandy shore below the cliffside ruins attracts beach bums with cultural pretensions.

Oceanfront accommodations in Tulum run from rustic sand-floor cabañas to upscale luxury suites—and everything in between.

Beachfront at the Cancún Hilton.

Underwater Yucatán

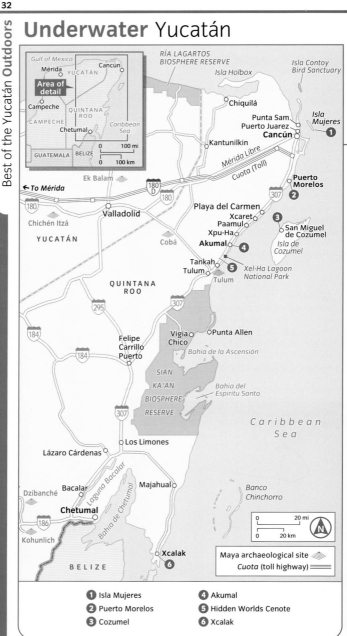

1 Isla Mujeres
2 Puerto Morelos
3 Cozumel
4 Akumal
5 Hidden Worlds Cenote
6 Xcalak

The Great Mesoamerican Reef—the 474km (294-mile) ribbon of coral adorning the Caribbean coast from Cancún to Belize—is the world's second-longest. Brimming with a diversity of organisms, it's home to 450 species of fish and 80 types of coral alone. Its barrier and fringe reefs are common enough, but its kidney-shaped Chinchorro Reef, off Xcalak, is the largest coral atoll in the Americas. It's also distinguished by *cenotes*—sinkholes or wellsprings unique to the Yucatán, with its fragile limestone makeup. START: **Isla Mujeres. Total trip length: 380km (236 miles).**

A Note on Hotels & Restaurants

For additional information on sights, shops, and recommended hotels and restaurants on Isla Mujeres, see p 102; on Cozumel, see p 96.

Isla Mujeres is 19km (12 miles) offshore from Cancún. Take the people ferry from either of two docks in Puerto Juárez, just north of downtown Cancún.

1 Isla Mujeres. The protected waters that separate Isla Mujeres from Cancún afford wonderful snorkeling and dive opportunities. Diverse enough to be an all-day excursion, El Garrafón Park is the most popular spot for beginners. Its reef, close to shore, sparkles with colorful fish swimming in and out of nooks and crannies. You can also take a launch to reach Manchones Reef or the reef around the lighthouse in the bay. Seemingly everybody will offer you trips as you arrive on the ferry.

A sunken 1-ton bronze cross, in memoriam to those lost at sea, is a favorite dive destination on Manchones Reef. So is Isla's world-famous Cave of the Sleeping Sharks, where sharks seem to float completely stationary in the currents. You can arrange **sport-fishing** trips at the Fishermen's Cooperative, near the ferry.

Take Highway 307 approximately 25km (16 miles) south of Cancún.

2 Puerto Morelos. This village is one of the few along the coastline that predates Cancún. An offshore reef shelters the coast and, in turn, is protected as a National Marine Park. Experienced snorkelers report that Puerto Morelos has better coral and fish than the widely regarded Chankanaab Park on Cozumel. Divers go down in several locales where the reef drops off, as well as in the *Ojo de Agua*, where fresh water enters the sea from the ocean floor.

You can arrange fruitful **fishing** trips at the central pier. If you can handle luxury, spend the night at Puerto Morelos's premier hotel, the **Ceiba del Mar** (see "The Riviera Maya's Best Spas," p 62). And while

A couple explores a Yucatecan coral reef.

A Yucatecan Gray Angelfish.

you're lapping up luxury, dine at the Riviera Maya's best gourmet restaurant, **John Gray's Kitchen** (Av. Niños Héroes; ☎ 998/871-0665).

Cozumel is 19km (12 miles) off the coast from the ferry dock in Playa del Carmen, which is about 70km (43 miles) south of Cancún on Highway 307.

❸ **Cozumel.** Jacques Cousteau's groundbreaking film about the stunningly beautiful garland of reefs off Cozumel's western shore helped

A snorkeler off the shores of Cozumel.

stake its reputation as *the* place to drift-dive. Underwater visibility can reach as far as 250 feet (75m), and excellent dive and snorkel spots abound. Snorkelers can go by launch on offshore excursions or stay near the beach at Chankanaab National Park. Experienced divers favor the Paraiso, Chankanaab, Yucab, Palancar, Columbia, and Maracaibo reefs, which parallel the leeward coast.

You can arrange **sport-fishing** trips through travel agents or directly through charter boats at the harbor, north of the ferry dock.

Approximately 122km (76 miles) south of Cancún on Highway 307, look for signs for "Playa Akumal."

❹ **Akumal.** Akumal's fabulous reef protects an idyllic half-moon bay, around which condominiums, private villas, boutique hotels, and beachfront restaurants have sprouted. It was already an established community in the 1950s, when Mexican divers made it their base after they found the wreck of *Mantanceros,* the Spanish galleon that sank in 1741. Now, Akumal's three bays and coral reefs are a playground for North Americans, many of whom populate the residential resort year-round.

Snorkelers plumb the reefs, while beginners start out in the natural Yal-ku Lagoon. Stay at the lagoon-side garden boutique hotel ★★ **Qué Onda** (☎ 984/875-9101; www.queondaakumal.com) and enjoy the good life at the upstairs/downstairs beachside ★ **La Buena Vida Bar & Restaurant.**

Take Highway 307 approximately 136km (84 miles) south of Cancún.

❺ **Hidden Worlds Cenote.** Discover hidden worlds (☎ 984/877-8535; www.hiddenworlds.com.mx; $30 snorkel tour) by diving and snorkeling in this series of lighted *cenote*

An adult Sargassum Triggerfish off the shores of Cozumel.

caverns. The water is crystalline but quite chilly. The protruding rock formations are so impressive that the caverns made an appearance in the IMAX movie, *Journey into Amazing Caves.* It's off the highway about 2km (1.25 miles) south of Xel-Ha Park. From the reception office, visitors journey to the various cave spots in a "jungle mobile" truck. Some walking is involved, so bring comfortable shoes. Scheduled snorkel and dive tours take place at 9 and 11am, and 1, 2, and 3pm. Thrill seekers can also ride jungle **zip-lines** above the treetops. ⏱ *4 hours.*

About 45 minutes south of Felipe Carrillo Puerto, turn left in Limones for Majahual and the Xcalak Peninsula. Drive 50km (31 miles) to an Army Guard house. Straight ahead is the town of Majahual. Turn left and go 55km (34 miles) more to Xcalak.

6 Xcalak. Lesser-known than its close neighbor, the Belize Cays, Xcalak offers equally great diving at a lower price. Thirty-two kilometers (20 miles) off the coast, the curious Chinchorro Reef is nearly the size of Cozumel Island. Chinchorro, which means "fishing net," features a shallow interior, ideal for snorkeling, and more than 30 shipwrecks. Only licensed operators can take divers to this national treasure, which was partly damaged when a ferry wrecked on the atoll during Hurricane Wilma in 2005.

Xcalak itself is a weather-beaten dive and fishing town, with a certain *je ne se quoi (no sé qué?)* among travelers in search of that elusive beach-bum culture. But you can also stay just north of town in classy comfort at ★★ **Casa Carolina** (☎ 983/839-1958; www.casacarolina.net), a bed-and-breakfast that runs dive trips from its wooden dock.

Divers at Hidden World Cenote.

The Best Yucatán **Golf Courses**

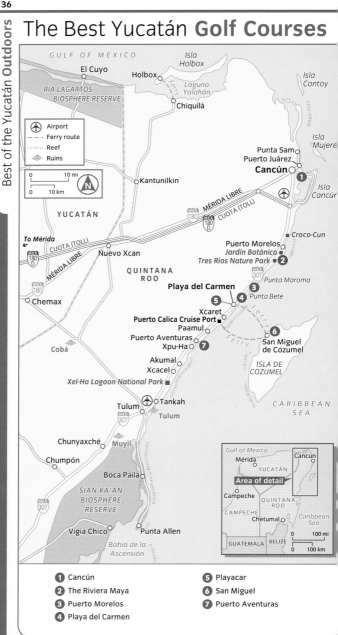

1. Cancún
2. The Riviera Maya
3. Puerto Morelos
4. Playa del Carmen
5. Playacar
6. San Miguel
7. Puerto Aventuras

Got balls? In recent years, the Riviera Maya has developed some challenging and visually appealing golf courses, with jungle roughs, water hazards, dazzling oceanfront views, and other exotic features. Several courses were laid out by the sport's most renowned architects, including the Nicklaus Design Group. Remember that midday golfers get the hot sun; early birds get the warm. Bring your own clubs or rent. A good source for all things golf is www.cancungolf.org.

A Note on Hotels & Restaurants

For additional information on sights, shops, and recommended hotels and restaurants in Cancún, see p 136; on the Riviera Maya, see p 75; on Playa del Carmen, see p 120.

❶ **Cancún.** Cancún currently fits four major golf courses into its 23km (14-mile) borders. Two new courses are under construction. **Puerto Cancún** is the centerpiece of a new, self-contained resort community between the Hotel Zone and downtown. And the impressive **TPC La Roca Country Club** promises to have the largest driving range in Latin America. La Roca is between the downtown and the airport on Highway 307.

The Hotel Zone's first established and most popular course is ★ **Pok-Ta-Pok Club de Golf** (☎ 998/883-1230; www.cancungolfclub.com), designed by Robert Trent Jones, Jr. This 18-hole, par-73 golf course is 6,721 yards.

The ★★ **Melia Cancún Golf Club** (☎ 998/885-1114) is an 18-hole, par-54 course, with a total length of 1,818 yards. It's on the grounds of the Melia Hotel at Km 16 on Kukulcán Boulevard.

The 9-hole ★ **Cancún Oasis Golf Club** (☎ 998/885-0867) has a par-27 course, with a maximum length of 888 yards. Short and sweet.

Robert Trent Jones, Jr., designed the ★★ **Caesar Park Hotel Golf Club** (☎ 998/881-8016), an 18-hole, par-72 championship course. It's 6,767 yards long, with an on-site pro shop, practice green, and driving range.

It's not exactly in the Hotel Zone, but ★★★ **Moon Palace**'s 7,165-yard, par-72 Jack Nicklaus Signature Golf Course (☎ 998.881.6000; www.palaceresorts.com) is just south of Cancún city, down Highway 307 near Bahia Petempech.

❷ **The Riviera Maya.** The Nicklaus Design Group created **El Manglar Golf Course** (☎ 984/206-4043; www.albatrossgolf-courses.com) on the Riviera Maya (Km 48, Hwy. 307). Known to have difficult greens, this challenging executive course is 2,923 yards with a par of 54.

❸ **Puerto Morelos.** The par-72, P. B. Dye–designed course at the

The Cancún Golf Club at Pok-Ta-Pok.

Teeing off at the Westin Resort & Spa Cancún.

★★ Iberostar Playa Paraiso Golf Club (☎ 984/877-2847; www.iberostar.com) features narrow fairways, undulating greens, and deep bunkers with dramatic vertical movement. It's south of Puerto Morelos on Highway 307.

④ Playa del Carmen. The **★★ Camaleón Mayakoba** (☎ 984/206-3088; www.fairmont.com/mayakoba/recreation/golf) is a challenging 18-hole course a few kilometers north of Playa del Carmen. Designed by Greg Norman, it's on the grounds of the luxury Mayakoba

Hotel. A boat ride on the hotel's canal system takes you to the first tee of this stunningly beautiful course, which bends through the vegetation and features long stretches of Pebble Beach–like oceanfront vistas.

⑤ Playacar. Just south of downtown Playa del Carmen is **★★ Playacar Golf Club** (☎ 987/873-0624; www.palaceresorts.com). This Robert Von Haggy course is as difficult to play as it is beautiful to view. It's a par-72 and 7,202 yards long. Errant shots into the jungle are definitely drop balls—or *mulligans*.

⑥ San Miguel. Another Nicklaus Design–built beauty is the environmentally sensitive showcase course at **★★★ Cozumel Country Club** (☎ 987/872-9570; www.cozumel countryclub.com.mx). It opened north of San Miguel in the island's lowland forest and features jungle roughs.

⑦ Puerto Aventuras. The **Puerto Aventuras Golf Club** (☎ 984/873-5109; www.puerto aventuras.com) is a par-36, 9-hole course designed by Thomas Leman. Look out for iguanas, deer and tropical birds as you make your way through the jungle-based course. ●

The Playacar Golf Club, near Playa del Carmen.

4 The Best Special-Interest Tours

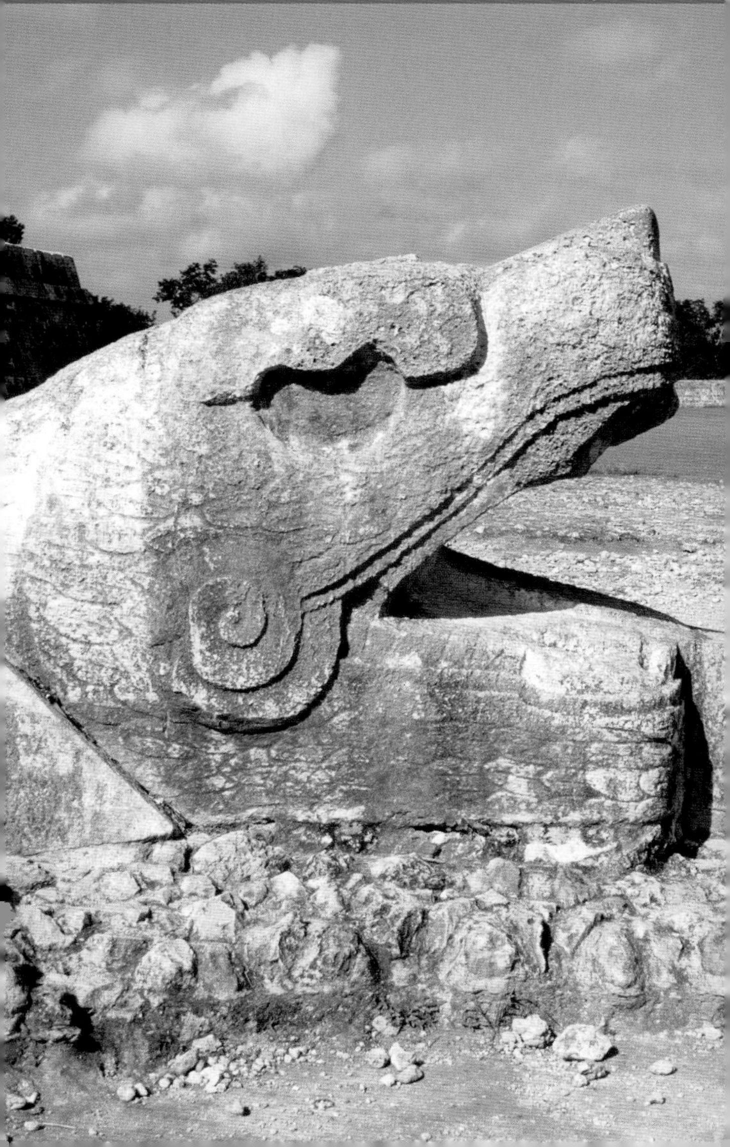

The Yucatán for **Ecotourists**

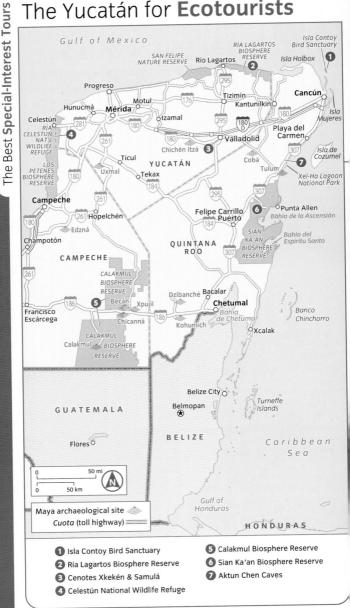

Maya archaeological site 〰️
Cuota (toll highway) ═══

1 Isla Contoy Bird Sanctuary
2 Ría Lagartos Biosphere Reserve
3 Cenotes Xkekén & Samulá
4 Celestún National Wildlife Refuge
5 Calakmul Biosphere Reserve
6 Sian Ka'an Biosphere Reserve
7 Aktun Chen Caves

Previous page: Plumed serpent head at the ball court, Chichen Itza.

denic beaches aside, the Yucatán is nothing short of ground zero for this geologic age—the crash pad for the asteroid that rocked the earth 65 million years ago, effecting the climate changes that annihilated the dinosaurs. The resulting underwater scar—the Chicxulub Crater—is just one of the peninsula's many features, including species of wildlife found nowhere else on earth. It's understandable that more and more developers want a piece of this extraordinary region, but the law curbs development in most of the following wildlife sanctuaries; many even limit the number of visitors they entertain. What's unlimited are the Technicolor birds, wildly fertile jungles, surreal *cenotes,* even jaguars and crocodiles. START: **Take the ferry from Isla Mujeres or from Cancun's Hotel Zone to reach Isla Contoy. Total trip: 1,200km (744 miles).**

① ★★ kids Isla Contoy Bird Sanctuary. Tiny Isla Contoy (☎ **998/884-7483;** www.islacontoy. org) is an uninhabited island off the coast of Cancún, set aside as a bird sanctuary and National Wildlife Reserve in 1981. Lush vegetation covers this oddly shaped, 6km (3.75-mile) -long parcel of land, which harbors more than 70 bird species and a host of marine and animal life. The island's nesting birds include pelicans (who will grub food from your boat), brown boobies, frigates, egrets, terns, and cormorants. Flocks of flamingos arrive in April, and from June through August turtles also nest in the sand dunes at night.

It's best to reach Contoy by boat from Isla Mujeres, but the number of daily visitors is limited. For about $50, you can arrange a launch at the **Fisherman's Cooperative** on the waterfront for the 45-minute journey. Many prefer the slightly slower trip on Capitán Ricardo Gaitán's wooden-hulled boat, the **Estrella del Norte.** Gaitán's office is on Avenida Madero (☎ 998/877-0434; $40 per person). As you sail, the crew unfurls fishing lines to catch your lunch. En route, you get to stop and snorkel over an open-water reef.

Isla Contoy also features a small museum (no address, no phone), walking paths, and a panoramic lookout tower. ⏱ *4 hrs.*

Approximately 105km (65 miles) north of Valladolid, at the end of Route 296, on the Yucatán's north shore.

Pink flamingos at Rio Lagartos.

Cenote Xkekén near Valladolid.

② ★ **kids Rio Lagartos Nature Reserve.** If it weren't for the thousands of flamingos that nest and feed in the river lagoons between a barrier island and the sea, the inhabitants of hardscrabble Rio Lagartos would still be eking out a living only as fishermen, living off the capricious whims of Neptune. But ecotourists and bird-watchers now flock here too, to see the pink and white birds, generating a second source of income for local residents.

The 48,564-hectare (1.2-million-acre) Rio Lagartos Nature Reserve was established in 1979 to protect the largest nesting population of flamingos in North America. It's the balance of mineral salts in the water that causes the delicate birds' soft pink color.

Boat launches depart from the village harbor to visit the colonies. You can arrange tours in advance through travel agents or **Eco-Colors** (☎ 998/884-3667) in Cancún. Or drive up from Valladolid early in the morning for the best

viewing. Enter the town and drive to the waterfront, where you can make tour arrangements at the guide's white kiosk. Hawkers often approach your car, soliciting you to board their boats. The cost is approximately $50 to $70 per person, depending on the length of your trip.

Breeding season runs from April through June, so you can't get too near the birds' mud nests, which protrude above the shallow waterline. The rest of the year, boat captains skillfully move in close enough that you can photograph the birds without scaring them away.

Be sure to wear insect repellent, a hat, and sunscreen. Bring water, a snack on longer journeys, and a camera with a zoom lens.

Take Route 180 (Calle 39) approximately 4km (2.5 miles) west of Valladolid. These *cenotes* are near the town of Dzitnup.

③ ★★★ **kids Cenotes Xkekén & Sammulá.** A series of steps, made from slightly slippery hewn rock, leads down into the cavern of **Cenote Xkekén** (Ish-kay-*ken*), the most fascinating and beautiful of Yucatán's countless underwater caves.

Also known as Cenote Dzitnup, this large underground cavern is illuminated by well-hidden artificial light, and a round hole in the roof shines a sunlight spotlight onto the translucent blue water below. The shaft of light penetrates the clear water to its very depths, and the colors are intense, making for a surreal scene. A $3 admission allows you to swim, but do not wear sunscreen because it damages the ecosystem.

Try to avoid arriving when tour buses are in the parking lot; a horde of people detracts from the experience. The parking lot has several stands selling souvenirs and some handicrafts made by the local people of Dzitnup.

Cenote Samulá, across the road, is an equally inspiring sight in a similar setting; a large cavern with intense blue water—part of the deep underground river that flows under Valladolid.

Cenote Samula near Valladolid.

Cenotes Xkekén and **Samulá** are like nothing you've seen before; only the *cenote* in the Aktun Chen cave rivals them. ⏱ *4 hrs.*

From Mérida, drive west on Route 25 through Caucel, Hunucmá, and Kinchil and follow the signs west on Route 281. It's about a 1½-hour drive.

Portals to the Underworld

The Yucatán Peninsula is a flat slab of limestone that millions of years ago absorbed the force of the giant meteor thought to have extinguished the dinosaurs. The impact sent shock waves through the brittle limestone, creating an immense network of fissures that drain rainwater away from the surface. The vast subterranean basin, which stretches for miles across the peninsula, is invisible but for the area's many *cenotes*—sinkholes or natural wells that exist nowhere else in nature. Many are perfectly round vertical shafts; others are in caverns that retain a partial roof, often perforated by tree roots. To the Maya, they were passageways to the underworld. Indeed, they look sacred: Quiet, dark, and cool, they are the opposite of the warm, bright world outside.

A long-legged Reddish Egret.

4 ★★ **kids** **Celestún National Wildlife Refuge.** After a hurricane once disrupted the Rio Lagartos breeding and feeding grounds, flamingo colonies settled on Yucatán's west coast in Celestún's brackish lagoons. Fortunately, Mexico formed the Celestún National Wildlife Refuge to protect them, on 6,070 hectares (15,000 acres) of coastal beach and mangrove wetlands.

Fresh water from scores of underwater *cenotes* mixes with salty water from the Gulf of Mexico in this long, shallow estuary, which provides perfect feeding and breeding conditions for flamingos. The estuary *(ria)* is 50km (31 miles) long, protected from the sea by a narrow strip of land. The boat ride along this corridor allows you to see the birds filtering the bottom mud for the small shrimp-like crustaceans and particular insects that make up the bulk of their diet.

Fun Fact

Ancient Romans considered pickled flamingo tongues to be a delicacy, and in the Andes flamingo fat was once believed to cure tuberculosis. Any modern nature lover will tell you the birds are more of a delicious sight than a dish.

Launches leave from the co-op at the bridge, where you can park, have a snack, and purchase tickets for the hour-long trip (about $45 per boat and $2 per person). The fewer people in the boat the better, because the *ria's* waters can get very shallow in spots. Longer trips are available from the beach in town. These boats go around the tip of the sand peninsula and visit an extra colony on the way. On either trip, ask to stop and swim at the *cenote* in the woods. The trees growing from underwater give it a swampy look, with clear, dark, fresh water that filters up from underground.

The beach in Celestún village is good, so consider an overnight stay at the new **Hotel Manglares** (☎ 988/916-2156; www.hotel manglares.com.mx) in the downtown, 300 meters (984 ft.) north of La Palapa Restaurant. It features lovely individual bungalows and ocean-view rooms with balconies. Any of the seafood restaurants that line the beach are excellent, but avoid La Palapa, which is a tour-bus stop.

Take Route 186 to the entrance 52km (32 miles) west of Xpujil; the ruins of Calakmul are another 60km (37 miles) south on a single-lane, bumpy road.

⑤ ★★★ Calakmul Biosphere Reserve. This protected forest, stretching into neighboring Guatemala, is the Yucatán's last virgin forest. In 1989, Campeche set aside almost 13% of the state—72,441 hectares (179,000 acres) on its side of the border—as a wildlife preserve.

Calakmul, named after the astonishing ruined city within its borders, boasts a wide diversity of flora and fauna, including sacred jaguars, margays, myriad plant species, 230 species of birds, *coatis*, pacas, monkeys, tapirs, armadillos, fox, and deer—not to mention several incredible ancient Maya cities overtaken by jungle.

Naturalists and avid nature photographers will find its topographical *aguada* fascinating. About 27km (17 miles) down the forest road from the highway, after the warden's hut, a path on the right leads to a natural depression in the ground, which collects and stores water during the rainy season from June to September. It holds the water into the dry season, and, night and day, during both seasons, the jungle's animal population comes to this water hole to drink. For your efforts—which include being sucked dry by mosquitoes or bitten by

snakes and scorpions—you might be lucky enough to spot a rare jaguar. Those with a deep interest in Pre-Columbian civilization will enjoy the fabulous ruins.

Arrange a tour in Campeche with **Expediciones Ecoturísticas** (☎ 981/816-0197); in Xpujil with the Tourist Information Office (☎ 983/871-6064); or in the Maya village of 20 de Noviembre (no phone, no English). For self-guided entrance, admission to the park is about $6 a car, $2 per person.

Stay the night in Xpujil or in **Hotel Puerta Calakmul** (Rte. 186; no phone) at the Biosphere's entrance from the highway. It's best to get an early start (by about 7am).

About 130km (81 miles) south of Cancún, turn left at the Tulum traffic light, toward the beach, and then right (south) on the Boca Paila Road. The biosphere begins a few miles down the road.

⑥ ★★ kids Sian Ka'an Biosphere Reserve. More accessible to tourists than Calakmul, the Sian Ka'an Biosphere (meaning Birth of the Sun in Maya) features 526,110 hectares (1.3 million acres) of land and watery lagoons teeming with wildlife, just south of the beaches

Ecotourism & You

The Yucatán Peninsula has seen an explosion in the number of companies that organize nature and adventure tours. Two well-established outfits with solid track records are **Ecoturismo Yucatan** in Mérida (☎ 999-920-2772; www.ecoyuc.com) and **Ecocolors** in Cancún (☎ 998/884-3667; www.ecotravelmexico.com). Even if you don't book with these companies, you can still do your part to minimize environmental impact. When in the water, always use biodegradable sunblock; *never* touch coral; and, if you see a turtle, don't swim above it since this blocks its access to fresh air.

of Tulum teeming with tanned tourists.

The pride of Quintana Roo's environmental movement, Sian Ka'an was created in 1986 to protect the mid-state region of tropical forests, savannas, mangroves, canals, lagoons, bays, *cenotes,* and coral reefs inhabited by hundreds of birds as well as land and marine animals.

The best way to see the core sights of this expansive nature reserve is through a guided tour. **EcoColors** in Cancún (☎ 998/884-3667; www.ecotravelmexico.com; tours $146 per person) offers several active day-tour options with transportation, which includes hiking, biking, kayaking, boat rides, and floats down a canal between

lagoons past the overgrown ruins of a Maya "customs house."

If one day isn't enough, plan to stay the night onsite at the comfortable beachfront jungle lodge run by the environmental group **Centro Ecológico Sian Ka'an** (☎ 984/871-2499; www.cesiak.org). Proceeds fund conservation programs.

Nearly 1,200 species of animals call Sian Ka'an home, including giant crocodiles and a plethora of birds, including blue and white herons, roseate spoonbills, cormorants, hummingbirds, snowy egrets, storks, kingfishers, and big black vultures. You can obtain more information about the biosphere from the **Amigos de Sian Ka'an** (☎ 998/848-2136; www.amigosdesiankaan.org),

The Sian Ka'an Biosphere Reserve.

Yucatán Parrots are endemic to the region.

a nonprofit organization set up by local environmentalists to help Mexico's federal and state governments govern this delicate ecosystem. It's a perpetual, delicate responsibility, as financial pressure to open the beaches to development is quite strong.

Theoretically, the number of visitors allowed into the biosphere at any one time is limited, but enforcement is lax, and the law has lots of loopholes. Don't take a jeep or all-terrain vehicle tour if you really care about the environment.

A visit to Sian Ka'an is not too strenuous or dangerous, and it makes a rewarding day trip—even for those who can't distinguish a crane from a cormorant.

Take Highway 307 approximately 84km (52 miles) south of Cancún.

7 ★★ kids Aktun Chen Caves. Discovered in the jungle by *chicle* workers, who used it as a refuge during hurricanes, Aktun Chen is a labyrinth of stunning caves and a brilliant green *cenote,* an underground river, and brilliantly sharp stalactites and stalagmites. Geological features including underground pools and large chambers have been carefully preserved.

The 1-hour-long escorted tour is well lit and not overly claustrophobic; footing is good, but the tour requires a fair amount of walking. A small zoo showcases local fauna, and several of the critters run free on the grounds.

The admission price is a little high ($35 for adults and $25 for kids under 10; includes entrance to the caves and *cenote*), which is typical of Quintana Roo attractions. But this is a unique natural wonder worth the price, especially given that the tours are in English as well as in Spanish. The caves are up a dirt road, about 3 or 4km (2 miles) from the highway at Km 107. ☎ *984/877-8550. www.aktunchen.com. Open daily 9am–5pm.*

The Yucatán for **Families**

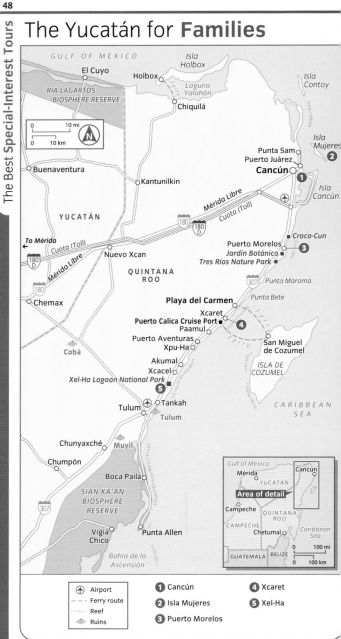

Airport ✈

Ferry route - - -

Reef

Ruins ◈

1 Cancún

2 Isla Mujeres

3 Puerto Morelos

4 Xcaret

5 Xel-Ha

Kids and water go together like peanut butter and jelly. And so the most basic secret to happy family travel, anywhere you venture in the Yucatán, is to give your children a daily dunk in the hotel pool or ocean waves. Here are a few other local attractions we've found to be especially child-friendly. START: **Cancún (the Hotel Zone is a few kilometers from the airport). Total trip: 80km (50 miles).**

Travel Tip

For additional information on sights, shops, and recommended hotels and restaurants in Cancún, see p 129; on Isla Mujeres, see p 102.

1 Cancún. Cancún is a magnet for children of all ages, but all-inclusive hotels are the best fit for the young set—including teenagers, who seem to take the "all-you-can-eat" feature as a direct challenge.

Many large hotels that cater to families offer some form of "kids clubs." For a fee, they will supervise and entertain children during the day while their parents play. Frequently they offer evening babysitting services as well.

For watery thrills and spills, consider ★ **Wet N' Wild Parque Nizuc** (Km 25; ☎ 998/881-3030; www.cancuntravel.com/wetnwild.asp; admission $45 adults, $39 children

under 11; Open daily 10am–5:30pm; AE, MC, V), at the southern end of the hotel zone. It's a fun place to enjoy numerous pools, waterslides, and rides, and also snorkel with manta rays, tropical fish, and tame sharks. You also have the chance to swim with dolphins through ★ **Dolphinaris** (☎ 998/849-4757; www.dolphindiscovery.com; prices start at $75 for a 50-minute interactive program). All activity prices include entry to Wet N' Wild, an educational introduction, and a 30-minute swim.

The ubiquitous ★★ **Jungle Tour,** a personal watercraft tour of the lagoon, is better for older youth. A 2½-hour tour takes you into the lagoon and out to a shallow reef, which includes some snorkeling. Several marinas offer this tour; kids will enjoy the WaveRunner, which grants them their own vessel, as opposed to the trips that seat two people single file.

Water fun in Playa del Carmen.

Mexican marionettes in Cancún.

A cheap boat trip would be the **car ferry,** where kids can run around on the upper deck, from Punta Sam to Isla Mujeres. See fish in the **Aquarium,** at La Isla Shopping Plaza, or eat fish sticks at the **Rainforest Café,** at Forum by the Sea shopping center, Km 9. ⏱ *2 days.*

Isla Mujeres is 13km (8 miles) off the coast of Cancún. Take the Ultramar Ferry from either of two docks in Puerto Juárez (40 pesos), north of Cancún's downtown, or a catamaran from the hotel zone's Embarcadero (about 150 pesos). Reach the Juárez ferry from downtown on any bus marked P. Juárez or P. Sam, north of Tulum Avenue.

② Isla Mujeres. The unhurried island of Isla Mujeres is a fun ferry ride away from Cancún's Hotel Zone, Puerto Juárez, or even the car ferry from Punta Sam; the slow ride over allows kids to see a lot on the upper deck, but departures are less frequent, at 8 and 11am, and 2:45, 5:30, and 8:15pm.

La Isla is a safe place to wander the streets or let kids play in the water. The beaches at the north end are wide, and the water is shallow and warm. But for an all-day excursion, choose ★★ **Garrafón Park** (☎ 998/193-3360; www.garrafon. com; packages start at $69 for adults and $50 for children). This park spills down from the road on several terraces to lovely swimming beaches that offer snorkeling on a close-in reef. Other attractions in the park include restaurants, a gift shop, kayaks, hammocks, tubes, and the exciting zip-line ride over the water.

You can also rent a **golf cart,** from one of many vendors on the island to reach the **lighthouse** and **Maya ruin** on the eastern tip.

The best swimming beaches for children are **Playa Lancheros,** where you can buy lunch and swim free, and the **North Beach,** which is fairly shallow. Tweens and teens enjoy a boat trip to the bird sanctuary of **Isla Contoy** (p 41).

Take Highway 307 approximately 25km (16 miles) south of Cancún.

Turn left at the traffic light to reach the town of Puerto Morelos.

❸ Puerto Morelos. The sleepy village of **Puerto Morelos,** a half-hour south of Cancún, boasts wonderful snorkel trips to its living reef. Come into town to the main *muelle* (pier) and arrange for the 1½-hour trip. The reef—so precious it garnered National Park status—is right offshore, so travel time from the pier is about 5 minutes each way. The rate is $25 per person, which includes a $5 park fee.

After donning life jackets, flippers, mask, and snorkel, you'll enter the water to drift and swim over a kaleidoscope of colors. Below you are giant brain coral, fantastic fans that wave in the current, and lots of fish—big and small, multicolored, striped, and electric blue. Have lunch at the Hotel Ojo de Agua's beachside restaurant, on Avenida Rojo Gomez, or base your vacation in this family-friendly town at an all-inclusive beachfront resort like Paradisus (☎ 998/872-8383; www.paradisus-riviera-cancun.com).

On the highway, 4km (2.5 miles) north of the Puerto Morelos traffic light, is ★ **CrocoCun** (☎ 998/850-3719; www.crococunzoo.com), a big zoo for ugly prehistoric crocodiles and other native Yucatán animals. The new Reptile House has many species of serpents, including rattlesnakes and boa constrictors that once roamed the local jungle. Kids will also like the creepy-crawly tarantulas, frisky spider monkeys, and wild pigs.

Less than half a kilometer (one-third mile) south of the traffic light, accessed from the far right lane, is a road under an arch known as the **Ruta de Cenotes,** which leads to the Maya village of Centro Vallarta. Along the route are several *cenotes*, which charge a few dollars admission

for a dip, and the activity park ★ **Selvatura.** This Costa Rican–inspired park features jungle zip-lines. They also have a large *cenote*, and hiking and mountain-bike rides that especially appeal to older kids.

Horseback riders of all abilities, from age 6 and up, will enjoy the American-owned ★★ **Loma Bonita Ranch** (☎ 998/887-5465; www.rancholomabonita.com), just south of Puerto Morelos. Five-hour packages include 2 hours of riding through the mangrove swamp to the beach, where you can relax and swim. The cost is $65 for adults, $57 for children 6 to 11, including lunch, soft drinks, a guide, insurance, and a horse, of course.

Take Highway 307 2km (1.25 miles) south of Playa del Carmen.

❹ ★★ Xcaret. Unleash Mother Nature on Disneyland and you'd get something like **Xcaret** (*Ish*-car-et;

Horseback riding is among the many activities at Xcaret.

Costumed performers at Xcaret Ecopark.

☎ 998/883-0470; save 10% at www.xcaret.com)—a guaranteed favorite among the junior set. The entrance to this eco-themed recreational park leads to a small area with pink flamingos and brightly marked red, blue, yellow, and green parrots. A series of wide palm- or jungle-lined paths meanders away to the 25 different sights and activities available.

Walk straight ahead for the two river trips, which are a great way to start your day. **The Underground River float** is the most popular and the most crowded. Carved through limestone caverns illuminated by natural skylights, the cool-water river flows 6m (20 ft.) below ground level. The **Mayan Village River** drifts along to the Mayan Village, where artisans create handicrafts. Several small waterfalls and a thick bamboo forest punctuate this journey.

Xcaret offers several optional activities that are not included in the all-inclusive price. Six programs to swim with dolphins—an experience of a lifetime—are aimed at both adults and children. After a short educational briefing, swimmers

enter the water to pet and play with the dolphins, culminating in a wild ride in which a pair of dolphins lifts the child from the water.

Snorkel and dive tours are available, as is Seatrek, which allows you to walk on the bottom; and Snuba, which allows you to dive without a tank. Reserve in advance or visit the booths as soon as you arrive. Good for nonswimmers.

Other major attractions scattered around the grounds are the Coral Reef Aquarium, several minor archaeological sites, Jaguar Island, a reproduction Mexican graveyard decorated for **Day of the Dead** celebrations, and the Mayan Village, where you can watch artisans work in various media.

Kids who are into horses or riding will dig the afternoon **Charrería** show, performed by cowboys and riders from the Mexican state of Jalisco. The **Voladores de Papantla** also has lots of kid appeal: Totonac Indians from Veracruz perform this death-defying pre-Columbian ceremony on a pole high above the ground.

No matter how cranky the kids are by late afternoon, don't leave without seeing **Xcaret Spectacular Night** (admission is included in your entrance fee). This full-blown show features 300 costumed performers tracing Mexico's history and culture through music and dance. Wait until you see the burning ball game—an ancient version of field hockey played with oil-soaked balls, struck with short sticks by young men in loincloths; it's still played by some indigenous peoples in Mexico.

Funky decorated buses provide transportation from Cancún's Xcaret terminal on Kukulcán at Km 9; reservations are not mandatory but are recommended. The all-inclusive cost for a day, including transportation, is 931 pesos per adult (special discount of about 200 pesos if you show up after 4pm in the summer or 3pm in the winter). Tickets for kids under 11 are about 20% off.

Take Highway 307 18km (11 miles) north of Tulum, 13km (8 miles) south of Akumal.

⑤ ★★★ **Xel-Ha.** The clear-water lagoons of **Xel-Ha** (Shell-*ha;* ☎ 998/ 884-9422; www.xel-ha.com; admission $36–$75), which means "the place where the water is born," are a subaquatic snorkel paradise run by the managers of Xcaret—but on a more subdued scale. Snorkeling the river and lagoon is the main attraction here—often combined with a visit to the Tulum ruins just a few minutes away by car.

Visitors swim and snorkel in clear water surrounded by thick jungle. Buy an all-inclusive ticket (including meals), or you can rent snorkel equipment for a comfortable float in the calm, fish-filled water. A mini-train delivers you to the beach.

Other attractions include a plant nursery, an apiary for local birds, hives of stingless Maya bees, a turtle camp, and a lovely walking path along the lagoon. What kids love best is the swim with dolphins at **Dolphin's World.** It's very popular, so book as soon as you arrive, if possible (☎ 998/883-0524; $140).

One of the coast's most treasured places, Xel-Ha is well worth a few hours or even a full day's visit—though be warned that in high season it can be overcrowded. **Eco-tip:** Do not wear sunscreen in the water: Wash it off first since it's bad for the marine ecology. Safe sunscreen is sold inside the park.

Aquatic dancing dolphins.

The **Pre-Columbian** Yucatán

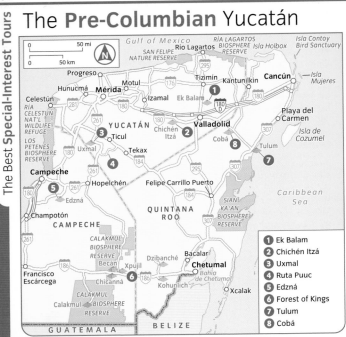

1 Ek Balam
2 Chichén Itzá
3 Uxmal
4 Ruta Puuc
5 Edzná
6 Forest of Kings
7 Tulum
8 Cobá

Three of the Yucatán's five UNESCO World Heritage sites are Maya ruins: Chichén Itzá, Uxmal, and Calakmul. These sophisticated structures continue to dazzle, displaying the Maya's revolutionary innovations in astronomy, which helped them perfect an accurate calendar system and register annual solstices and equinoxes in their civic architecture; letters, making them the only indigenous people of the Americas with a written history—recorded in part in the *stelae* that still stand at some of the following sites; and architecture, which brought us numerous construction techniques still in use today, from corbel arches to honeycombed roof combs. Most of the following ruin sites have accommodations nearby, so you can start exploring first thing in the morning before the crowds descend. START: **Ek Balam is 13km (8 miles) north of the Cuota on the road from Valladolid to Tizimin. Total trip: 1,200km (744 miles).**

1 **Ek Balam.** The compact "Black Jaguar" ruin **Ek Balam** was considered a minor archaeological site until diggers unearthed the great Acropolis pyramid. What they found was a Chenes-style serpent-mouth

entrance to an interior tomb that the Maya had carefully covered over with dirt when they abandoned the city. It's a magnificent work of art, with intricately carved figures. Other structures on-site include La

Rodonda, the oval palace seemingly made of stone drums. Enter the walled site through a four-sided arch, which may have been a ceremonial entry from a *scabe* (sacred road) to the wealthy city. Ek Balam is a gem that's rarely crowded. Stay in Valladolid or onsite at the appealingly rustic **Genesis Retreat** (☎ 998/852-7980; www.genesis retreat.com). *See p 77 for more on Ek Balam.*

Take the road from Tizmin to Valladolid (295) back 13km (8miles) until you reach route 180. Head west for 45 km (28 miles), and take the exit for the town of Pisté.

② ★★★ **Chichén Itzá.** Chichén Itzá, a half-hour drive west of Valladolid, is the Yucatán's most famous and perhaps most fabulous Maya ruin, despite the near-constant throng of admirers it attracts. Go early to avoid the worst of the heat and crowds, and stay for the evening light show.

The talk of the town is **El Castillo** (the castle), an imposing pyramid that dominates its surroundings. The mathematically inclined Maya built it as a giant physical calendar—with 364 steps plus a platform on top and 52 panels on each side—and aligned it to the sun for both equinoxes. The stairway's shadow during the spring equinox forms the shape of a serpent, and thousands of people come to celebrate.

In the largest **ball court** in the Americas—where the Maya played a precursor of soccer/basketball to the death—the acoustic properties render a whisper audible from one end to the other. The imposing playing field has sloped sides and large stone rings that were goal markers. On the southeast corner, two temples, built one over the other, are collectively called the **Temple of the Jaguars.** The lower one has a wonderful carved mural of the city's founding, and the upper one, now off-limits, has faded paintings that depict triumphs in warfare.

Death was obviously an integral part of Maya life, as demonstrated by the **Temple of Skulls,** outside the ballcourt on the plaza, and the **Cenote of Sacrifice.**

The Chac Mool altar atop the Templo de los Guerreros at Chichén Itzá.

The Sacred Cenote at Chichén Itzá, where many sacrificial victims met their deaths.

An archaeological dive into the spectacularly deep *cenote* yielded bones of sacrificial victims, including children (who just as likely may have fallen in).

In the main plaza, the **Group of a Thousand Columns** and **Temple of Warriors** depict a Toltec-Maya style reminiscent of Greco-Roman architecture. At the top of the Warriors Temple—where you can no longer climb—is the famous **Chac Mool:** This ubiquitous statue features a Maya God in recline, with his hands on his stomach cupping a dish used to hold hearts ripped from live sacrifices.

The temple derives its name from the depictions of over 200 warriors carved on columns in front of the entrance. The Group of a Thousand Columns, which once supported a roof to create colonnaded hallways and rooms, may have had more functional than ceremonial uses.

The **Caracol** (meaning "conch shell" or "snail") is one of the most fascinating structures in Chichén. Seen from afar, it looks like a modern celestial observatory, which was probably its purpose. The rounded tower is unlike other Maya structures in that its entrances, staircases, and angles are not aligned with one another. Though window

slots in the walls are aligned with the sun's equinoxes. A stone spiral staircase gave the structure its name.

Stay overnight at the opulent **Hotel Mayaland** (☎ 998/887-2495; www.mayaland.com), with magnificent gardens and king-size rooms, or on the highway to the east at the economical ★ **Dolores Alba** (☎ 985/858-1555; www.doloresalba.com), which has bragging rights to a one-of-a-kind, *cenote*-style swimming pool.

Take the cuota 115 km (71.5 miles) west of Chichén Itzá until you reach Mérida (2 hrs). Head south on route 261 for 80 km (50 miles), about 90 minutes.

A carving at Chichén Itzá.

3 ★★★ Uxmal. The grand ruins of Uxmal (pronounced *Oosh-mahl*) lie 80km (49.5 miles) southeast of Mérida in the heart of a rich archaeological area that includes four other important Maya sites: **Sayil, Kabah, Xlapak,** and **Labná.** Uxmal's rich geometric stone facades are perhaps the most beautiful on the peninsula. As a ruin, it rivals Chichén Itzá in grandeur. Unlike Chichén, however, Uxmal features two very large pyramids: the **Pyramid of the Magician** (aka Pyramid of the Dwarf), an unusual oval-shaped pyramid with massive rounded ends, built in layers over five earlier structures, and the humongous, partially restored **Great Pyramid.**

Other important buildings include the 70-odd-room **Nunnery Quadrangle,** a four-building complex named because of its austere-looking living quarters. The exterior walls, built in the Puuc style with plain bottoms and elaborately decorated upper halves, feature marvelous carvings.

The long, imposing **Governor's Palace** is one of the Maya world's most beautiful buildings, set on a hill atop a platform and decorated with a mosaic, lattice-pattern facade with masks of Chac and other gods. The entire structure is aligned to Venus. The Maya architects who built it also played on the principles of optical illusion by making the two ends slightly lower than the middle. A perfectly straight roofline would have seemed to dip in the center when seen from one end.

The amazing **Dovecote,** or House of Pigeons, is also a long building, crowned with nine triangular crests with roof combs of square holes. It dates from around 800 A.D. and was part of a large, horseshoe-shaped complex.

A good way to see Uxmal is to arrive late in the day, stay overnight, and attend the 8pm light show (ask for English headphones). You can use your ticket to reenter to see the ruins early, before it gets hot. Stay at the venerable **Hacienda Uxmal** (☎ 997/976-2011; www.mayaland.com), or in nearby Santa Elena at the lovely **Flycatcher Inn B&B** (☎ 997/102-0865; www.flycatcherinn.com).

Continue south on route 261 for 24km (15 miles) until you reach Kabah. There are signs for the rest of the ruta.

4 ★★ Ruta Puuc. *Puuc* means hill country, and this route gets its name from the tall hills to the north. A string of ruins south and east of Uxmal makes a rewarding minitour (total trip: 31km/19 miles), or can be used as a path to return to Mérida through small Maya villages and towns. Head south from Santa Elena to the nearby abandoned city, Kabah. Farther south, turn left for the other Puuc ruins; straight ahead leads to Campeche.

Steps at Uxmal.

Ruta Puuc ↑ To Mérida

The ancient city of **4A Kabah** lines both sides of the roadway, so you can't miss it. Park right, enter left. The most notable building is the extraordinary **Palace of Masks,** named for its decorative motif: 250 elephant-nose masks of the rain god, Chac, blanket the exterior. On the other side of the road is what's left of the **Great Temple** and an arch through which a ceremonial *sacbe* (road) connects with Uxmal.

Maya for "place of ants," **4B Sayil** contains a massive masterpiece of Maya architecture, **El Palacio.** Like a classical Greek building, El Palacio is simple and elegant in design, yet imposing *in situ.* The 90-room building stretches across three sweeping levels with a wide central stairway. In front is a circular *chultún,* or

catch basin for rainwater (this is a very dry part of the Yucatán). Sayil is also noted for its many stone phalluses, carved in honor of Yum Keep, the phallic deity. The next ruin is **Xlapak,** 5km (3 miles) east.

The ruins of **4C Labná** are best known for the magnificent corbelled **arch** that was once part of a more elaborate structure. It is the best-preserved arch portal in the Yucatán and gives a hint of how impressively decorated they were. Carvings on one side depict *najs,* traditional Maya houses still dotted around the Yucatán today. The large Puuc-style **palace** is similar to Sayil's but is not in equally good condition. Check out the **Chac mask,** with a carved head in its mouth.

Travel Tip

If you've got the time, continue on that road another 25km (16 miles) to the Loltún Caves, where artifacts of the Yucatán's earliest human inhabitants have been found. It's damp, dark, and close, but very interesting. Tip the guide. To get back to Mérida, retrace your steps or follow signs for 1km (two-thirds

of a mile) to Oxkutzcab and then north to Ticul and Muna.

Continue south along route 261.

5 ★★ Edzná. Easily accessed from Campeche city (40km/25 miles), the impressive ruins of Edzná are dominated by a large plaza called the **Great Acropolis.** Atop this massive platform are several pyramid structures; the most prominent is the **Pyramid of Five Stories.** This pyramid commands a panoramic vista of the expansive ceremonial grounds in the **Great Plaza.** The size of this open grass plaza, complete with an immense viewing stand, hints at Edzná's importance as a Maya ceremonial city.

The structures on the Acropolis face inward to a smaller plaza that was designed so sound would echo off the buildings. And the Pyramid of Five Stories is aligned so that a straight line from its steps follows the line of the setting sun on August 13, the date the Maya were created.

Next to the **Small Acropolis,** a lesser temple platform, dating to the pre-Classic era, is the **Temple of the Stone Masks.** Two huge stucco faces of the sun god, Kinich Ahau, flank the main stairway. The one facing east is a young face, representing dawn. The one facing west is an old man, representing sunset.

Edzná is a great place to wander around for an hour or two, with a guide or on your own. It's all the more amazing when you consider that there are more giant unexcavated ruins about 1km (less than a mile) away. *See p 90 for hotels and restaurants in Campeche.* 🕐 5 hours.

A portal at Labná on the Ruta Puuc.

Labná tops a hill on the Ruta Puuc.

Continue south on Route 261 150km (93 miles) to Route 186 near Francisco Escárcega then head east for 172km (103 miles) on 186 until you reach Xpujil.

6 ★★★ **Forest of Kings.** A stunning array of Maya ruins, strung like pearls along the border of Mexico, Belize, and Guatemala, are known collectively as the "Forest of Kings." They can be accessed off the long, straight road between Chetumal in Quintana Roo and Escárcega in Campeche. This is a tour for adventurous travelers with a fascination with lost Maya cities.

Forest of Kings

The ruins closest to Chetumal are **6A Dzibanché** and neighboring **Kinichná,** two Classic-era cities whose impressive buildings and isolation make a visit more like an exploration. Dzibanché's **Main Plaza,** part of a complex of three sprawling open areas, is home to **Structure II,** a huge pyramid that housed a Maya lord's tomb. It is one of the Maya world's more memorable cities and shouldn't be missed.

The easy-to-reach **6B Kohunlich** site is famous for its Classic-era structure known as *Los Mascarones* (the masks), resplendent with stone faces that represent the ages of the sun. The masks date to circa 500 A.D., although the buildings show a mishmash of styles and periods of occupation. Recent excavations make a circuit of the site possible.

The small ruins of **6C Chicanna, Becán,** and **Xpujil** are all clustered about halfway across the peninsula

outside the town of Xpujil (pronounced *ish*-poo-heel). Xpujil is also a good base from which to explore the Calakmul Biosphere and Rio Bec ruins. Chicanna features a really cool, *Chenes*-style monster-mouth doorway. *Becán,* like a walled city with a moat, contains massive towers and an enclosed plaza. Xpujil boasts the Maya equivalent of skyscrapers. These are easily reached from the roadway.

The international nature preserve of Calakmul Biosphere holds many ruins, notably **6D Calakmul** and **Rio Bec,** a collection of abandoned sites in the jungle that are difficult to access but well worth the trouble. These are principally for those with a die-hard interest in archaeology and nature, or for anyone who wants to go where few have gone before. It's best to take a guide from **Xpujil** or, if you speak Spanish, from the village of **20 de Noviembre.**

From Chetumal take Route 307 north for about two and a half hours until you start to see signs for Tulum. Make a right turn for the ruins just after you pass town.

7 Tulum. Tulum ruin, 131km (81 miles) south of Cancún, is a walled ceremonial city that the Maya still occupied when the Spanish landed in 1517. Its principal attraction is its location, location, location. The pyramid of **El Castillo** and the **Temple of the Wind** sit atop a bluff overlooking the Caribbean Sea, and first-time visitors are stunned by the beautiful view over the water to the east. Fittingly, Tulum's Maya name was *Zama* (place of the dawn).

Below the structures are some small horseshoe-shaped beaches, very popular among visitors who come to take a long swim after a short visit to the ruins. Climb down the new wooden stairs to the sandy shore. Try and visit early or late in the day: Tulum is the third most visited archaeological site in Mexico after Teotihuacán and Chichén Itzá, and it can get hot and very crowded. *See p 75 for other sites, hotels, and restaurants in Tulum.*

Head west on Highway 5 for approximately 39km (24 miles). The highway is newly completed, so your trip should take around 30 minutes.

8 ★★ **Cobá.** Directly inland from Tulum is the expansive Maya site Cobá, a relatively unexcavated city that covers 108 sq. km (42 sq. miles). Until the rise of other large cities in about 1000 A.D., Cobá dominated the lowland Maya culture. It's next to two lakes, which is rare in the Yucatán. Visitors come upon the structures in jungle clearings connected by wide

A facial carving at Kohunlich in the Forest of Kings.

paths dappled by shade from the forest. It's a long walk between structures, so consider hiring a *triciclo* (three-wheeled bicycle pedaled by a Maya) if it's hot. You can do that after you visit **La Iglesia** pyramid, not far from the entrance. Of the major sites, Cobá is the least reconstructed and may disappoint those who expect another Chichén Itzá.

Cobá does boast a steep, 42m (138-ft.) -high pyramid, **Nohoch Mul,** which towers over the jungle. The site is also known for still-standing carved stelae, scattered throughout the excavated areas.

Stay and dine and watch the sunset from the very pleasing **Villas Arqueológicas** hotel on the lake (☎ 222/273-7900; standard rooms start at $59 a night; AE, MC, V).

The ruins of Becán against the clouds in the Forest of Kings.

The Riviera Maya's Best **Spas**

1. Cancún
2. Puerto Morelos
3. Playa Maroma
4. Playa del Carmen
5. Puerto Aventuras
6. Tulum

A health-conscious, luxury spa vacation recommends itself in the Riviera Maya, given the region's mind-bending beauty and the relaxing pace of Mexican life in general. And so it should come as no surprise that some splendid spas have opened recently. Most feature some sort of *temazcal,* the ancient Maya equivalent of a sweat lodge, using herbal-infused waters.

Travel Tip

For additional information on sights, shops, and recommended hotels and restaurants in Cancún, see chapter 7; on Playa del Carmen, see p 120.

1 Cancún. In downtown Cancún, in the middle block of Avenida Yax-chilan, **★★ Xbalamqué** (☎ 998/884-9690; www.xbalamque.com) has good-value accommodations as well as a day spa. The friendly, intimate spa is near a lovely little pool

and surrounded by tropical gardens. Xbalamqué offers an unpretentious environment, a yoga room, and a full-service beauty salon.

★★★ Aqua (Km 12.5.; ☎ 800/343-7821 in the U.S.; www.fiesta americana.com) has raised the bar for quality, with a stunning, stylish, and sensual new hotel and spa. Sophisticated travelers appreciate chic decor, buzz, and the modern amenities. The intimate spa is among the hotel's most notable attractions, offering a blend of Eastern, pre-Columbian, and Western health and beauty treatments. Outdoor Pilates, Tai Chi, and yoga classes are held daily, and massage cabins are available on the beach.

In the hotel zone, ★★ **JW Marriott** (Km 14.5; ☎ 888/813-2776 in the U.S.; www.marriott.com) offers rejuvenating spa treatments in a huge Maya-inspired luxury spa facility high above the sparkling Caribbean Sea. It affords guests a high-quality health and fitness experience in Cancún's largest private spa.

The gorgeous ★★ **Westin Resort** (Km 20; ☎ 888/625-5144 in the U.S.; www.starwoodhotels.com) boasts **Heavenly Spa,** a full-service luxury spa facility. With strikingly austere architecture and an impressive use of stone and marble, the Westin is one of the most elegant resorts in Cancún. The high-class spa emphasizes its Yucatán inspirations with a signature Mayan Mystic Massage treatment.

One of Cancún's most appealing spas is ★★ **Le Meridien** (Km 14;

☎ 800/543-4300 in the U.S.; www. lemeridiencancun.com), which features the elegant **Spa del Mar.** The Spa of the Sea—a sophisticated European-style facility—includes steam and inhalation rooms, saunas, Jacuzzis, plunge pools, Swiss showers, a waterfall whirlpool, and 14 specialized treatment rooms. It's natural that a seaside spa like Meridien would specialize in hydrotherapy to wash away your cares.

❷ **Puerto Morelos.** Small boutique hotel **Ceiba del Mar**'s (☎ 998/872-8060; www.ceibadel mar.com) holistic and aromatherapy spa's signature treatment is a ★★ **Top' Nikte** massage (Maya for cocoon). It begins with a 50-minute relaxing massage, followed by a body wrap of soft cotton soaked in an infusion of aromatic herbs. They also feature Temazcal, an ancestral indigenous ritual created to purify and renew the mind, body, and spirit. The sweat lodge's steam uses herbal aromatherapy.

A treatment at Le Meridien Spa.

An outdoor massage at the Cancún Meridien.

By contrast, the steam room at ★ **Desire Resort** (☎ 998/872-8293; www.desirecancun.com) can get a little, er, steamy. Desire exemplifies one of the hottest new concepts in hotels—an all-inclusive, hedonistic lifestyle resort and spa. The adults-only, couples-only hotel is clothing optional, except in places such as the dining room. My favorite of their traditional spa offerings is the hot-stone massage, which uses heated smooth stones as deep heat therapy—a good way to loosen the muscle tightness brought on by sucking in your stomach all the time. It's a very popular resort among those who are comfortable in their own skin.

❸ **Playa Maroma.** The stunning beach at Playa Maroma, south of Puerto Morelos, is home to the ★★ **Maroma Hotel** (☎ 998/872-8200; www.orientexpresshotels.com). The Maroma has always been an exclusive getaway destination; a frequent host to the wealthy and well-known. Although Orient Express Hotels has recently expanded the number of rooms, the intimate ★★ **Kinan Spa** is still a good place to be touched by human hands. Kinan means "energy of the sun" in Maya.

Facing the sea in alleged astrological harmony, the spa offers a variety of relaxing treatments. One that's sure to stimulate and perhaps whet your appetite for more is the couples-only Aphrodisia Chocolate Invigoration, a very sensual massage.

❹ **Playa del Carmen.** A few kilometers north of Playa, the ★★★ **Mayakoba** (☎ 800/257-7544 in the U.S.; www.fairmont.com) is a new super luxury resort in the exclusive Fairmont chain of worldwide hotels. Inspired by local Maya healing traditions using indigenous plants and herbs, their Willow Stream Spa is renowned for its natural setting and for pampering treatments. They're also sensitive to sore muscles or sore feelings from the hotel's challenging golf course.

A pleasing day spa in the center of downtown Playa del Carmen, the serene ★ **Spa Itzá** (☎ 984/803-2588; www.spaitza.com) is in a secluded garden in the Calle Corazon district on 12th Street, just off 5th Avenue. Their array of massages includes shiatsu, floor massage, deep tissue, lymphatic drainage, and their Itzá Special, a blend of deep tissue, Swedish, and shiatsu.

The **Royal Hideaway** (☎ 800/999-9182 in the U.S.; www.royalhideaway.com) is an all-inclusive resort on a great beach in Playacar, an exclusive planned community just to the south of downtown Playa del Carmen. Their beauty salon and spa offers French-trained estheticians to consult on skin care and a variety of indulgences such as Hawaiian Lomi Lomi massages.

❺ **Puerto Aventuras.** The "Port of Adventures" features a unique, water-inspired spa, aptly named ★★ **Casa del Agua** (☎ 984/873-5184; www.casadelagua.com). Originally built as a luxurious private beachfront home, the Water House features intimate B&B suites as well as complete day-spa services. Book

The Fiesta Americana Resort in Cancún.

a room in this tropical paradise villa or rent it in its entirety for the utmost privacy. All individualized spa services are by appointment only; schedule them prior to your arrival and receive a 10% discount. Although it's not a new wrinkle in skin care, its especially relaxing to get wrapped up in seaweed and packed in rainforest mud.

6 Tulum. Along the incredible beaches in Tulum, ★★★ **Maya Spa Wellness Center** (☎ 800/123-3278; www.maya-spa.com) is a holistic spa in idyllic surroundings. Rustic, tropical cabaña accommodations are available at its affiliated EcoTulum hotels: Cabanas Copal, Azulik, and Zahra. They are all clothing optional.

The rustic spa center features a Temazcal, a unique Maya sweat lodge ceremony that purges the body of noxious toxins. The spa's holistic activities program features yoga exercises, Maya astrology, corn readings, crystal therapies, and treatments performed by self-proclaimed local shamans who use indigenous plants. They also offer a

lucid dreaming course and a flotation chamber. What a trip.

An early hideaway spot, 7km (4.5 miles) down the Boca Paila Road, is the famous ★ **Ana y José Hotel & Spa** (☎ 998/887-5470; www.anayjose.com). This beautiful bungalow beachfront hotel was one of the first hostelries on the edge of the Sian Ka'an Biosphere, a protected nature reserve. Originally offering isolated rustic cabanas and a small eatery, the hotel now features modern rooms without sacrificing the sense that you've gotten away from it all. Over the years, Ana and José continued to grow with the demand and now feature the Om Spa as part of their amenities. As if the idyllic setting isn't relaxing enough, guests can enjoy spa therapies such as their "Mayan Secret." This unique offering features a relaxing massage using clay mud from a *cenote,* followed by a fruit body wrap. As part of the mystique, they burn copal incense, which the Maya use in religious ceremonies.

Mud facials are a popular spa treatment in the Yucatán.

Extreme Yucatán

Gulf of Mexico

Mérida
YUCATÁN
Cancún

Area of detail

Campeche

CAMPECHE

QUINTANA
ROO

Chetumal

Caribbean
Sea

GUATEMALA   BELIZE

0   100 mi

0   100 km

RÍA LAGARTOS
BIOSPHERE RESERVE

Isla Holbox

Isla Contoy
Bird Sanctuary

Chiquilá

Punta Sam
Puerto Juarez
Cancún

Isla
Mujeres

Kantunilkin

Mérida Libre

Cuota (Toll)

**Puerto
Morelos**

Ek Balam

307

←To Mérida

180
D

180

Playa del Carmen

Xcaret   ❶

180

Valladolid

Paamul
Xpu-Ha

San Miguel
de Cozumel

Chichén Itzá

YUCATÁN

Cobá

Akumal ❷

❸

Isla de
Cozumel

Tankah

Xel-Ha Lagoon
National Park

Tulum ❹

Tulum

QUINTANA
ROO

295

307

184

Felipe
Carrillo
Puerto

Vigia
Chico

Punta Allen

Bahía de la Ascensión

184

SIAN
KA'AN
BIOSPHERE
RESERVE

Bahía del
Espíritu Santo

Caribbean
Sea

307

Los Limones

Lázaro Cárdenas

Dzibanché

Bacalar

Majahual

Banco
Chinchorro

186

Chetumal

Kohunlich
❺

BELIZE

Xcalak

0   20 mi

0   20 km

N

Maya archaeological site ≋
Cuota (toll highway) ═══

❶ Playa del Carmen
❷ Akumal
❸ Aktun Chen

❹ Tulum
❺ Forest of Kings

You can leave your surfboard at home, but don't forget your parachute, your kitesurfing equipment, or your biodegradable sunscreen. You might be surprised to learn that as idyllic as the beaches are in the Yucatán, they don't produce many surfable waves. Don't fret; there are plenty of other activities you can take part in that will make you feel like you've just caught the "big one." If you don't surf, even better—many of these adrenaline activities are just as fun for the spectator. START: **Take Highway 307 for 70km (43 miles) south of Cancún. Total length: approximately 700km (434 miles).**

A Note on Hotels & Restaurants

For additional information on sights, shops, hotels, dining, and nightlife in Playa del Carmen, see p 120.

1 Skydiving in Playa del Carmen. Most visitors' very first glimpse of the region is of its azure waters and pristine white beaches, seen from the sky above on a flight into town. If you want to take your flight experience one step further, consider jumping out the next time you're in that aircraft. ★★ **Skydive Playa** (☎ 984/873-0192; www.skydive cancun.com; $229 for a tandem dive,

$130 for the video) offers visitors the choice of tandem dives with experienced guides or solo advanced freefall dives (6-hour training required).

Take Highway 307 approximately 37 km (23 miles) south of Playa del Carmen.

2 Diving in Akumal's Underworld. Been wondering what lurks beneath the surface of the legendary *cenotes*? If you've got an openwater diving certification, you can find the answers on a SCUBA diving experience unique to the Yucatán. ★★★ **Akumal Dive Adventures**'s (☎ 888/425-8625 in the U.S.; www.akumaldiveadventures. com) certified guides take divers

Windsurfing, or "sailboarding" at Cozumel Island.

through *cenotes* to a underwater caverns filled with ancient stalactite and stalagmite formations. If you're not certified, rent snorkeling gear from Akumal Dive and explore the *cenotes* closer to the surface.

Continue south on 307 for approximately 3 km (2 miles). The site is in front of the Bahia Principe hotel. If you hit Xel Ha, you've gone too far.

③ Canopy Touring in Aktun Chen. It's a bird, it's a plane, it's. . . you! Canopy touring, or zip-lining, is popular in resort destinations around Latin America as a fun, eco-friendly way to experience the local flora and fauna. Participants are strapped into a harness similar to those used in rock climbing and hooked up by a pulley-like device to a series of cables strung across the jungle ceiling. The result is a Tarzan-like tour (or Superman-like, if you remember to bring your tights). For information, call ☎ **984/877-8550** or visit www.aktunchen.com.

Gear Up

Before you strap on a water ski, jump on a wake board, or step on a skateboard, you'll probably want to make sure you've got the right gear for your

Kiteboarding, Tulum.

adventure. At **Koko Dogz,** Avenida Nader Plaza (☎ 998/887-3635; www.kokodogz.com) in Cancún, you can find everything from body boards to sunglasses. It's also a popular gathering spot for local extreme sports enthusiasts. You can also rent windsurfing equipment at their second location in Puerto Morelos on the beach by the Hotel Ojo de Agua.

Keep going south on route 307 to the hotel zone of Tulum. The school is on the right hand side of the strip.

④ Kiteboarding in Tulum. What do you get when you combine windsurfing, snowboarding, paragliding, and wakeboarding? An adrenaline sport called kiteboarding. The rider gets on a board that is propelled into the air by wind in its sail. Learn how to attempt gravity-defying tricks from Tulum's **Mexico Kan Tours' kiteboarding school** (☎ 984/140-7870; www.mexicokan tours.com); the wind season is long there—from November to June—and the water is warm enough that you don't need a wetsuit.

Approximately 122km (76 miles) south of Cancún on Highway 307. Continue south on Highway 307 until it joins Highway 186 going west. Turn left at the exit for Francisco Villa.

⑤ Adventure in the Forest of Kings. Normally all-inclusive hotels and heart-pounding adventure don't mix. But **Explorean Kohunlich** (☎ 800/504-5000 in Mexico; www. explorean.com), in the middle of the jungle, has managed to buck that trend. Included in the nightly room price are daily adventure activities like rappelling down a 70m (230-ft.) cliff, kayaking up Rio Hondo, or biking to the Dzibanché ruins. *For more information on the Explorean, see p 83.* ●

5 The Best **Regional Tours**

The **Riviera Maya**

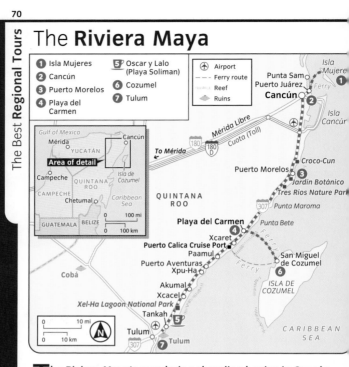

1. Isla Mujeres
2. Cancún
3. Puerto Morelos
4. Playa del Carmen
5. Oscar y Lalo (Playa Soliman)
6. Cozumel
7. Tulum

✈ Airport
--- Ferry route
Reef
Ruins

T he Riviera Maya's wandering shoreline begins in Cancún and runs along the azure Caribbean Sea south to Tulum. These are some of the world's most beautiful beaches, with warm blue waters and white sand never hot to the touch. Although all-inclusive resorts are intruding on formerly isolated shores, beach lovers can still find paradise in smaller boutique hotels. START: **From Cancún, Take Avenida Bonampak north from Kukulcán Boulevard and turn right on Avenida Lopéz Portillo, 3km (2 miles) to the Punta Sam ferry. Better yet, ditch the car and take either ferry from Puerto Juárez, 1km (¾ mile) before Punta Sam. Catch any bus marked "Puerto Juárez" from Avenida Tulum, downtown. Total trip: 140km (87 miles).**

A Note on Hotels & Restaurants

For additional information on sights, shops, and recommended hotels and restaurants in Isla Mujeres, see p 102; Playa del Carmen, see p 120;

Cozumel, see p 96; and Cancún, see p 129.

1 **Isla Mujeres.** The tiny, picturesque island of Isla Mujeres (Island of Women) is visible from Cancún's

Previous page: A burro in traditional gear, Cozumel.

shore, but the lovely fishing village of La Isla is much more relaxed; streets are cobblestone; buildings are limited to three stories, so less comes between you and the beach.

The island is known for its endearing hospitality, and accommodations vary from rustic to posh-boutique. Many visitors arrive from Cancún's hotel zone on catamaran boats from Playa Linda, but I prefer the less expensive people ferries that run from Puerto Juárez, just north of downtown.

Isla Mujeres is well known for its snorkeling, sunbathing on powdery white beaches, and swimming. Gift, jewelry, and beachwear shops rub shoulders with economical ethnic and seafood restaurants. The downtown is made for walking, but rental golf carts and motorbikes are the preferred way to see the rest of the island. The southern and western shores are home to the nature-themed amusement park ★★ **Garrafón,** the pirate Mundaca's ruined hacienda, a turtle research center, a swim with dolphins, dramatic cliffs with a Maya ruin, and a lighthouse. The northern and western beaches afford the best swimming and spectacular sunsets, while the rough and rocky Caribbean shoreline is perfect for shell collecting.

Take the car ferry back to Punta Sam, just north of the people ferry at Puerto Juárez, and drive 7km (4.5 miles) to downtown Cancún.

❷ **Cancún.** Mexico's most popular resort city continues to draw hordes of year-round vacationers to its ideal weather, clear blue waters, and fine white beaches. A relatively new vacation destination, it has developed quickly since the late 1970s because of its proximity to the United States. (New York, for example, is less than 3½ hours away by plane.)

Cancún's downtown is vibrant, attracting shoppers, diners, and budget-conscious travelers; but the Hotel Zone—on a 27km (17-mile)-long, pencil-thin island shaped like a figure "7,"—is what people mean when they say "Cancún."

Sprinkled along the line of big resort hotels are more intimate accommodations, gourmet restaurants, nightclubs and bars, shopping malls, golf courses, marinas offering watersports and, of course, gorgeous beaches. The Isla Mujeres Bay beaches on the short side of the figure 7 are calmer, with swimming in warm, protected waters. Facing the Caribbean, beaches are dramatically beautiful—check out **Playa Delfines** at Km 17—but there can be heavy surf.

Some visitors use the Hotel Zone as a base to explore more of the Yucatán and Riviera Maya, taking any of the many day trips available. *See p 131.*

Drive south from Cancún 36km (22 miles) on Highway 307 and turn left at the traffic light; go 3km (2 miles) to the square.

Garrafon Natural Reef Park on Isla Mujeres.

A palapa on the beach at the Westin Resort & Spa in Cancún.

③ Puerto Morelos. If the high-energy atmosphere of Cancún or Playa isn't for you, try **Puerto Morelos.** This small fishing-village-turned-bedroom-community attracts low-key tourists who don't need their pleasures spoon-fed.

The **snorkeling** here is as good as, if not better than, the more famous spots on Cozumel. Just a few hundred yards off the broad white beach is a colorful coral reef with a large variety of curious fish. Another attraction for active tourists is **wind- and kitesurfing** inside the reef's protected waters.

The town offers visitors diverse lodging: rustic wooden cabañas facing the mangroves, modern hotels, beachfront condos, and apartments and private homes available for a week or longer.

Take Highway 307 for 32km (20 miles) south to Playa del Carmen.

④ Playa del Carmen. If an urban, somewhat bohemian beach destination sounds like fun, join the many Europeans and North Americans who pack the city of **Playa del Carmen** on the Riviera Maya. Playa is *the* "in" place for shopping, dining, people watching, and more shopping around the main drag,

Fifth Avenue (Quinta Avenida), which runs over a kilometer in length and is packed with people, day and night. Oh yeah, there's also a gorgeous beach somewhere beneath all those tanned bodies.

Just a dozen years ago, Playa was best known as the departure point for the ferry to Cozumel, only 19km (12 miles) across the channel. A few hotels, some shops, and a couple of restaurants filled the needs of its transient visitors. Then, somebody noticed its gorgeous beach, reef for snorkeling, and turquoise waters, and wondered why bother to go anywhere else?

A vacation in Playa appeals to travelers who are young or young at heart who want to soak up sun, suds, and the social scene. Day-trippers or overnight visitors appreciate the multinational food selection and shopping options—everything from fun junk to fine jewelry.

About halfway down the Riviera Maya coast, Playa is good for archaeological excursions or day trips to places such as nearby Xcaret. But for unique, off-track ecotours of the jungle and the coast, try ★★ **Playa's Alltournative,** Fifth Avenue, between Km 12 & 14 (☎ 984/873-2036; www.alltournative.com).

One of the last places for lunch on a deserted beach, with no other buildings in sight, is **5 ★★ Oscar y Lalo's** (☎ 984/804-4189) on Playa Soliman, Km 241.5, south of Playa. Swim in the sea or their cenote, snooze in a hammock, snorkel the reef, sea kayak, or just hang out. The beer is cold and the fresh fish is prepared as you like it.

Ditch the car and take the people ferry from Playa to Cozumel. Long-term vacationers can send their car via the ferry at Puerto Calica, 14km (9 miles) south of Playa.

6 Cozumel. Cozumel ranks among the top five dive destinations in the world, given the towering reefs that line its southwest shore. The downtown gets crowded during the day with cruise-ship passengers, but the mornings and evenings belong to locals and island guests.

Less than 10% of warm and cozy Cozumel is developed, principally around the island's only town, San Miguel. The eastern, windward side and northern shore are virtually uninhabited; the southern leeward coast, facing west, features occasional beach clubs and some all-inclusive hotels.

The Main Plaza and adjacent side streets are full of gift and flea-market shops peddling handicrafts, beachwear, and souvenirs; restaurants with tempting dining pleasures; and some economy hotels that cater to divers. Avenida Melgar is the major north/south road paralleling the harbor. Several popular jewelry and diamond shops and the original Los Cinco Sols gifts can be found there. Farther north leads to the international airport and the **Cozumel Country Club** golf course (☎ 987/872-9570; www.cozumelcountryclub.com.mx).

Take a taxi to Chankanaab Park for a day of snorkeling, picnicking, and swimming with dolphins, or visit one of the beaches south of town. Divers and open-water snorkelers have ample choice of approved tour providers. Rent a car or motorbike to do the loop road around the entire island; the windward side is wildly fascinating with a few seafood restaurants right on the beach.

Visitors can fly here directly, connect in Cancún, or take the half-hour ferry ride from Playa, mentioned earlier.

Take Highway 307 for 63km (39 miles) south to Tulum.

A Golden Iguana at Laguna Chankanab National Park in Cozumel.

An Olmec head in Chankanaab Natural Park in Cozumel.

7 Tulum. When people say "Tulum," they could be talking about the *pueblo* on the highway, the ruined Maya city at the edge of town, or the beaches along the Boca Paila Road. Tulum *pueblo* doesn't have much besides some worthwhile restaurants and economy hotels. But it's close enough to the beach (3km/2 miles) to attract budget-minded travelers. A new airport and road to the beach are fueling rapid development as well as concern from environmentalists.

The ruins of the walled city of Tulum are Mexico's most visited archaeological site; thus, busloads of cruise passengers and tours make an intimate visit difficult. Tulum looks its best early in the morning or late afternoon, when it's less hot, sunny, and crowded. Stand on the edge of the cliff (you can no longer climb the pyramid) and look over the ocean to experience the area's beauty. Bring a swimsuit to cool off on the beach below. *For detailed information, see p 60.*

The Boca Paila Road, which runs along the shore into the Sian Ka'an Biosphere, has sprouted hotels like coconut palms along its white sand. It's a beachcomber favorite, but you can still find pockets of paradise and some lonely stretches. Accommodations range from rustic, sand-floor cabañas to small luxury hotels, and several enticing beach-shack eateries are perfect for long lunches or romantic dinners. Electricity turns off at 11pm.

Beachfront at the Occidental Grande in Cozumel.

Where to **Stay & Dine**

★★★ **Ana y Jose** TULUM *MEXI-CAN* This landmark hotel and restaurant lures travelers down the Boca Paila Road, toward the Sian Ka'an Biosphere, with rustic and luxury accommodations, a fine white-sand beach, and a Mexican restaurant. Even though it has a small pool with a waterfall and candlelit *al fresco* dining, Ana y Jose's is best known for its quiet privacy and gorgeous beach. *Boca Paila Rd.* ☎ *984/871-2476. www.anayjose. com. 23 units. Suites $248–$399. Entrees 180–250 pesos. MC, V. Restaurant 7:30am–10pm.*

★★ **Bodo's** PUERTO MORELOS *INTERNATIONAL/SEAFOOD* The world is so small these days, it's hardly surprising to find a fabulous little German restaurant in a Mexican beach town. With linen-covered wood tables in an air-conditioned storefront, Bodo's shines with such delicious dishes as Weiner Schnitzel and other European specialties. Plus there's always fresh fish, shrimp, or lobster on the menu. *Av. Javier Rojo Gomez.* ☎ *998/180-8920. Main courses $10–$25. No credit cards. Open Thurs–Tues 2–10pm.*

★★ **Ceiba del Mar** PUERTO MORELOS *INTERNATIONAL* The large, well-appointed rooms here are in white, three-story, *palapa*-roofed buildings trimmed in natural wood. Each features a balcony or terrace facing the beach. Ceiba boasts a free-form infinity pool, two quality restaurants, and luxury spa facilities, including a *temezcal* (Maya sweat lodge). *North Rd. Km 1.5.* ☎ *877/545-6221 in the U.S. or 998/872-8060. www.ceibadelmar.*

Mariachis in Playa del Carmen.

com. All-inclusive rates start at $200. AE, MC, V.

★★ **Pelícanos** PUERTO MORELOS *SEAFOOD* This informal covered dining patio overlooks the beach and fishing pier—especially nice when it's hot and the sea breeze is up. While it's not always locally caught *mariscos,* everything they serve is well prepared and tasty. *On the corner of Square & the beach. No phone. Entrees $8–$15. MC, V. Open daily for breakfast, lunch, & dinner.*

★★★ **Zamas** TULUM *SEAFOOD* One of the most popular cabaña hotels along Tulum's white-powder beaches, Zamas offers romantic beachfront accommodations in rustic but cute *palapa* bungalows spread along a rocky beach. Qué Fresco is their renowned seafood restaurant. *Boca Paila Rd.* ☎ *984/877-8523. www.zamas.com. Beachfront $150–$175, oceanview $180, garden $120–$145. MC, V.*

The **Central Yucatán**

1 Valladolid   3 Río Lagartos
2 Ek Balam   4 Chichén Itzá

0 ___ 20 mi
0 ___ 20 km

Just 2 hours away from Cancún's airport—but a world away from prepackaged vacations—the center of the Yucatán peninsula offers travelers a chance to explore ancient Maya ruins, Spanish Colonial–era history, ecotourism opportunities, and a town that time forgot. It's ideal for a short tour when you have a week or less.
START: **Take the Cuota toll road from Cancún, just south of the airport entrance on Highway 307, or follow Avenida Lopéz Portillo west from downtown until it becomes the Mérida Libre, Highway 180, a slow road through Maya villages. Valladolid is 152km (94 miles) from Cancún. Total trip: 296km (184 miles) from Cancún.**

Travel Tip

For additional information on sights, shops, and recommended hotels and restaurants in Valladolid, see p 124.

1 **Valladolid.** Colonial and quaint, Valladolid is a vital city about half-way between Cancún and Mérida. It

played a central role in the history of the Yucatán, first as the Maya city of Zací, conquered by Conquistadors, and then during the bloody Caste War of the 1800s, when the Maya revolted against their Yucatecan oppressors and sacked the city.

These days it makes an interest-ing, quick stop on the way to the Maya ruins, or a rewarding base for your Central Yucatán travels. Highlights of downtown Valladolid include its pretty **Main Plaza,** where Maya women sell handicrafts under large shade trees, and the **Cathedral of San Gervacio,** a huge, thick-walled church facing the plaza. The surrounding buildings date from the late 16th and 17th centuries, and many now house shops and eateries. Stop in **Yalat** on calles 39 and 40 for some of the finest local art and handicrafts available, or **Mercado de Artensanías de Valladolid** at calles 39 and 44 for less elegant, less expensive stuff.

On the corner of the Main Plaza, the **Palacio Municipal** features historical painted murals and a good view of the park.

On the busy corner of calles 40 and 41, ★★ **Portales Restaurant** (no phone) has occupied its spot under the Moorish arches for over 100 years. Sit outside and sip a refreshing horchata (rice-milk drink) while the world passes by.

A few blocks from the center of town is the **Cenote Zací,** offering a profound look into the watery underworld, and, in the opposite direction, the **Church of San Bernardino** and the **Ex-Convento of Sisal,** a religious complex with some of the oldest Catholic structures in the Western Hemisphere. Approach the church from **Calle 41A,** a beautiful colonial street known as the "Walkway of the Friars."

Only a few kilometers west of Valladolid, on the road to Chichén Itzá, are **Cenote Xke'ken** and **Samula,** two fascinating caverns where an underground river forms a subterranean lake. See p 42.

Driving directions to Ek Balam: Leave Valladolid on Calle 40 north, cross over the *Cuota,* and after 12km (7.5 miles), look for signs on the right.

The Palacio Municipal in Valladolid.

❷ **Ek Balam.** About 15km (9.5 miles) north of Valladolid off the road to Río Lagartos is a turn for the Ek Balam (Black Jaguar) ruins. These impressive Maya ruins have yet to be discovered by swarms of bus-tour groups from Cancún, which means a visit here is unhurried. When Ek Balam's large pyramid was first excavated in 1999, archaeologists discovered a huge, well-preserved monster-mouth entrance into a tomb.

Well before the Spanish arrived, Ek Balam's Maya built a wall in front of the monster-mouth entry and filled it in with dirt and rubble. Because Maya cities were regularly abandoned and then repopulated, they probably planned to return and uncover it again. The huge pyramid at Ek Balam, a different style than Chichén's, is in excellent condition, well worth a visit and a climb. From the top, the pyramid at Cobá is visible. For more details about Ek Balam, see p 54.

A fisherman and tern in Rio Lagartos.

Stay in Valladolid or nearby at the pleasant rustic hotel, ★★ **Genesis Retreat** (☎ 985/852-7980; www.genesisretreat.com), with a nice pool and friendly hosts.

Continue north from Ek Balam through the city of Tizimin, the center of horse and cattle country, and drive another 53km (33 miles), about 45 minutes, on a good road.

③ Rio Lagartos. The lush lagoons of Rio Lagartos, on the northern coast of the Yucatán, are home to thousands of pink flamingos that nest and feed in its shallows, making the area a popular bird-watching and ecotourism destination.

From the fishing village of the same name, arrange a 2- to 4-hour tour in a launch boat that visits several flamingo feeding grounds in protected national parkland.

The poorest section of the fishing village of Rio Lagartos is on the way into town. Men will approach your car offering trips as you enter;

it's OK to say yes, but verify the price with the authorized cooperative at the harbor kiosk. A 1-hour-plus excursion runs about 400 pesos. To see all the flocks in a 4-hour round-trip, the cost is about 650 to 700 pesos a boat.

A good side trip from the fork in the road before Rio Lagartos is nearby Las Coloradas, which features salt mountains that have been harvested by the Maya for more than a thousand years.

You'll have to return to Valladolid for better accommodations, but good seafood is available in Rio Lagartos at the restaurant in the **Punta Ponto hotel,** on the *malecón.* Drink with the men cantina-style at **Torreja,** next to the lighthouse. *For more information on Rio Lagartos, see p 42.*

Return toward Valladolid and drive west on the bypass until it rejoins Highway 180, *Mérida Libre.* You can also get on the *Cuota* for about 40km (25 miles) and exit at the next toll for Chichén Itzá.

④ Chichén Itzá. The ancient Maya city of Chichén Itzá is the crown jewel of Central Yucatán. These magnificent ruins can be seen in a few hours, or explored over 2 or more days, including an entertaining evening light show. It can get very hot and sunny in the open grass areas of the ruins, so wear a hat, carry a sunbrella and a bottle of water, and slather on the sunscreen beforehand.

The big attraction of these thousand-plus-year-old ruins is Chichén's towering central pyramid, **El Castillo.** To your left is the **Ball Court,** with its amazing acoustic characteristics, and the gruesome **Platform of the Skulls,** where carved stone faces of victims gaze out from their ill-fated lineup. The deep **Sacred Cenote,** where people were sacrificed to the underworld by being thrown over the side, is a long walk up a *sacbé* path.

Other highlights of Chichén include the Greco-Roman–looking **Group of a Thousand Columns;** the impressively large **Nunnery; El Caracol,** which looks almost exactly like a modern celestial observatory; and the **Temple of the Warriors,** with the original statue of Chac Mool presiding on

The macabre Platform of the Skulls, Chichén Itzá.

top—Mayanist scholars think it may have held human hearts, cut from living victims. You can no longer climb the platform, but the statue is visible from the ground.

Stay nearby this must-see site at the hotels just outside the back entrance, or in Valladolid, a half-hour drive away. *For more information on the Maya ruins & recommended hotels and restaurants near Chichén Itzá, see p 55.*

The Templo de los Guerreros at Chichén Itzá.

Campeche & **Southern Quintana Roo**

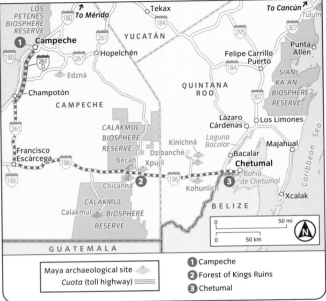

Maya archaeological site ≋
Cuota (toll highway) ═══

1 Campeche
2 Forest of Kings Ruins
3 Chetumal

Few tourists venture down this path, which leaves savvy travelers with an unheralded array of Maya ruins hidden in the jungle, a colonial-era World Heritage seaside city once fortified against frequent pirate attacks, ecotourism in Central America's largest biosphere, an inland lake of seven colors, and Chetumal city, gateway to Belize. START: **An airport serves Campeche from Mexico City and Cancún. First-class ADO buses depart Cancún's downtown bus station several times a day. To drive, take the Cuota to Mérida, then head south on Highway 261. Or reverse this itinerary and drive south from Cancún on Highway 307 through Bacalar to Chetumal, then head west on Highway 186 to Escarcega, and then north on Highway 261 to Campeche. Round-trip length: 425km (264 miles), Campeche to Chetumal.**

A Note on Hotels & Restaurants

For additional information on sights, shops, and recommended hotels and restaurants in Campeche, see p 90.

1 **Campeche** (495km/307 miles SW of Cancún). The delightful city of Campeche, on the Gulf coast around 2 hours south of Mérida, was designated a **World Heritage Site** in 2000 by the United Nations. It is a living-history museum, with narrow cobblestone streets and colonial-era buildings awash in authentic period colors.

Campeche is conveniently compact; most of what you want to experience is within **Centro Historico's ramparts,** built to deter pirate attacks. Not all the walls have survived, but the **Baluartes**—firing positions that once bristled with cannons—make for an interesting walking tour. Begin at the **Parque Principal,** Main Plaza, and see the imposing **Cathedral de la Concepción.**

The **Baluarte de la Soledad** is a Museum of Maya *stelae* or carved pillars. At the **Puerta de Tierra** (land gate), original 18th-century guns still guard the city entrance. Three times a week, a **Light and Sound Spectacular** takes place here; performers walk on the balustrade and stage a swordfight. The **Baluarte de San Carlos** houses the city museum, with an 18th-century dungeon harkening back to when the site was a military prison.

On a flanking hill, high above the city, sits **Fuerte San Miguel,** a well-preserved 18th-century fortress overlooking the harbor. Its excellent little **museum** features a priceless Maya jade mask and artifacts from the ruins of **Calakmul** (p 60).

Campeche is surprisingly close to the great Maya ruin of **Edzná.** This classical site boasts a religious complex known as the **Great Acropolis,** which rises above a very large open-air ceremonial plaza. The acropolis contains five flanking pyramids, built in varying styles. The most prominent—the **Pyramid of Five Stories**—doubled as a royal palace.

Drive out from Campeche on Avenida Pedro Moreno, toward the airport, and take the toll road, Highway 261, for Champoton. Turn left (east), in Escarcega, on Highway 186 for Xpujil and Chetumal. Ruins are accessed from this main road across the peninsula.

❷ Forest of Kings Ruins. The southern part of Quintana Roo and Campeche states is home to many impressive, rarely visited Maya ruins. In Campeche's 71,600-hectare (179,000-acre) **Calakmul Biosphere Reserve** lie the ruins of **Rio Bec,** including the city of **Calakmul.** Look for the single-lane entrance road on your right at Km 97, west of Xpujil. It's a multiday effort to see, so if that's too much, visit the more easily accessed ruins on the border of Campeche and Quintana Roo: **Chicanna,** with a great Chenes monster-mouth doorway; **Becán,** which features towers

Traditional Yucatecan architecture in Campeche.

The Baluarte San Carlos in Campeche.

and a moat; and **Xpujil,** which boasts a Maya version of skyscrapers. All are close to the road, and you can visit each in a half-hour without doing them a disservice.

The ruins near Chetumal are **Dzibanché** and **Kinichná,** two nearly deserted classic-era sites within walking distance of each other, but well off the highway. **Kohunlich** is a ruined lowland city known for its **Pyramid of the**

The Maya site of Xpujil in Quintana Roo.

Masks. These stucco face designs date from around 500 A.D.

Continue west on Highway 186 until it joins Highway 307. Turn right (south) for Chetumal, or left (north) for Lake Bacalar.

3 Chetumal (379km/235 miles south of Cancún). The capital of the state of Quintana Roo is Chetumal, a rather undistinguished-looking city on Belize Bay. Despite its governmental status, it has a less Mexican, more *laissez-faire* Caribbean attitude, enhanced by its wooden houses and proximity to English-speaking Belize.

Known as the cradle of the Mestizo race, Chetumal is where the first Spanish-Maya children were born. A lengthy and inviting *malecón* (boardwalk) wanders along the broad bay, and Chetumal's wonderful **Museum of the Maya** (☎ 983/832-6838) is a must-see. Downtown on Avenida Héroes, it offers a comprehensive look at the Yucatán's history and a multistory, wheeled Maya calendar. North of Chetumal is the large ★★★ **Laguna Bacalar,** or Lake of Seven Colors. **Fort Bacalar,** in the town of the same name, makes a brief but interesting historical stop. You can bypass Chetumal's downtown by staying on the lakeshore.

Where to **Stay & Dine**

★★ **Chicanna Ecovillage** XPUJIL/ CHICANNA   Across the highway from the Chicanna Maya ruins, this ecologically themed resort welcomes guests to well-appointed accommodations in South Pacific–worthy thatched-roof buildings. Each holds four ample bedrooms (upstairs units are better), with outside balconies or patios. All feature two double beds, solar hot water, and the liberal use of polished native hardwoods throughout. A very good restaurant is onsite; before dinner, guests sit and socialize on its veranda. *Hwy. 186 opposite the Chicanna Ruins.* ☎ *981/811-9192. www.chicannaecovillageresort. com. 1,300 pesos. AE, MC, V.*

★★★ **Explorean Kohunlich** KOHUNLICH/CHETUMAL   The tall, pyramid-shaped thatched roof of the all-inclusive resort's central lodge rises above the jungle just outside the classic Maya ruins of Kohunlich. This boutique hotel features a long, thin infinity pool, saunas, and other luxury amenities in a colorful jungle-garden setting. Luxury guest villas have king-size beds, designer toiletries, complimentary thick cotton robes, and private patios. *Kohunlich Ruins Rd.* ☎ *877/397-5672 in the U.S. or 800/366-6666. www.theexplorean. com. $250 all-inclusive. AE, MC, V.*

★★ **Holiday Inn Puerta Maya** CHETUMAL   The Holiday Inn in downtown Chetumal offers standardized, dependable comfort in the heart of the city. Its rooms, with low ceilings, can be described as small, but we find them to be intimate and cozy. Large, restful beds, cable television, and tile bathrooms with good

towels make up for what the rooms lack in size. The hotel has a nice shady pool but a forgettable restaurant. Dine across the street at Los Cocos instead. *Av. Niños Héroes No. 171.* ☎ *983/835-0400. www.ichotels group.com. $78. AE, MC, V.*

★ **Hotel Laguna** BACALAR/CHETUMAL   This funky hotel is a time warp back to the 1970s, when it was built. With a gorgeous location on a hill that slips down to the Laguna Bacalar, it has large bedrooms with two double beds and private balconies with white wrought-iron furniture. The tropical garden grounds are manicured and very inviting. Walls of the common areas are quirkily decorated in seashells—apparently brought in by the trailer load and affixed to the walls. The restaurant walls are adorned with hand-painted *dichos* (sayings or maxims) in Spanish, in case you need some life advice. This place remains a personal favorite. *Hwy. 307.* ☎ *983/834-2206. www.hotellagunabacalar.com. 34 units. 750 pesos double. MC, V.*

★ **Hotel Los Cocos** CHETUMAL MEXICAN   Down the street from the Museum of the Maya, this notable capital hotel features overly large bedrooms and simple but comfortable furnishings. Each room is tidy, and the staff here is very helpful, albeit in Spanish. The hotel's open-air, street-side Mexican restaurant is the best place to dine in town; tasty dishes, reasonable prices, and excellent service are its hallmarks. *Av. Niños Héroes No. 134.* ☎ *983/832-0544. www.hotelloscocos.com.mx. 80 units. $60–80. AE, MC, V.*

The **Western** Yucatán

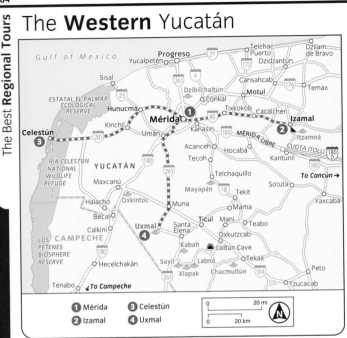

1 Mérida   **3** Celestún

2 Izamal   **4** Uxmal

```
0          20 mi
0          20 km
```

Travelers seeking adventure, history, colonial architecture, ruined or restored *haciendas,* lost Maya cities and culture, natural wonders, unspoiled beaches, and plentiful birds have flocked to the Western Yucatán since long before Cancún was even a twinkle in a developer's eye. The western part of the peninsula includes some of the most wondrous destinations in North America, beginning with the city of Mérida. START: **Take the Cuota toll road from Cancún (about 4 hrs.) or the slower (6-hr.) free route, Highway 180, Mérida Libre, past many small Yucatán villages. Mérida is 306km (189.75 miles) west of Cancún. An international airport serves Mérida with flights from select U.S. cities, Mexico City, and Cancún. Round-trip length: 480km (298 miles) return to Mérida.**

A Note on Hotels & Restaurants

For additional information on sights, shops, and recommended hotels and restaurants in Mérida, see p 108.

1 **Mérida.** "One fiesta was hardly ended when another began," wrote Mérida's first North American tourist, John Lloyd Stephens, in 1841. In that respect, things haven't changed much in the peninsula's largest, most cosmopolitan city, the capital of Yucatán State. Every day or evening, Mérida offers cultural happenings, and weekends in the city are like one long holiday. Urban enthusiasts will thrive on Mérida's relatively busy pace, but the sheer volume and magnitude of the traffic may turn off others.

Francisco de Montejo, the conqueror of the Yucatán, founded Mérida in 1542. The Spanish built it from the dismantled pyramids of the Maya city of T'ho, whose foundations lie beneath the modern streets. The **Centro Historico,** heart of the city, expands out from the shady **Main Plaza,** where frequent fiestas and celebrations take place. Most of Mérida's highlights are conveniently contained within a 12-square-block area.

If you see nothing else of the city, visit the hulking fortress cathedral facing the plaza. The **Catedral de San Ildefonso,** finished in 1598, is considered perhaps the finest Spanish-built structure in the Americas. Nearby is Montejo's family home, **Casa de Montejo,** with its friezes of Conquistadors crushing the heads of Maya warriors underfoot.

Other attractions around the square include the **Contemporary Art Museum** (☎ 999/928-3258); **Municipal Palace,** host to weekly folklore dances and musical performances; and the **Governor's Palace,** with a great view of the park, the cathedral, and huge interesting mural paintings and portraits on the second story. The corner of calles 61 and 60 is also a great place to hire a *casela* (horse-drawn buggy) for a romantic tour of the downtown.

Up Calle 60, discover Mérida's finest theater, **Teatro Peón Contreras.** This opulent Italianesque monument was built in 1908, in imitation of the finest European

The golden cityscape of Ixamal.

theaters of that era. North of Calle 47, find the fashionable **Paseo de Montejo,** a broad, Champs d'Elysee–style boulevard lined with mansions, some converted to offices and restaurants. One of the largest homes is now the **Anthropology Museum.**

Mérida was influenced by indigenous Maya, who still come to their ancient city for market; by the French during the Second Empire; by the influx of Lebanese at the turn of the 20th century; and by the influx of tourism made easier by Cancún's popularity. Mérida offers the best of the old and new worlds. Lively arts, theater, culture, and music—attractions partly fueled by a large North American expatriate population—make Mérida the place to begin and end a tour of the western Yucatán.

Smaller side roads lead to Izamal; the most direct route is Route 80 through Tixkokob, turning for Cacalchén rather than continuing straight toward Motul. Or a faster

Salt harvested via ancient Mayan methods from the salt ponds at Celestún.

way is to retrace Highway 180 east to Kantunil, where the *Cuota* begins, and follow the signs north to Izamal.

② **Izamal** (about 80km/50 miles west of Mérida). Once a holy city for the pre-Columbian Maya, **Izamal** is perhaps the most traditional of Yucatecan cities. Famous for having all its buildings painted gold, the massive **Convento de San Antoñio de Padua** dominates the town and its people. Built in 1561 by the Franciscans, on the base of what was a humongous Maya pyramid, it boasts the second-largest central courtyard outside of the Vatican.

Surviving pyramids are scattered around the town that grew up around them. The most notable is the 35m (115-ft.) **Kinich Kakmo** (Fire Macaw), which occupies an entire city block. Don't miss a ride around town in a classic "Victoria" horse and buggy or the striking 16th-century wall paintings in the Convento.

Frequent buses run to Celestún from the station on Calle 71, 64/66, and travel agents sell daily escorted tours. To drive, follow

Calle 57 west until it becomes 59A and continue straight, following signs for Hunucmá and then Celestún.

③ **Celestún** (about 80km/50 miles east of Mérida). Even the most jaded urbanite can't help but admire the beauty of hundreds of delicate pink-white flamingos when they take flight over the shallow lagoons of **Celestún Nature Reserve,** which is located 1½ hours west of Mérida.

Celestún village is situated on the Gulf of Mexico, nearly surrounded by marshy lagoons. Several large colonies of pink flamingos migrated here to nest and feed after Hurricane Gilbert changed the lagoons around Rio Lagartos. Flamingo colors depend on the salt content of the water they strain through their beaks as they feed; without salt, they're white.

Celestún is still predominately a fishing community, where 7.5m (25-ft.) launches line the dirty estuary harbor. But many former fishermen now pilot their boats for tourists instead.

You can hire a launch (the fewer people in the boat, the better) at the **Unidad Reception Center,** at the bridge to the entrance to the village. The boats will get close, but not too close, to the flocks of birds. On the way back, be sure to have your boatman stop at the *cenote* beside the lagoon, so you can take a quick dip. Launches also leave from the beach and reach the lagoon via the river mouth, visiting another colony along the way.

Take Highway 261 from the zoo south to the city of Uman, continuing toward Muna. Take the bypass road that goes around Muna, just before Uxmal, or drive directly through town to Uxmal Ruins.

Piramide del Adivino (Pyramid of the Magician), Uxmal.

4 Uxmal (about 80km/50 miles south of Mérida). Rising above the almost flat topography of the Yucatán, the Puuc Hills (*pook,* which means hill country in Maya) herald your approach to Uxmal, one of the most intriguing ruins of the ancient Maya. Like Chichén Itzá, Uxmal (oosh-*mahl*) is an impressive ruin with huge pyramids and fascinating structures noted for their rich geometric stone facades. Where Chichén is grandiose and crowded, Uxmal is beautiful and much less visited.

The **Pyramid of the Magician** (also known as the **Pyramid of the Dwarf**) is the first structure you'll see when you enter the grounds. Its distinctive steep, rounded sides are unique, and the far side features an ornate doorway with 12 stylized masks of the rain god Chac.

The **Nunnery Quadrangle** resembled a convent to the Spanish, hence its name, but it may have housed warrior princes in training in its 70-odd cubicle rooms.

In terms of its size and intricate stonework, the **Governor's Palace** is a gem of Maya architecture. It's three levels tall, with a long mosaic facade. Its central doorway is aligned with Venus. Next to it, the massive **Great Pyramid** affords a wonderful view from the top of its nine stories.

A series of smaller but very interesting ruins lines a road known as the **Ruta Puuc,** a short drive south (see p 58).

Uxmal makes a good day trip, but we suggest an overnight stay to do it justice. This way you can work in the Ruta Puuc ruins and Uxmal's evening light show as well. *For more details, see p 57.*

Where to **Stay & Dine**

★★★ Eco Paraíso Xixim

CELESTÚN   Located well out of town, this ecological-themed resort on 112 hectares (280 acres) features generous, private rooms in attractive individual cabañas, with porch patios, steps from a deserted beach. A shade portico covers the pool, and the common room is good for socializing. The hotel recycles its water and waste, grows its own vegetables, and offers much-needed eco-friendly mosquito repellent. *Antigua Carretera a Sisal Km 9.* ☎ *988/916-2100. www.ecoparaiso. com. 15 units. $200 double, including 2 meals per person. AE, MC, V.*

★★ Ecohotel Flamingo Playa

CELESTÚN   This hotel stands out only for its quiet location on the broad Gulf Beach on the northern edge of town where shell collecting is a favorite pastime. An appealing pool faces the beach, but the clean rooms are very basic: beds, fan or air-conditioning, and bathroom. The congenial manager offers a basic breakfast on a card table in front. *North road along the beach.* ☎ *988/916-2166. 6 rooms. $50. No credit cards.*

★★ Flycatcher Inn B&B SANTA

ELENA/UXMAL   This pleasant little bed-and-breakfast, with helpful hosts, is a short drive from the ruins of Uxmal along the road to Kabah and the Ruta Puuc. The rooms are quiet, attractive, and spacious, with queen-size beds and wrought-iron headboards. New rooms are available in charming casitas outside the main house. *Carretera Uxmal-Kabah. No phone. www.flycatcherinn.com. $40 double, $50 suite. No credit cards.*

★★★ Hacienda Temozón

TEMOZON SUR   This magnificent 17th-century estancia presides over acres of rainforest with subtropical gardens, cenotes, and infinity plunge pools, 24 miles (38.6km) from Mérida. Built in 1655, Temozón was the region's most productive livestock estancia, and later the region's top producer of sisal (henequén). Meticulously restored in 1997, it's now a luxury Starwood property committed to employing local workers and using locally grown organic produce in the open-air restaurant. Spacious Spanish colonial–style rooms have 18-foot ceilings; Spanish-tile floors and baths; hammocks positioned to catch natural breezes; and large, plush iron beds with white linens adorned daily with fresh flowers. The Casa del Patrón suite has hosted many global heads of state. *KM 182 Carretera Merida-Uxmal.* ☎ *888/625-5144 or 999/923 8089. www.haciendas mexico.com. 28 units. Doubles from $325. AE, MC, V.*

★★★ Kinich Kakmo IZAMAL

REGIONAL/MEXICAN   Near the large pyramid of the same name, this Yucatecan restaurant attracts tourists to its shady *palapa* dining area set in gardens behind a gift shop. Arrive in style in a horse-drawn buggy, called a "Victoria" to see tortillas made and cooked by hand in a smoky Maya hut. Order either the *pollo pibil* or *cochenita pibil;* the former is chicken, the latter, pork, cooked in banana leaves. *Calle 27 between 28 & 30. No phone. Entrees $3–$8. No credit cards.*

★★ Macan Che IZAMAL   The

best accommodations in Izamal are at this appealing B&B that features individual cabañas, decorated with worldwide travel themes, and set apart in shady tropical gardens. They have a small pool, a good paperback library, and a full breakfast that is included in the rates. *Calle 22 (between 31 & 33).* ☎ *988/954-0287. www.macanche.com. $50 w/breakfast. No credit cards.* ●

6 Charming Cities & Towns

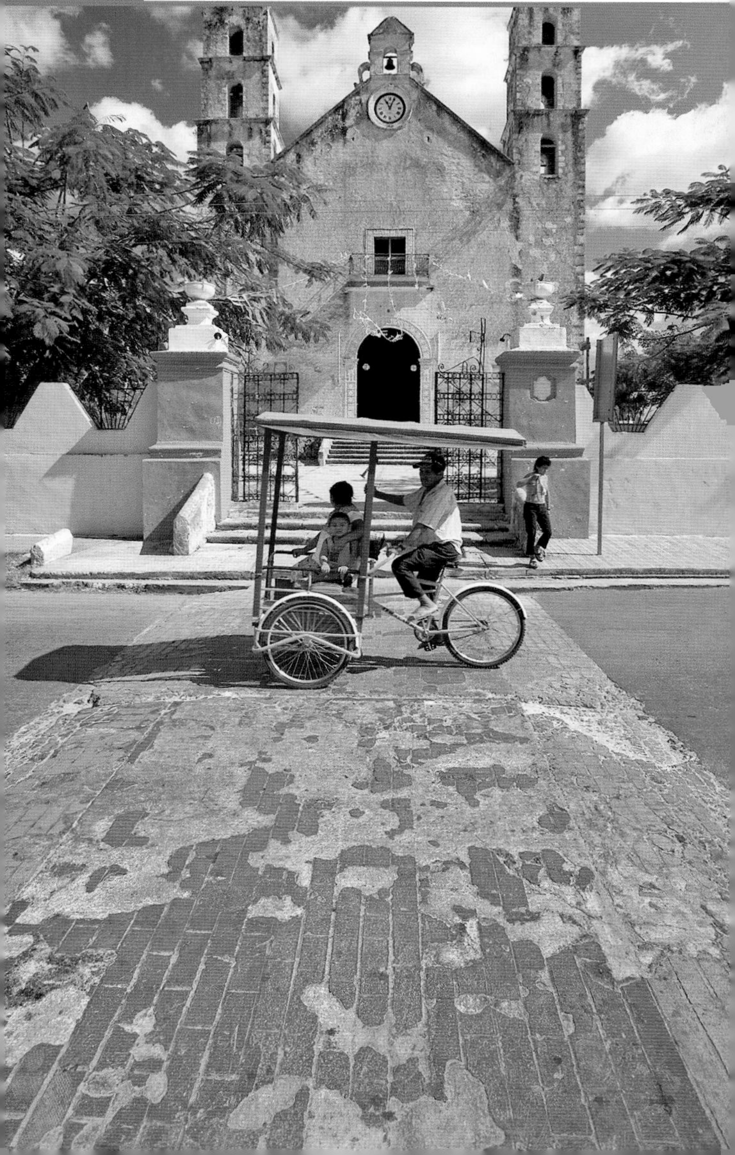

Campeche

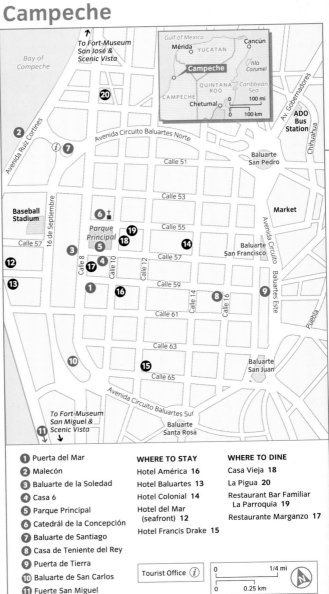

1 Puerta del Mar
2 Malecón
3 Baluarte de la Soledad
4 Casa 6
5 Parque Principal
6 Catedrál de la Concepción
7 Baluarte de Santiago
8 Casa de Teniente del Rey
9 Puerta de Tierra
10 Baluarte de San Carlos
11 Fuerte San Miguel

WHERE TO STAY

Hotel América 16
Hotel Baluartes 13
Hotel Colonial 14
Hotel del Mar (seafront) 12
Hotel Francis Drake 15

WHERE TO DINE

Casa Vieja 18
La Pigua 20
Restaurant Bar Familiar La Parroquia 19
Restaurante Marganzo 17

Tourist Office ⓘ

0 ————— 1/4 mi
0 ————— 0.25 km

Previous page: The Catholic cathedral in Izamal.

With narrow streets, high sidewalks, and period color on the 17th- and 18th-century homes in its walled center, Campeche is the best-restored colonial city in Mexico. UNESCO named it a World Heritage Site in 2000, and its cinematic Spanish Colonial streets have appeared in a number of Mexican films. Yet it's still well off the beaten path of most tourists to the Yucatán—despite the fact that it's a historic treasure box, compact and ideal for exploring on foot. START: **Campeche is SW of Mérida on Highway 180. You can also get here from the Ruta Puuc/Uxmal area on Highway 261. Trip length: 257km (159 miles) from Mérida; 100km (62 miles) from Ruta Puuc/Uxmal.**

① **Puerta del Mar.** One of four major entrance gates into the city—which the Spanish walled and fortified in the late 1600s against pirate attacks—the *Puerta del Mar* (Sea Gate) once opened onto a dock. Over the years, the waterfront was gradually filled and relocated to its present position farther west. The park in front of the gate hosts occasional fairs. 🕐 *30 min. Calles 8 & 59.*

② **Malecón.** Stretcing along the waterfront for more than a kilometer, the *malecón* is a long, paved walkway popular with Campechanos and tourists alike. A favorite walking and running path, the *malecón* broadens in places to make room for contemporary sculpture and restful seating—a popular place to watch the sun set over the Gulf. *Av. Ruíz Cortines.*

③ **Baluarte de la Soledad Baluartes.** Armed defensive bastions flank the entrance gates to the city. This one, north of the Sea Gate, is now a museum of Maya *stelae*. Its salons showcase carved stone hieroglyph tablets found in Campeche ruins; many are badly worn, but line drawings highlight their design. Explanatory text is in Spanish. The outdoor water fountains are illuminated in the evening. 🕐 *30 min. Calles 57 & 8. Open Tues–Sat 9am–8pm, Sun 9am–1pm. Admission $3.*

④ **Casa 6 (Seis).** The city's main tourist office and cultural center is in this wonderfully restored Moorish-style mansion opposite the park. Rich period furniture is on display in various rooms, and photographs of other restored colonial buildings in

Campeche's main plaza.

The Baluarte San Carlos.

Campeche are on exhibit in the striking, arched-roof patio. ⏲ *25 min. Calle 57 (opposite the park). Open 9am–9pm. Free.*

⑤ Parque Principal. Campeche's pretty central plaza is the center of city life, despite its small size. In the middle is **El Kiosko,** a gazebo bandstand that becomes a restaurant in the evening. Bus tours of the city leave from in front of the park, hourly or so on weekends, from Calle 10. ⏲ *30 min. Calles 8, 10, 59, & 57.*

⑥ Cathedral de la Concepción. The dominant facade of Campeche's cathedral faces the park. Its tall twin towers were built slowly over 2 centuries: One is known as the "El Colonial" because it was completed during colonial times; the other as "La Campechano," finished after independence. Inside, it's quite austere. ⏲ *15 min. Calles 55 & 10. No phone. Admission free.*

⑦ Baluarte de Santiago. Take respite from the heat in the middle of a traffic circle, where a green botanical garden fills the former military fortification. Flower power, baby. ⏲ *15 min. Av. 16 de Septiembre & Av. Circuito Baluartes Norte. Admission by donation.*

⑧ Casa de Teniente del Rey. An interesting collection of Maya cultural artifacts found a home in this former Conquistador's house. The spoils: jade jewelry from Calakmul and a wooden plank headdress, used to slant a baby's head to the oblong shape the Maya considered beautiful. ⏲ *40 min. Calle 59 (between calles 14 & 16). Open Tues–Sat 8am–2pm and 5–8pm. Sun 9am–1pm. Admission $3.*

Crafts Fair

Shoppers will find the best handicrafts from around the state in the official city arts building, **Tukulná,** on Calle 10 between calles 59 and 61. It's a beautifully restored structure with a small coffee shop. Also look in the specialty craft store, **Típica Naval,** on Calle 8 between calles 59 and 57, for wooden sailing ship models—a Campeche folk art tradition.

⑨ Puerta de Tierra. Campeche's icon, the Land Gate is the largest surviving portion of the old city ramparts. Thick wooden doors, built

Catedral de la Concepción in Campeche.

in 1732 to repel pirate attacks, later protected refugees of European ancestry from Maya attacks in the 19th-century Caste War. Original 18th-century guns still guard the gate. In the entryway, the 5-ton French cannon from 1732 was found in 1990. On Tuesdays, Fridays, and Saturday nights at 8pm, a **Light and Sound Spectacular** includes actors walking on the balustrade and sword fighting at the Baluarte de San Juan (buy tickets in advance). ⏱ *30 min. 1½ hr. for the show. Calle 59 at Circuito Baluartes. No phone. Open Tues–Sun 8am–8pm. Admission $3.*

The streets of Campeche.

⑩ **Baluarte de San Carlos. Museo de la Ciudad.** The Museum of the City is housed in the oldest baluarte, built in 1686 to protect the wall's vulnerable southern exposure. Principally concerned with the construction of Campeche's fortifications, it has an intriguing collection of old maps and a scale model of the city from way back when. ⏱ *30 min. Circuito Baluartes Sur & Av. Justo Sierra. Open Tues–Sat 8am–2pm and 5–8pm. Sun 9am–1pm. Admission $3.*

⑪ **Fuerte San Miguel.** A visit to Campeche would not be complete without a glimpse of Campeche's best-preserved, most photogenic fort, built to end pirate attacks. With the original 18th-century cannon on its parapets, it's easy to imagine a swashbuckling movie being filmed here. On a mountaintop overlooking the harbor, 4km (2.5 miles) south of the city, the site is graced by refreshing breezes and a super view of the sunset. The museum in the interior houses the exquisite jade mask found in the Maya ruins of Calakmul, creative Maya pottery, and the prow of an ancient mariner's vessel. ("By thy long gray beard and glittering eye, now wherefore stoppest thou me?") ⏱ *1 hr. Ruta Esencia. No phone. Open Tues–Sat 9am–8pm and Sun 8am–noon. Admission $3.*

The Ruins of Edzná

The breathtaking Maya ruins of Edzná, only 50km (31 miles) west of the downtown, boast a huge ceremonial grass courtyard, complete with stadium-style seats and a unique astronomical phenomenon—when a *stele* is illuminated by a beam of light to signal the start of planting season. Even if you're just passing through Campeche, don't miss these ruins. See p 58 for more details.

Charming Cities & Towns

Where to Stay

★★★ **Hotel América** HISTORIC CENTER   A bit more modern and distinguished than the Colonial is this hotel in a Spanish-style mansion, where individual rooms surround an open, tiled courtyard with Moorish arches. Hacienda artifacts, such as hand tools and wooden carts, accent its Mexican decor. Rooms are midsize and comfortable with soft lighting. One block south of the main plaza, the América offers private parking. *Calle 10 (near 59).* ☎ *981/816-4588. www.hotel americacampeche.com. 52 units. Doubles $45. MC, V.*

★★ **Hotel Baluartes** SEAFRONT Facing the Gulf, across the street from the del Mar, is Campeche's original "luxury" hotel, Baluartes. The cheerful rooms were recently refurbished with new tile floors, beds, and furniture. Despite the remodeling, the Baluartes retains its 1960s feel—which is fairly modern, considering you're in Campeche. *Av. Ruiz Cortines.* ☎ *981/816-3911. www.baluartes.com.mx. 104 units. Doubles $60. AE, MC, V.*

★★ **Hotel Colonial** HISTORIC CENTER   This is the best bet if you're looking for a family-run, colonial-era hotel that time has seemingly forgotten—and you don't mind funky. The former family residence of a colonial governor appointed by the King of Spain, Brigadier don Miguel de Castro, the Colonial is neat and clean but careworn. Each room has high ceilings and original tile floors made to imitate Oriental rugs. *Calle 14 no. 122 (between calles 57 & 55).* ☎ *981/ 816-2222. 30 units. Doubles $25; $35 with A/C. No credit cards.*

★ **Hotel del Mar** SEAFRONT This four-story landmark facing the Gulf is rightly Campeche's best and most popular hotel—with its large rooms, big cool pool, oceanfront views, excellent restaurant, popular nightclub, and attentive staff. Make reservations here for the Chicanna Ecolodge, near Xpujil on the road back to Chetumal. See p 60 for details of the Forest of Kings ruins. *Av. Ruiz Cortines.* ☎ *981/811-9192. www.delmarhotel.com.mx. 145 units. Doubles $125. AE, MC, V.*

★ **Hotel Francis Drake** HISTORIC CENTER   A welcome treat in the historic center, this new boutique hotel in a beautifully restored mansion features restful, midsize rooms, a quality restaurant serving seafood and Mexican fare, and air-conditioning. Named after the English admiral who purportedly raided the city as a pirate, the Drake is reasonably priced and one of the best values in town. *Calle 12 (between calles 63 & 65).* ☎ *981/811-5626. www.hotel francisdrake.com. 24 units. Doubles $70, suites $80–$93. AE, MC, V.*

The lobby of the Hotel América.

Where **to Dine**

★★★ **Casa Vieja** HISTORIC CENTER *CUBAN/MEXICAN* When you'd like something other than seafood, head to this romantic "Old House" restaurant overlooking the Park. Choose a table in one of the intimate rooms decorated with Campechano memorabilia and old photos, or on a dreamy second-floor veranda with a view of the street and park below (our preference). *Calle 10 no. 319.* ☎ *981/811-1311. Entrees $6–$16. No credit cards. Open Tues–Sun 9am–2am, Mon 5:30pm–2am.*

★★ **La Pigua** GUADELOUPE *SEAFOOD* La Pigua, named after a kind of shrimp, offers a fresh selection of seafood delicacies—including a shrimp "caviar"—in a dining room filled with cool greenery. This famous restaurant is open only for lunch—which in Campeche means all afternoon. Walk north from Baluarte de Santiago; it's a block and a half past the circle. *Av. Miguel Alemán 179A.* ☎ *981/811-3365. Entrees $9–$17. AE, MC, V. Daily noon–6pm. Reservations suggested.*

★★★ **Restaurant Bar Familiar La Parroquia** HISTORIC CENTER *SEAFOOD/MEXICAN* Given its central location and large menu, this restaurant would have qualified for our "Take a Break" sidebar, but it's such a venerable dining institution we'd be remiss not to give it a full listing. La Parroquia has a plain dining room with a diner-like menu, but it's *the* place in Campeche for families, friends, lovers, and strangers to meet, greet, eat, or just sit around with cold beers in hand. Open 24 hours a day. *Calle 55 no. 9 (between calles 10 & 12).* ☎ *981/816-8086. Entrees $4–$12. No credit cards. Daily 24 hrs.*

★★ **Restaurante Marganzo** HISTORIC CENTER *SEAFOOD/MEXICAN* With waitresses wearing colorful costume dresses that swirl brightly when they turn, this special little restaurant is a long-time favorite of tourists and locals alike. Seating is in a tiered dining room at tables with starched white linens. Fresh seafood dominates the varied menu: Try any of the baby shark dishes, such as *pan de cazón:* layered tortilla, shark, and tomato sauce—a Campechano delicacy. Open early until late, near the Sea Gate. *Calle 8 no. 267 (near the Puerta del Mar).* ☎ *981/816-3899. Entrees $6–$15. AE, MC, V. Daily 7am–11pm.*

Campeche After Dark

They'd roll up the streets after the sun goes down here if they could. Campeche isn't known as a party town, except for occasional street festivals around Mexican and religious holidays. **Lafitte's,** a nautical nightclub and bar in the Hotel del Mar (see "Where to Stay," p 94), draws a mixed crowd. A teen and young adult weekend hotspot is **KY8,** a nightclub near the Sea Gate on calles 8 and 10, and **La Parroquia** (see "Where to Dine," p 95) is open 24 hours for food and drink.

Cozumel

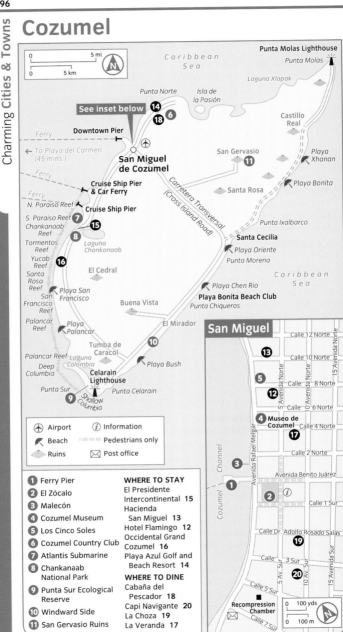

See inset below

0 — 5 mi
0 — 5 km

Caribbean Sea

Punta Molas Lighthouse
Punta Molas

Laguna Xlapak

Punta Norte · Isla de la Pasión

Castillo Real

Downtown Pier

Ferry

← To Playa del Carmen (45 mins.)

San Miguel de Cozumel

San Gervasio ⓫

Playa Xhanan

Cruise Ship Pier & Car Ferry

Ferry

Santa Rosa

Playa Bonita

N. Paraíso Reef

Cruise Ship Pier

Carretera Transversal (Cross Island Road)

S. Paraíso Reef ❼

Punta Ixalbarco

Chankanaab Reef ⓯

Tormentos Reef ❽

Laguna Chankanaab

Santa Cecilia

Playa Oriente

Yucab Reef ⓰

Punta Morena

El Cedral

Caribbean Sea

Santa Rosa Reef

Playa Chen Río

San Francisco Reef

Playa San Francisco

Buena Vista

Playa Bonita Beach Club
Punta Chiqueros

Palancar Reef

Playa Palancar

El Mirador

San Miguel

Calle 12 Norte

Calle 10 Norte

Palancar Reef Deep Columbia

Laguna Colombia

Tumba de Caracol

⓱

⓮

Playa Bush

⓭

Punta Sur

Celarain Lighthouse

❾

Shallow Columbia

Punta Celarain

Calle 8 Norte

⓹

Calle 6 Norte

⓬

Calle 0 Norte

5 Avenida Norte

10 Avenida Norte

15 Avenida Norte

❹ Museo de Cozumel

Calle 4 Norte

⓱

Calle 2 Norte

❸

Avenida Benito Juárez

❶

❷ ⓘ

Calle 1 Sur

Cozumel Channel

Avenida Rafael Melgar

Calle Dr. Adolfo Rosado Salas

Calle 3 Sur

⓳

5 Av. Sur

10 Av. Sur

15 Avenida Sur

Calle 5 Sur

⓴

Recompression Chamber
✉

0 — 100 yds
0 — 100 m

Calle 7 Sur

Legend:

✈ Airport
🏖 Beach
≋ Ruins
ⓘ Information
━━━ Pedestrians only
✉ Post office

❶ Ferry Pier
❷ El Zócalo
❸ Malecón
❹ Cozumel Museum
❺ Los Cinco Soles
❻ Cozumel Country Club
❼ Atlantis Submarine
❽ Chankanaab National Park
❾ Punta Sur Ecological Reserve
❿ Windward Side
⓫ San Gervasio Ruins

WHERE TO STAY
El Presidente Intercontinental **15**
Hacienda San Miguel **13**
Hotel Flamingo **12**
Occidental Grand Cozumel **16**
Playa Azul Golf and Beach Resort **14**

WHERE TO DINE
Cabaña del Pescador **18**
Capi Navigante **20**
La Choza **19**
La Veranda **17**

Widely considered the top dive destination in the Western Hemisphere, Mexico's largest island attracts tens of thousands of divers each year seeking to plumb its towering reefs. Even landlubbers shouldn't miss a loop around the island to see its dramatic, deserted windward side. San Miguel, Cozumel's only town, is home to specialty shops, restaurants, and hotels. Thousands of 1-day cruise-ship passengers stop here, but they rarely make it farther than the waterfront shopping area. START: **Cancún or Playa del Carmen. Trip length: Cozumel is 19km (12 miles) off the coast from the Playa del Carmen ferry dock, about 70km (43 miles) south of Cancún on Highway 307.**

Travel Tip

For more information on diving opportunities in Cozumel, see p 34.

① Ferry Pier. Island life begins where the ferries run from Playa del Carmen. After disembarking, passengers can expect hawkers to solicit them to rent cars or motorbikes, or to book fishing or snorkeling trips. ⏱ *1 hour. Av. Rafael Melgar.*

② El Zócalo. All around San Miguel's main plaza, or *zócalo,* are many jewelry, gift, and handicraft shops and a variety of dining choices. In fact, the central downtown caters to shoppers and diners. Cruise-ship passengers who never leave the enclosed air-conditioned shopping malls at their dock miss out. On Sundays, local residents congregate to socialize, often accompanied by live music. *Av. Rafael Melgar.*

③ Malecón. North and south of the ferry pier, paralleling Avenida Rafael Melgar, an appealing walkway *(malecón)* winds along the waterfront. It's a popular stroll in the morning or evening and a good place to watch the sunset or ships in the harbor. *Av. Rafael Melgar.*

④ kids Cozumel Museum. The history of Cozumel is presented in this modest museum in what was the island's first luxury hotel, which opened in 1936. Natural-history exhibits feature local flora and fauna, including endangered species, topography, and the coral reef that put Cozumel on the map. An exhibit tells the story of Cozumel from pre-Columbian through modern times, including pirates of the Caribbean. *Salas* house Maya artifacts found at the ruins and colonial-era cannons, swords, and shipwreck paraphernalia. ⏱ *30 min. Av. Rafael Melgar (between calles 4 & 6).* ☎ *987/872-1475. Admission $3.*

A horse and buggy stops by the sea in Cozumel.

On the breezy second-floor balcony of the City Museum, overlooking the harbor across the straits to Playa del Carmen, **Café del Museo** is an inexpensive little coffee shop that opens for breakfast and lunch and offers the island's best all-around light dining value.

⑤ Los Cinco Soles. Cozumel's largest air-conditioned store offers weary travelers lots of quality gifts and Pancho's Backyard, a pleasant Mexican restaurant. Best of all, they have wonderfully clean bathrooms, open to the public. The building originally served as a *chicle* resin (used for the first chewing gum) warehouse in the early 1900s and, from 1960 to the1980s, as a hotel. *Av. Rafael Melgar (Calle 8).* ☎ *987/ 872-0132. www.loscincosoles.com.*

⑥ Cozumel Country Club. It takes a lot of balls to play this golf course, where shots into the rough become part of the jungle or disappear into a wide inland lagoon. The Nicholas Design Group carved this challenging, 18-hole course out of Cozumel's thick jungle and low-growing mangroves. The result is

Iglesia de San Miguel in Cozumel.

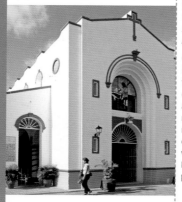

Local handicrafts at a store in Cozumel.

spectacular and a sheer pleasure to play. It's a naturally gorgeous course that won an ecological award for conservation efforts. The country club features an outdoor restaurant, on-course beverage carts, and equipment rental. *Carretera Santa Pilar.* ☎ *987/872-9570. www.cozumelcountryclub.com.mx.*

⑦ kids Atlantis Submarine. Forget *Das Boot* and go for a fascinating dive in an air-conditioned submersible boat. It dips as deep as 30m (98 ft.) for views of Cozumel's incredible reef formations and colorful schools of fish. 🕐 *1 hr. Carretera Sur Km 4.* ☎ *987/872-5671. Open Mon–Sat 9am–2pm.*

⑧ kids Chankanaab National Park. If you're looking for a place to spend the day on a lovely stretch of beach with full facilities, Chankanaab is a solid choice. Its name means "Small Sea" in Maya, referring to the lagoon full of petrified coral. Botanical gardens with shady walking paths surround the lagoon. It gets crowded when cruise-ship passengers arrive, so get here early to stake out a *palapa* and rent snorkel gear. Swim with dolphins at **Dolphin Discovery** (☎ 987/869-0314; www.dolphindiscovery.com; packages start at $78). They also have a swim with sea lions ($60) and a sea lions show ($5), for which reservations are not necessary. ⏲ *2 hrs. (families may want to spend the entire day). Carretera Sur. Admission $10. Open 8am–5pm.*

⑨ Punta Sur Ecological Reserve. A trip into Punta Sur helps support conservation efforts, but it's of limited interest if time is tight. This ecological park has a small museum dedicated to marine navigation, the small Maya ruins of Caracol, a large lagoon, lighthouse, and wild landscape. Bring your own snorkel gear. In summer, turtles nest on the natural beaches, and you can assist conservation efforts (☎ 987/872-2940). Next to the entrance is the Paradise Café, a reggae bar and restaurant with a cool blowhole in the rocks. ⏲ *2 hrs. Southern tip of the island. Admission $10. Open 9am–5pm.*

⑩ Windward Side. Cozumel is a barrier island, developed on only about 6% of its land. A trip along its dramatic, deserted, windward Caribbean side is a must. The shoreline is jagged, pocketed with rock pools. Swimming is dangerous except in a few small coves where rustic eateries have sprung up. Drive or taxi the loop around the southern half of the island in either direction. ⏲ *1–2 hrs. round-trip. Eastern Shore Rd.*

⑪ San Gervasio Ruins. These are the ruins of a Maya holy city where indigenous women once came to worship the moon goddess of fertility, Ixchel. Cortéz's conquest of Mexico began here in 1519, after he sacked the ruins and then celebrated Mass. The five crudely built temples are connected by raised stone walkways, called *sacbes* in Maya. It's rarely crowded. ⏲ *1 hr. Carretera Transversal (Av. Benito Juárez). Admission $6. Open 9am–5pm.*

Water World

Cozumel's reefs are truly amazing underwater mountain ranges —steep walls of coral, rock, and sponge that drop into an abyss, with colors and coral textures that rival the fall foliage of New England. After a Jacques Cousteau film in 1954 publicized the reef system, Cozumel became one of the top dive destinations in the world.

The most famous reef dives are *Yucab,* a deep descent into more than a thousand coral formations of as high as 18m to 24m (60–80 ft.) high; *San Francisco,* riddled with tunnels and large yellow tube sponges that hang over the depths; *Santa Rosa,* full of fish hiding in caves and delicate coral fans that sway in the current; *Palancar,* Cozumel's best-loved dive site, with enormous canyons of coral reef; and *Punta Sur,* with its giant cave, *Garganta del Diablo* (Devil's Throat).

Where to Stay

★★★ El Presidente Inter-Continental Cozumel SOUTH OF TOWN Expansively remodeled after Hurricane Wilma, the Presidente continues to set Cozumel's luxury standards. It boasts a long, inviting beach with good snorkeling, two huge swimming pools with whirlpools, and gorgeous tropical gardens. The oversize rooms have a tasteful decor. The beachfront, ground-floor rooms with private patios are the best on the island. Two full restaurants offer delicious dining. *Costera Sur Km 6.5.* ☎ *800/327-0200 in the U.S. or 987/872-9500. www.cozumel.intercontinental.com. 253 units. Doubles $360–$675, suites from $850. AE, DC, MC, V.*

★ Hacienda San Miguel SAN MIGUEL On a quiet side street, this appealing, Mexican hacienda-styled small hotel offers comfortable, fair-size rooms with a garden, central courtyard, and superb location—far from the noise but close enough to walk to the action downtown. A separate town house is $150. *Calle 10 Norte 500 (between Rafael Melgar & Av. 5).* ☎ *987/872-1986. www.haciendasanmiguel.com. 11 units. Studios $90, junior suites $100, suites $165; rates include continental breakfast. AE, MC, V.*

★★ Hotel Flamingo SAN MIGUEL The Flamingo is a place to escape the rush of the larger hotels. The restaurant bar "Aqua" offers several interesting and delicious dishes prepared by a chef from Chile. On the weekends they host live Cuban music with dancing. Original Cuban art and mosquito netting set the Havana-like mood. A separate top-floor penthouse sleeps four. *Calle 6 Norte (near Av. 5).* ☎ *987/872-0299. www.hotelflamingo.com. 22 units. Doubles $65–$75. AE, MC, V.*

★★★ kids Occidental Grand Cozumel SOUTH OF TOWN The Tourist Board awarded the Occidental Grand a "Gran Turismo" rating—Mexico's highest. This "village" style all-inclusive beachfront hotel has thatched *palapa* roofs and guest quarters arranged so pools and activity areas are central. The beach is pretty, and the hotel prides itself on its four restaurants, two huge swimming pools, a kids' club, and a dance club. *Carretera Chankanab Km 17.5.* ☎ *800/907-9500 in the U.S. or 987/872-9730. www.occidentalhotels.com. 255 units. Doubles $150–$229. AE, DC, MC, V.*

Sunset at the Occidental Grand.

Where **to Dine**

★★★ Cabaña del Pescador (Lobster House) NORTH END

LOBSTER This island legend serves lobster the way it should be served: boiled with a hint of spices, accompanied by rich butter and sides of rice, veggies, and bread. Lobster is the only dish on the menu, priced by weight. The owner's brother has an equally ambient restaurant next door, El Guaycamayo. *Carretera Santa Pilar Km 4 (across from Playa Azul Hotel). No phone. Lobster by weight $19–$30. No credit cards. Open daily 6–10:30pm.*

★ Capi Navigante SAN MIGUEL

SEAFOOD Without paying extra for a view of the water, dine on the freshest seafood in one of Cozumel's first *mariscos* restaurants, opened in 1975. Specialties such as crab legs and butterfly shrimp are made from family recipes. A favorite among locals, El Capi is proud of its "Langosta Capi," lobster cooked with secret spices. Attentive service in a simple nautical setting, but the live mariachis can be a bit loud. *Calle 10 Sur (between calles 3 & 5).*

☎ *987/872-1730. Entrees $7–$35. MC, V. Open noon–10pm.*

★ La Choza SAN MIGUEL *MEXICAN*

This local favorite is under a big thatched *palapa* with large open windows. Crowds come for the inexpensive Yucatecan food. Platters of poblano chiles stuffed with shrimp and *pollo en relleno negro* (chicken in a blackened chili sauce) are among the specialties. *Calle Rosado Salas 198 (Av. 10 Sur).* ☎ *987/872-0958. Entrees $9–$15. AE, MC, V. Open daily 7am–11pm.*

★★ La Veranda SAN MIGUEL *SEAFOOD/CARIBBEAN* Choose the

Veranda for dinner if you're tired of fried fish and Mexican food. The inventive menu emphasizes tropical ingredients and offers delicious West Indian and European-infused *nouvelle* cuisine in a magical setting. Both indoor or outdoor veranda dining areas are airy and appealing. The mango fish is delicate and fruity. *Calle 4 (between calles 5 & 10).* ☎ *987/872-4132. Entrees $14–$20. MC, V. Open daily 4:30pm–midnight. Reservations recommended.*

Cozumel After Dark

For a more lively evening, enjoy the salsa bands at Pura Vida, from Wednesday to Sunday. Go early for free dance lessons (☎ 987/878-7831. Av. Rosado Salas and Av. 5 Sur). Oldies but goodies might like **Tony Rome's** (☎ 987/872-0131; also on Av. Salas near Av. 5). Performing Sinatra and Bennett, Tony does two shows nightly, at 7:30 and 9:30pm. **Carlos 'n' Charlie's** and a **Señor Frogs** also have outposts on Cozumel. Jello shots, anyone?

Isla Mujeres (Island of Women)

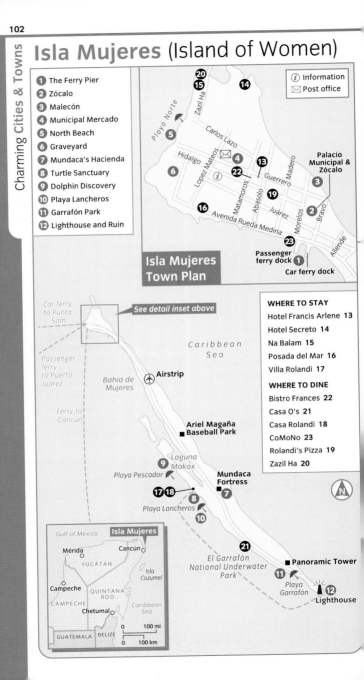

1. The Ferry Pier
2. Zócalo
3. Malecón
4. Municipal Mercado
5. North Beach
6. Graveyard
7. Mundaca's Hacienda
8. Turtle Sanctuary
9. Dolphin Discovery
10. Playa Lancheros
11. Garrafón Park
12. Lighthouse and Ruin

(i) Information
✉ Post office

Isla Mujeres Town Plan

Palacio Municipal & Zócalo

Passenger ferry dock
Car ferry dock

WHERE TO STAY
Hotel Francis Arlene 13
Hotel Secreto 14
Na Balam 15
Posada del Mar 16
Villa Rolandi 17

WHERE TO DINE
Bistro Frances 22
Casa O's 21
Casa Rolandi 18
CoMoNo 23
Rolandi's Pizza 19
Zazil Ha 20

Car ferry to Punta Sam

See detail inset above

Caribbean Sea

Passenger ferry to Puerto Juárez

Bahía de Mujeres

Airstrip

Ferry to Cancún

Ariel Magaña Baseball Park

Laguna Makax

Playa Pescador

Mundaca Fortress

Playa Lancheros

El Garrafón National Underwater Park

Panoramic Tower

Playa Garrafón

Lighthouse

Isla Mujeres

Gulf of Mexico

Mérida
Cancún
YUCATÁN
Isla Cozumel

Campeche
QUINTANA ROO

Chetumal
Caribbean Sea
CAMPECHE

GUATEMALA   BELIZE

0   100 mi
0   100 km

I n 1517, when Francisco Hernández de Córdoba landed on this sliver of an island off the coast of Cancún, he found figurines of women littering the shore, inspiring the name the island bears today. The statues—believed to have been offerings to Ixchel, the Maya goddess of fertility and the moon—suggest this land was sacred to the Maya, whose resident descendants still fish bonito, mackerel, and kingfish from the warm waters. Now Isla Mujeres still feels like a small fishing village, with cobblestone streets, lively independent shops and restaurants, and no buildings higher than the height of a royal palm (three stories). START: **To reach Isla Mujeres from Cancún, take the Ultramar Ferry from Puerto Juárez (40 pesos), north of Cancún's downtown, or a catamaran from the Hotel Zone's Embarcadero (150 pesos). If you drive, take the car ferry from Punta Sam, 2km (1.5 miles) north of Puerto Juárez. Trip length: Isla Mujeres is 13km (8 miles) off the coast.**

① **The Ferry Pier.** The island's pulse is the parade of passenger boats that run back and forth, from 6am to 12:30am, from the mainland to either Puerto Juárez or the new Puerto Cancún terminal next door. The pier is rife with hawkers and seafood restaurants. Walking is the best way to explore: Any of the narrow cobbled streets lead into the heart of the city, barely 4 blocks wide and 7 long. ⏱ *30 min. Av. Rueda Medina.*

② **El Zócalo (Central Square).** Find a pickup game of basketball or volleyball, or groups of local residents sitting and chatting under the Zócalo's scraggly trees. Around the square is the police station, Catholic church, and supermarket. *Avs. Madero & Hidalgo.*

③ **Malecón.** This seafront, paving-stone walkway meanders along the dramatic Caribbean shore. Built in the late 1980s to make the town more attractive after Hurricane Gilbert's destruction, the walk was hit hard again by Hurricane Wilma in 2005. *Avs. Guerrero & Madero.*

④ **Municipal Mercado.** This warehouse-like market was once where local residents did all their shopping, pre-Cancún. Some

An aerial view of Isla Mujeres.

A beach bar on Isla Mujeres.

merchants still peddle wares from inside stalls on weekends, but now the market is better known for the inexpensive little eateries under its arches. Most open early for breakfast and lunch. *Av. Guerrero. Market open weekends from 8am until dark; eateries open daily 6am until dark.*

5 kids North Beach. A favorite among sunbathers (some of them topless), Playa Norte is blessed with La Isla's widest beaches. The sand here—like all the Yucatán's Caribbean shoreline—doesn't get hot to the touch in the sun. The North Beach's warm, shallow water affords the best swimming for kids, and its beach bars are a prime spot to watch the sunset. *Av Lopéz Mateos.*

Travel Tip

When you want to explore more of the island than the downtown, rent a golf cart ($16/hr.) or motorbike from any of the many vendors around town, and follow the shore road around the island. Go slowly and watch for traffic.

6 Graveyard. Brightly decorated with flowers and colorful mementos of those who have passed, Isla's

pocket-sized graveyard is a jumble of above-ground tombs and monuments with praying angels. Look for the pirate Mundaca's memorial tombstone with a carved skull and crossbones and the saying (translated from Latin): "As you are now, so once was I. As I am now, so you will be." (Walk straight in about 4m/13 ft., turn right, and walk 3m/10 ft. or so.) *Av. Lopéz Mateos (between Hidalgo & Juárez). Open daily until sunset.*

7 Mundaca's Hacienda. Fermín Mundaca de Marcheaga was a lovelorn pirate and slave trader who gave up the sea in the mid–19th century and built once-beautiful gardens on this hacienda, in an effort to win the love of a young *trigueña* (brunette). Unfortunately for him, he was not to her taste. Unfortunately for visitors, not too much taste has gone into the garden restoration. Mundaca's memorial tombstone is in the local cemetery in Mérida (see below), where he died and is buried. *North end, about Km 4. Admission $2. Open 10am–6pm.*

8 kids Turtle Sanctuary. Isla's sandy shores have long been a breeding ground for endangered turtles. The most abundant species is the green turtle, which weighs as much as 450 pounds. Isla's fishermen once slaughtered the enormous, lumbering creatures; in the 1970s, they decided to protect them instead by creating the *Centro de Investigaciones,* an ecological sanctuary. With all the development nearby, the sanctuary is needed now more than ever. ⏱ *1 hr. Sac Bajo.* ☎ *998/877-0595. Admission $3. Open daily 9am–5pm.*

9 kids Dolphin Discovery. I have mixed feelings about the ubiquitous dolphin swims along the Riviera Maya. But the joy on participants' faces and the respect they gain for the sea-dwelling mammals go a long

A hut on Isla Mujeres.

way to mitigate my misgivings. Make advance reservations for this educational fun time, only $100. Arrive an hour before your appointment for the educational video. ⏲ *1 hr. or longer. Sac Bajo.* ☎ *998/877-0207. www. dolphindiscovery.com. Open daily 8am–4pm.*

⑩ kids Playa Lancheros.
Choose a spot under a palm tree, or a table under a shady *palapa,* and enjoy cold drinks and cheap food. Swim in sheltered waters and order the beach shack specialty, *Tikin-Xic,* a charcoal-grilled fresh fish filet, spiced with *achiote.* The free beach has parking and plenty of safe swimming, a restaurant/bar, plus a chance to get in the water with a sand shark; tips accepted. *Carretera Garrafón. No Phone. Open all day. Free admission.*

⑪ kids Garrafón Park. Garrafón
is a National Marine Park with a reef close to shore and full of colorful fish—perfect for beginning snorkelers—and a relaxing day park that spills down to the water's edge, with snorkeling, "Snuba" (a tankless version of scuba in which you breathe through a long hose), ziplines, tanning decks, live music, inviting swimming pools, shady hammocks, souvenir shops, snack bars, and two restaurants. Outside the entrance is a Panoramic Tower ($6) with a bird's-eye view of the island. ⏲ *2 hrs. (families may want to spend the entire day). South end.* ☎ *998/884-9422. Admission $30 or all-inclusive $60. Open 9am–5pm.*

⑫ Lighthouse and Ruin. At
dawn, the sun first touches Mexican land at this tall, rocky, headland bluff on the southeastern tip of the island. Here, overlooking the sea, the ancient Maya built a temple to Ixchel, female goddess of fertility. Destroyed by Hurricane Gilbert, it has since been restored; follow the cement path past anachronistic contemporary sculptures. A modern lighthouse is on higher ground. ⏲ *20–30 min. Southern tip.*

Ruins of a Mayan Temple Against the Sea in Isla Mujeres.

Where to Stay

★ **Hotel Francis Arlene** DOWN-TOWN   The peach-color Francis Arlene maintains a family-friendly ambience, handy kitchenettes, and reasonable prices. Built around a shady courtyard, a block in from the *malecón,* this neat little hotel has 26 rooms, 14 of them air-conditioned. A few have ocean views; all are comfortable with tile floors and tiled bathrooms. *Guerrero 7 (5½ blocks inland from the ferry pier, between Abasolo & Matamoros).* ☎ *998/877-0310. www.francisarlene.com. 26 units. Doubles $55–$65. No credit cards.*

★★★ **Hotel Secreto** NORTH END A virginal white-on-white decor distinguishes this ultra-modern boutique hotel from other beachfront island digs. Nine suites overlook a small garden pool with tropical gardens, and an outdoor living area offers comfy couches and dining. One of the best beaches in the Caribbean, on a half-moon cove. *Punta Norte (behind the Convention Center).* ☎ *877/278-8018 in the U.S., 998/877-1039 in Mexico. www.hotel secreto.com. 9 units. Doubles $190–$260 w/continental breakfast. MC, V.*

The Hotel Secreto on Isla Mujeres.

★★ **kids Na Balam** NORTH END One of Isla's most popular hotels, the "Black Jaguar" is best known as a sanctuary for yoga, meditation, and sunny libations at its ★ Palapa Bar. On a wide, palm-lined beach with shallow waters, it offers rooms facing the ocean or across the street in a garden with a small swimming pool. Garden rooms are newer, but all have a terrace or balcony and hammocks. *Calle Zazil Ha 118.* ☎ *998/877-0279. www.na balam.com. 31 units. Doubles $165–$275. AE, MC, V.*

★★★ **Villa Rolandi Hotel & Beach Club** SAC BAJO   This Swiss-Italian hotel offers pampering in superb luxury accommodations, an infinity pool, and a beachfront gourmet restaurant. Each oversize, Mediterranean-style suite has an ocean view, private balcony or large terrace, plus an individual whirlpool. *Fracc. Lagunamar, SM 7, Mza. 75, Locals 15 & 16.* ☎ *998/877-0100. www.villarolandi.com. 20 units. Doubles $360–$425 w/breakfast & lunch or dinner, plus transportation from Cancún. AE, MC, V.*

Where to Dine

Bistro Frances DOWNTOWN *EUROPEAN* This storefront features economical and delicious meals. Open for breakfast or dinner only, it's casual with a French flair. *Av. Matamoros. No phone. Entrees $4–$11. No credit cards. Open 8am–noon & 6–10pm.*

★ **Casa O's** GARRAFON *SEAFOOD/ MEXICAN* This romantic *palapa* restaurant is on a hill overlooking the bay and the lights of Cancún. Their signature dish is live spiny lobster, and diners choose their own catch. *Carretera Garrafón (south end of Isla Mujeres, on the road to Garrafón).* ☎ *998/888-0170. Entrees $10–$35. MC, V. Open daily 1–11pm.*

★★★ **Casa Rolandi** SAC BAJO *ITALIAN/SEAFOOD* This is the island's best restaurant, with a sophisticated Northern Italian menu, accompanying quality wines, and digs facing the beach in the Villa Rolandi Hotel. The maitre d' suggests the lamb, but they also do a good job with fresh seafood and Italian cuisine. *On the pier of Villa Rolandi, Lagunamar SM 7.* ☎ *998/ 877-0100. Entrees $9–$26. AE, MC, V. Open daily 11am–11pm. Reservations recommended.*

Miramar DOWNTOWN *SEAFOOD/ MEXICAN* Among the small fish restaurants next to the ferry dock, the modest Miramar is my favorite, in a clean and appealing seafront setting. Sit and watch the fisherman unload their catch. *Av. Medina. No phone. Entrees $5–$15. No credit cards. Open daily 7am–10pm.*

Rolandi's Pizza DOWNTOWN *ITALIAN* Rolandi's mini-empire of hotels and restaurants started with

Fish with tomatoes, onions, and achiote.

real brick-oven pizzas and Italian favorites. The extensive menu also features baked chicken, roast beef, seafood platters, and plenty of pasta. Always crowded. *Av. Hidalgo (Madero & Abasolo).* ☎ *998/877-0430. Entrees $4–$13. AE, MC, V. Open daily 11am–11:30pm.*

★★ **Zazil Ha** NORTH END *CARIB-BEAN/INTERNATIONAL* Dine among palm trees and gardens in the open-air dining area or upstairs in an enclosed veranda. The varied menu features excellent pasta, vegetarian options, and. Caribbean specialties. *Calle Zazil Ha 118 (in Hotel Na Balam at the end of Playa Norte).* ☎ *998/877-0279. Entrees $9–$16. AE, MC, V. Open daily 7:30–10:30am, 12:30–3:30pm, 6:30–11pm.*

Mérida

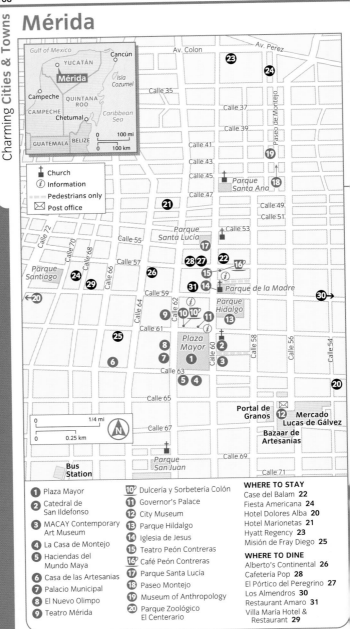

Gulf of Mexico

YUCATÁN

Cancún

Mérida

Isla Cozumel

Campeche

QUINTANA ROO

CAMPECHE

Caribbean Sea

Chetumal

GUATEMALA   BELIZE

0   100 mi
0   100 km

✝ Church
ⓘ Information
- - - Pedestrians only
✉ Post office

Av. Colon

Av. Perez

Calle 35

Calle 37

Calle 39

Paseo de Montejo

Calle 41

Calle 43

Calle 45

Parque Santa Ana

Calle 47

Calle 49

Calle 51

Parque Santa Lucía

✝ Calle 53

Parque de la Madre

Parque Santiago

Calle 72

Calle 70

Calle 68

Calle 66

Calle 55

Calle 57

Parque Hidalgo

Calle 64

Calle 62

Calle 59

Calle 61

Plaza Mayor

Calle 60

Calle 58

Calle 56

Calle 54

Calle 63

Calle 65

Portal de Granos

✉ Mercado Lucas de Gálvez

Bazaar de Artesanías

Calle 67

0   1/4 mi
0   0.25 km

N

Bus Station

✝ Parque San Juan

Calle 69

Calle 71

① Plaza Mayor
② Catedral de San Ildefonso
③ MACAY Contemporary Art Museum
④ La Casa de Montejo
⑤ Haciendas del Mundo Maya
⑥ Casa de las Artesanías
⑦ Palacio Municipal
⑧ El Nuevo Olimpo
⑨ Teatro Mérida

⑩ Dulcería y Sorbetería Colón
⑪ Governor's Palace
⑫ City Museum
⑬ Parque Hildago
⑭ Iglesia de Jesus
⑮ Teatro Peón Contreras
⑯ Café Peón Contreras
⑰ Parque Santa Lucía
⑱ Paseo Montejo
⑲ Museum of Anthropology
⑳ Parque Zoológico El Centenario

WHERE TO STAY
Case del Balam **22**
Fiesta Americana **24**
Hotel Dolores Alba **20**
Hotel Marionetas **21**
Hyatt Regency **23**
Misión de Fray Diego **25**

WHERE TO DINE
Alberto's Continental **26**
Cafeteria Pop **28**
El Pórtico del Peregrino **27**
Los Almendros **30**
Restaurant Amaro **31**
Villa María Hotel & Restaurant **29**

Strolling down the cobblestone streets of Mérida, its not difficult to imagine the city's distinguished past; step into one of its famed remodeled hacienda-style houses and the transformation will be complete. Mérida has European roots as old as the Spanish Conquest of the Americas. Older by a thousand years are its remains of Maya civilization, whose temples in the ancient city of T'ho provided the building blocks for Mérida's first colonial constructions. Stay for at least 2 days; it's an excellent base for exploring the region. START: Valladolid or Cancún. Mérida is west of Valladolid on either the Cuota or Mérida Libre, Highway 180. The toll road rejoins Highway 180 a little under an hour before reaching the city. It's west of Cancún on the toll road, about 6 hours on the Libre. Trip length: 154km (95 miles) from Valladolid; 320km (198 miles) from Cancún.

1 Plaza Mayor. Tall trees shade casual strollers, and vendors with handcarts peddle sweets in this block-sized park. The epicenter of cultural activity in town, the plaza is the meeting place for families, lovers, and old friends who sit side by side in S-shaped seats called *confidenciales*. Its cement walkways throng with people on Sundays for the Mérida en Domingo street fair and other festivals frequently hosted here. Events such as the dance along Calle 62 draw up to 1,000 people (7pm). A 2-hour-long, air-conditioned **bus tour** of the city leaves frequently from Calle 60, opposite the cathedral. *Calles 60, 62, 61, & 63.*

2 Catedral de San Ildefonso. Mérida's most recognizable landmark, the massive Catedral of San Ildefonso dominates the corner of calles 60 and 61, opposite the Main Plaza. In 1561, almost 20 years after founding the city, Spanish Conquistadors began building this severe, fortress-like cathedral using stone blocks torn down from Maya pyramids in the city of T'ho. Cool and dark inside, the plainly adorned cathedral is the oldest in the Americas, completed in 1598.

The interior is as simple as the exterior, but its altars are draped in colorful Maya-inspired embroidered fabric. The main altar is reputed to have the second largest *retablo* in

A street corner in Mérida.

Catedral de San Ildefonso.

the Americas. Over the side door on the right is a painting of Ah Kulum Tutul Xiu, chief of the Xiu clan, who joined forces with Francisco Montejo to defeat their rivals, the Cocoms. To the left of the main altar is *Cristo de Ampollas (Christ of the Blisters)*, a replica of an original carving made from a tree struck by lightning that burned but did not char. The original carving, looted in the Revolution of 1915, was from the early 1600s.

A life-size diorama of the Last Supper is on display in a side chapel (open daily 8–11am and 4:30–7pm). Prayer crosses brought by suppliers cover the Mexican Jesus, and outside the front entrance, impoverished suppliants beg worshippers for pesos. ⏲ *30 min. Calles 60 & 61.*

❸ **MACAY Contemporary Art Museum.** Contemporary Mexican artists have found a home in the *Ateneo Peninsular* (Athenian Peninsula), the former home of the bishop of Yucatán. Enter from the alleyway alongside the cathedral, known as the *Pasaje de la Revolución*—which, until the 1940s, was covered by a distinctive glass roof. Nine air-conditioned salons hold the permanent art collection of mostly Yucatecan painters, notably Fernando Castro

Pacheco and Fernando García Ponce. ⏲ *½ hr.–1 hr. Open Wed–Mon 10am–6pm. Admission $3.*

❹ **La Casa de Montejo.** In 1542, fresh on the heels of conquering the Maya at T'ho, Francisco Montejo, known as *El Mozo* (The Younger), began building this grand private home. It remained in the Montejo family for more than 450 years until it became bank offices in the early 1970s. Flaunting his military prowess and Spanish chauvinism, Montejo flanked the entrance to his home with bas-reliefs of two Conquistadors, standing triumphantly with their feet on the heads of two screaming Maya warriors. The inscription on the plaque underneath reads, "The Adelante Don Francisco Montejo caused this to be made in the year 1549." The interior garden courtyard is in the public area. ⏲ *15 mins. Calle 63. Open daily.*

❺ **Haciendas del Mundo Maya Boutique.** Inside Montejo's house is a shop featuring the products of the Haciendas Mundo Maya workshops, located in rural Maya villages throughout the Yucatán peninsula. *Calle 63.* ☎ *999/924-3070.*

❻ **Casa de las Artesanias.** The official home of local artisan vendors, this large handicrafts shop is in *Las Monjas* (The Nuns), a restored former monastery, a block and a half off the main square. This interesting vendor occupies the front rooms of the colonial building, which dates from the late 1500s, with a Moorish-style tower that was added in 1648. Shoppers will find generally higher-quality Yucatán-made crafts here, at slightly elevated prices. The monastery's back courtyard serves as a gallery with rotating folk and fine-art exhibits. ⏲ *1 hr. Calle 63 (between calles 64 & 66). Open Mon–Sat 9am–8pm, Sun 9am–1pm.*

❼ Palacio Municipal. City hall was built on the site of the last Maya building in Mérida to be dismantled. The mid-19th-century edifice has a second-floor balcony with views of the park. Sunday and Monday it hosts special—very special—all-day events during the town's biggest fiesta. *Calle 62 (between calles 63 & 61).*

Tourist Office

On Calle 60, between calles 59 and 57, is a helpful **tourist information office,** behind huge wooden doors next to the Peón Contreras Theater. They provide pamphlets, directions, and maps, and they answer questions in English.

❽ El Nuevo Olimpo. This modern "New Olympus" tries to recapture the panache of its predecessor by combining architectural styles and filling it with a bookstore, concert and gallery space, a round atrium, and a street-side coffee shop. Check the bulletin board in front for concert information; live music is performed almost nightly at 9pm. *Calles 62 & 61.*

❾ Teatro Mérida. An Edwardian Art Deco delight, this beautifully renovated chrome and glass-block

Cuzamá: Caballos, Culture & Cenotes

Unless you happened to be a henequén farmer with a habit for playing hooky in *cenotes* in your past life, chances are you've never experienced anything like Cuzamá. The small municipality just 65km (40 miles) south of Mérida is home to three cenotes—Chelentún, Chacsinic-Che, and Bolonchojol—which are along the small railway formally used to transport henequén leaves from the fields to the hacienda's machinery room. The rails still exist and visitors can hire a horse-drawn *troque,* or cart, for about 150 pesos for a daylong excursion that stops at each cenote. Each stop includes a descent down a wooden ladder that leads to an aqua paradise where visitors can feel at one with the gods of the Maya underworld. Be sure to pack a picnic lunch, water-resistant sandals, and snorkeling gear to ply the crystalline waters.

The horsedrawn cart to Cuzamá.

For more information on a 7-hour tour that includes transportation from Mérida and the price of the troque, visit www.yucatan.travel.

Sunday dancers in the Main Plaza.

former movie house is now a center-stage theater and cinema. If something is playing, don't miss it. *Calle 62 (between calles 61 & 59).* ☎ *999/924-0040. Admission usually $3, depending on the performance.*

Mérida can be hot, humid, and hard on the feet. When the mercury is high, nothing beats the refreshing ice cream and sherbet served at 🔟 **Dulcería y Sorbetería Colón** under the colonial arches of the old Casa del Alguacil (Magistrate's House), opposite the south corner of the Plaza. *Calle 61 (at 62). No phone.*

⓫ **Governor's Palace.** The seat of Yucatán's state government, the Palacio del Gobierno overlooks the entrance to the cathedral, at the corner of the Main Plaza. It's open to the public, and wandering around is encouraged. The building dates to 1892, with arches covering a walkway that connects the entire block. Decorating the walls of the interior courtyard, huge murals by Yucatecan artist Fernando Castro Pacheco depict Maya and Mexican history.

The second floor's front room, Salon de Historia, provides a good view of the cathedral, plaza, and more huge paintings by Castro. A musical performance takes place in the salon every Sunday at 11am. A small tourism office is to your left as you enter. ⏱ *30 min. Calles 61 & 60. Open Mon–Sat 8am–8pm, Sun 9am–5pm.*

⓬ **City Museum.** The newly remodeled and relocated *Museo de la Ciudad* occupies the former majestic post office palace. Explanatory English texts accompany exhibits on Mérida's history, including some fascinating old photos. ⏱ *30–45 min. Calle 65 (near 56). Open Tues–Fri 9am–8pm; Sat & Sun 9am–2pm. Free admission.*

⓭ **Parque Hildalgo.** On the east side of Calle 60, this popular little rectangular park was in the original city plan that Francisco Montejo laid out in 1542. It houses two venerable hotels with outside dining areas. That makes it a very popular place, at any time of the day, to grab a bite to eat and to people-watch. *Calle 60 at 59.*

A fruit stall in the Mercado Municipal in Mérida.

The streets of Mérida.

⑭ Iglesia de Jesus. This charming little church is one of Mérida's older buildings, built in 1618 by the Jesuit Order. The Jesuits lost a power struggle to the Franciscans—after a Jesuit-educated Maya Indian, Jacinto Canek, started a rebellion—and were expelled from the peninsula in 1761; but the educational institution they left behind became the present-day University of Yucatán.

The picturesque exterior is a favorite site for weddings. The faint markings on its exterior stone walls are Maya carvings from the temple that formerly stood here. A tiny, shady park to the side, *Parque de la Madre,* has a replica statue of Renoir's *Madonna and Child.* It's a favorite spot for jewelry vendors and artists, especially on Sundays. *Calle 60 (between calles 59 & 57).*

⑮ Teatro Peón Contreras. Designed in 1908 by Enrico Deserti, and built in the flush of wealth from the henequén trade, this magnificent theater is the city's main concert and performance center. It's noted for its opulent Carrara marble staircase and frescoed dome, restored to their original glory in the

Swing Time

Yucatán's most famous cottage industry is the production of hammocks made of cotton or nylon, woven by hand on wooden looms. You sleep in this style of hammock on the diagonal. The most durable and colorful variety are made from nylon, but the cotton ones are the most comfortable. You'll find both types sold in handicraft shops and by street vendors who come in from the nearby town of Tixcocob, where every family in town makes them. Quality counts, so buy the best ($35 and up); look for fine and plentiful string in the body. The merchandise at **Hamacas El Aguacate,** on Calle 58 at 73, 6 blocks south of the square, is consistently high-end.

Exterior ornament on Spanish colonial mansion.

1980s when Mérida's tourism trade substantially increased. If something's on, be sure to go. If not, peek inside at the lavish decor meant to rival the great European theaters of its time.

Horsing Around

The corner of calles 60 and 61, along the north side of the cathedral, is a good place to hire *caselas*—horse-drawn buggies—for a romantic tour of the Centro Historico. Listen for the clip-clop.

Most Wednesdays at 9pm, you can count on the Ballet Folklorico from the University of Yucatán to present a musical and dance interpretation of *Yucatán and its Roots*. Check the schedule for its roster of national and international stars. *Calle 60 (between calles 59 & 57). Admission to Ballet Folklorico $5.*

Wrought-iron tables with romantic market umbrellas accent the charm and appeal of 16 **Café Peón**

Contreras, an al fresco cafe in the heart of the historic center. Order a tall cappuccino, a light snack, or a cool drink to see or be seen on this pedestrian-only alleyway next to the tourist office and Contreras Theater.

17 **Parque Santa Lucia.** Santa Lucia Park was once the end of the stagecoach run in the early days of Mérida. Now it's the departure point for a 2-hour **Discover Mérida Trolley Tour** of the city, which leaves daily at 10am and 1, 4, and 7pm (about $8). It's narrated mostly in Spanish. Be sure to keep your head and arms inside on the narrow streets.

The tiny park is bordered by an arcaded terrace. Busts of Yucatán poets frame its small courtyard. Musical entertainment takes place on most weeknights. Every Sunday, a stamp and used-book flea market runs here from 10am to 2pm, with a police band performance at 11:30am. The park is best known for its Thursday-evening Yucatán Serenade, which starts around 9pm. Begun in 1965, it's a free

The Plaza Grande after dark.

Local handicrafts.

vocal and musical performance of typical Yucatecan and Mexican songs, poetry readings, and folk dancing. Very popular among locals and tourists alike.

The small church opposite the park, *Iglesia de Santa Lucia,* was built in 1575 for the African and Caribbean slaves who lived in the surrounding district. The area is a lot more upscale now. *Calles 60 & 55.*

⑱ **Paseo Montejo.** Mérida's most fashionable district is the broad, tree-lined boulevard *Paseo de Montejo,* and its surrounding northern neighborhood. Built in the boom times of the henequén industry, it is reminiscent of the Champs d'Elysee in Paris. It was once lined on both sides by stately, Belle Epoque mansions owned by Mérida's elite, but many have been converted into offices and fine restaurants. It's a popular place to hire a *casela* for a horse-drawn buggy ride—especially in the evening, when the remaining private homes turn on their lights, affording a glimpse of the luxurious interiors within. The Paseo begins at Calle 47 and parallels Calle 60, 7 blocks north of the Main Plaza. In the center of the traffic circle with Avenida Colón, a grand memorial by Columbian sculptor Rumulo Rozo, *Monumento a la Patria,* depicts Mexico's

Mérida After Dark

For all its cultural happenings, Mérida's historic center isn't particularly wild after dark, so young professionals frequent dance clubs and bars in the fashionable neighborhoods around the Paseo. Performing arts nightlife downtown can be found at the Teatro Peón Contreras, calles 60 and 57, and Teatro Ayala, calles 60 and 61; art cinema is shown at the Nuevo Olympio, Calle 62, on the square, and the Teatro Mérida, a half-block north.

If you don't take yourself seriously, **Pancho's** (☎ 999/923-0942; Calle 59 between calles 60 and 62) is a lighthearted cantina restaurant great for drinking, schmoozing, and good Tex-Mex grub. Waiters wear Pancho Villa mustaches, sombreros, and bandoliers. There's live music nightly. In the large dining room at ★ **Restaurant El Nuevo Tucho** (☎ 999/924-2323; Calle 60 between calles 55 and 57), patrons spontaneously get up to dance to the band. **La Habana** is a popular restaurant and cafe, open 24 hours, on the corner of calles 59 and 62.

Young men in traditional costume.

history in stone. *Paseo de Montejo (from Calle 47 to Av. Colón).*

⑲ Museum of Anthropology.

One of Mérida's most important scholarly resources, the *Museo Regional de Antropología,* is housed in a magnificent mansion halfway up the Paseo de Montejo. Enrico Deserti, the architect of the Teatro Peón Contreras, designed and built the place from 1909 to 1911 for General Francisco Cantón Rosado. Rosado relished its beauty for only a few years before he died in 1917; it subsequently served as the official residence of Yucatán's governors until it was converted to this museum. The lavish interior architecture warrants a tour of the inside.

The Anthropology Museum's main focus is the peninsula's pre-Columbian culture. Its permanent exhibitions, captioned only in Spanish, start with fossil mastodon teeth and then trace Yucatán's history from the earliest pre-Columbian cultural customs to the recent excavations of Maya ceremonial sites, as well as everyday contemporary life of the indigenous people.

Exhibitions illustrate a number of fascinating Maya customs. They used to tie boards to baby's heads, for instance, to reshape them in an oblong slant considered beautiful. They also filed or perforated teeth to insert jewels. Enlarged photos of excavations give visitors a different perspective on the ruined Maya cities. 🕐 *1½ hrs. Paseo de Montejo and Calle 43.* ☎ *999/923-0557. Open Tues–Sun 8am–5pm. Admission 41 pesos.*

⑳ kids Parque Zoológico El Centerario.

This zoo and young children's amusement park is on the western fringe of the colonial center of Mérida, at the end of Calle 59. It's packed with families on Sundays. Little kids love the narrow-gauge train that drives them around the shady park, and grown-ups love the walks. But animal lovers may bray at the confined conditions of many of the animals. Let's face it: The Bronx Zoo it's not. 🕐 *1 hr. Av. Itzáes & Calle 59. Admission $2.*

Where to Stay

★★ Casa del Balam HISTORIC CENTER House of the Jaguar features 51 appealing junior suites in the gorgeous ancestral home of the Yucatán's earliest pioneer families. Bedrooms are large with wrought-iron accents and Spanish furnishings. With its dependable quality and sensitive combination of old and new, the del Balam is the epitome of colonial class in the historic center, right next to the Teatro Peón Contreras. *Calle 60 (at 57).* ☎ *800/624-8451 in the U.S., or 999/924-2150. www.casa delbalam.com. 51 units. Doubles 1,345 pesos. AE, MC, V.*

★★ Fiesta Americana PASEO This stately hotel is a great place to stay if you've got business to attend to. Although it hasn't been used for its official purpose since Former U.S. President George W. Bush arrived in 2007, guests can book the helicopter pad for private events. *Paseo de Montejo 451 (near Colón).* ☎ *999/942-1111. www.fiesta mericana.com. 350 units. Doubles 1,000–2,000 pesos, presidential suite 6,999 pesos. MC, V.*

The Casa Principal.

Hotel Dolores Alba HISTORIC CENTER Attractive, comfortably large rooms, air-conditioning, an inviting swimming pool, and free parking are yours at this clean, family-run hotel, 4 blocks off the square. It's an excellent value, and they also

Hacienda Living

Symbols of lavish Mexican country estate living, haciendas (ranch estates) are scattered throughout the Yucatán peninsula, and they make for the most luxurious yet authentic accommodations in the peninsula. These large architectural gems fell into disrepair after the henequén trade went bust in the early 1900s. Luckily, many have come back to life as luxurious hotels, some with spa amenities that envelop guests in sensuous surroundings. A favorite among longtime visitors is the 17th-century **★★★ Hacienda Temozón** (☎ 999/923-8089; www.haciendasmexico.com), a great place to be pampered. Beautifully restored, the hacienda is located on lovely grounds, which include a remarkable eight cenotes. It's worth a visit just to dine at the restaurant on the premises. See p 88.

Get Cookin'

Chef David Sterling will teach you to cook authentic Yucatecan meals in a beautifully restored colonial home in the heart of the historic district, through his **Los Dos Cooking School** *(Calle 68 between calles 65 and 67; www.los-dos.com; doubles $1,725 for a 3-day workshop including meals and accommodation).*

have an economy hotel near Chichén Itzá. *Calle 63 (between calles 52 & 54).* ☎ *999/928-5650. www. doloresalba.com. 100 units. Doubles 545 pesos. No credit cards.*

★★ **Hotel Marionetas** HISTORIC CENTER   The dreamy gold and blue Marionetas is one of the most successful conversions of a colonial mansion into a boutique hotel. Intimate rooms, with colorful Mérida tile floors, are elegantly decorated and very comfortable. A stay at this hotel is a sensual pleasure. *Calle 49 (between calles 62 & 64).* ☎ *999/ 928-3377. www.hotelmarionetas. com. 8 units. $160. AE, MC, V.*

★★ **Hyatt Regency** PASEO   Rising 17 stories, the Hyatt is not hard to spot in Mérida's northern skyline,

1 block off the Paseo de Montejo, in the most fashionable neighborhood in town. Count on it for dependable Hyatt quality and quiet rooms. *Calle 60 (Av. Colón).* ☎ *800/223-1234 in the U.S., or 999/942-1234. www. merida.regency.hyatt.com. 289 units. Double $89–$190. AE, DC, MC, V.*

★★ **Misión de Fray Diego** HISTORIC CENTER   Behind a tall 17th-century wall and thick wooden portal, this small boutique hotel successfully combines a historical ambience with modern conveniences. Rooms surround a small central courtyard pool. *Calle 61 (between calles 64 & 66).* ☎ *866/639-2933 in the U.S. and Canada, or 999/924-1111. www.lamision defraydiego.com. 26 units. Doubles $95. AE, MC, V.*

Garden Palapa Mayan massage table.

Where **to Dine**

★★ **Alberto's Continental** HISTORIC CENTER *REGIONAL/SEAFOOD* Alberto's features romantic candlelit dining in a courtyard framed by Moorish arches and elegant *mudejar*-patterned tile floors. The restaurant is in a colonial-era building built with the stones of original Maya temples. Try the Lebanese sampler platter and stuffed fish Celestún. *Calle 64 (at 57).* ☎ *999/928-5367. Entrees 90–295 pesos. AE, MC, V. Open daily 1–11pm.*

★ **Cafeteria Pop** HISTORIC CENTER *MEXICAN* Plan a revolution under the noses of the bourgeois at El Pórtico next door. This cafe, frequented by Yucatán University students and academics, serves light meals and a bottomless cup of coffee. Opens early, closes late. *Calle 57 (between calles 60 & 62). No phone. Entrees 50–100 pesos. No credit cards. 6am–10pm.*

★★ **El Pórtico del Peregrino** HISTORIC CENTER *MEXICAN/REGIONAL* El Pórtico is a favorite among visitors for its central location, charm, comfort, and distinctive Mérida flavor. The interior features a lovely garden for dining *al fresco* and two air-conditioned dining rooms. They serve a good *pollo pibil*, chicken cooked in banana leaves until it falls off the bone. *Calle 57 (between calles 60 & 62).* ☎ *999/ 928-6163. Entrees 70–175 pesos. AE, MC, V. Daily noon–11pm.*

★★★ **Los Almendros** AROUND TOWN *MEXICAN/REGIONAL* Los Almendros is the birthplace of *poc chuc,* a grilled pork dish, but also try the *cochinita pibil,* pork cooked in banana leaf—both are mouth-watering Yucatecan favorites. *Calle 50A no. 493 (facing Parque de la Mejorada).* ☎ *999/928-5459. Entrees $6–$15. AE, MC, V. Daily 10am–11pm.*

★ **Restaurant Amaro** HISTORIC CENTER *MEXICAN/VEGETARIAN* This romantic restaurant with an open-air courtyard dining room, candlelit tables, and roving troubadours features vegetarian dishes on a mostly Mexican menu. Try the *queso relleno,* pepper stuffed with cheese. *Calle 59 (between calles 60 & 62).* ☎ *999/928-2451. Entrees 45–145 pesos. AE, MC, V. 9am–10pm.*

★★★ **Villa María Hotel & Restaurant** HISTORIC CENTER *INTERNATIONAL/BISTRO* This gorgeously restored 17th-century mansion hotel is the city's only authentic fine-dining bistro. It serves great cuts of meat and generous salads. Try the mouth-watering Moroccan Chicken in lemon, olives, and spices, with rice and dried fruit. *Calle 59 (at 68).* ☎ *999/923-3357. www.villamariamerida.com. Entrees 100–190 pesos. AE, MC, V. Mon–Sat 2pm–midnight, Sun 2–10pm. Reservations recommended.*

Liquid Lunch

Mérida and the Yucatán have a few homegrown liquors: **Montejo** and **Leon Negra** are two excellent beers brewed in Mérida, and **Xtabentun** is a Maya liqueur made from honey and anise. The best is Mérida's **Argaez** brand in a blue bottle.

Playa **del** Carmen

1 Ferry Pier
2 Central Plaza
3 Fifth Ave. (Avenida Quinta)
4 Coffee Press
5 Bus Station

WHERE TO STAY
Deseo Hotel 10
Hotel Playa Maya 7
Jungla Caribe Hotel
& Restaurant 9
La Tortuga 8

WHERE TO DINE
Casa Mediterránea 13
El Chino 12
John Gray's Place 11
La Tarraya Restaurant 14

Playa's growth in the last dozen years has been nothing short of phenomenal; it's a destination that's constantly growing and changing. But for all its development, Playa retains the feel of a small, pedestrian-friendly beach town with unique hotels, restaurants, and shops—despite the increasing preponderance of them. Those who knew it before may lament its growth from sleepy harbor village into a social and commercial mecca; those who come for the first time will be seduced by its lively tourist scene, fine beach, and European influence, with the region's most nonchalant acceptance of topless sunbathing. START: **Cancún. Trip length: Playa is 70km (43 miles) south of Cancún on Highway 307.**

1 **Ferry Pier.** The main ferry pier *(muelle)* for Cozumel is at the southern end of Playa del Carmen town; a bit farther south, you'll end up in Playacar, a planned development with all-inclusive hotels, residential town houses, and a golf course. Ferries depart hourly between 6am and 11pm (Ultramar boats are faster than Barcos Mexico). Purchase tickets at any of the kiosks. ⏱ *30 min.*

2 **Central Plaza.** Set up like a small park with a children's playground, the town plaza is a hangout for trinket vendors from Chiapas, fruit-salad sellers, and stoop sitters. The beach in front hosts

The streets of Playa del Carmen after dark.

sometimes-competitive hard-body volleyball and soccer games. *Av. 5 & Juárez.*

3 Avenida Quinta. Fifth Avenue begins here and feels like it may someday stretch all the way to New York, it's developing so fast. From morning until long into the evening, pedestrians stroll, shop, dine, drink, shop some more, and people-watch on Playa's signature street. The gorgeous colorful rayon *parejas* for sale in many shops used to be made right in Playa, but most come from Indonesia now. They're still a best buy by virtue of the huge selection and sexy styles. Shopping dominates the pedestrian-only avenue, but you'll also find a plethora of unique and rewarding restaurants, bars, and boutique hotels. Just a block off the beach.

Grab a cup of hand-pressed joe and a muffin at the **4 Coffee Press.** The town's favorite coffee stop sells paperbacks to read while you eat breakfast or lunch near the beach. *Calle 2 (between Fifth Ave. & the beach). No phone.*

5 Bus Station. If you're returning to Cancún or the airport, you won't have to wait long for buses, which arrive and depart every 10 to 15 minutes. They also stop at Puerto Morelos, and Mayab buses bound for Tulum depart here as well. *Av. Juárez & 5th Av. ☎ 987/803-0109. (For journeys to destinations farther afield, you'll likely use the station on Av. 20 [at Calle 12]; ☎ 998/884-5542.) The fare to the airport or Cancún is about $7.*

Playa After Dark

Fifth Avenue has a long lineup of bars; one of the most popular is ★ **Karen's Bar & Grill** between calles 2 and 4. Follow the sound of the crowd and canned music. A rock 'n' roll crowd frequents the age-old tropical beach bar, the ★ **Blue Parrot,** which hosts live music at night. It's on the sand at the end of Calle 12 (☎ 984/873-0083). The trendy ★★ **Mambo Café** (☎ 984/803-2656) swings to salsa on Calle 6 between avenidas 5 and 10.

Across the highway, ★ **Alux** (☎ 984/803-0713) is a unique nightclub in a large cavern with two dramatically lit chambers. The music is varied, with occasional belly dancers, and rarely a cover charge (open Tues–Sun 7pm–2am; take Av. Juárez across Hwy. 307 and go 2 blocks on your left).

Where **to Stay**

★★★ Hotel Deseo DOWNTOWN The Deseo is perhaps the most desirable hotel in a town where being hip is a *raison d'etre*. The adults-only environment was designed to foster socializing, and the open-air lounge plays a central role; it's faced on two sides by guest rooms and combines the functions of lobby, restaurant, bar, and pool. The raised platform also features a self-serve kitchen and daybeds for sunning or enjoying an evening drink. Clientele are predominately 25- to 45-year-olds. Rooms are comfortable, visually striking, somewhat luxurious, and sans TV. Under the thick, king-size beds, a pullout drawer holds nighttime necessities such as incense, earplugs, and condoms. *Av. 5 (Calle 12).* ☎ *984/879-3620. www.hoteldeseo.com. 15 units. Doubles $180–$200. AE, MC, V.*

★ Hotel Playa Maya DOWNTOWN Guests enter Hotel Playa Maya from the sandy shore, differentiating it from other lodgings on this busy street scene. A quiet location; reasonable prices; friendly, helpful management; and attractive, comfortable rooms also set it apart from the rest. Rooms are relatively large; a few have

The lounge at the Hotel Deseo.

private garden terraces with Jacuzzis, and others have balconies facing the beach. *On the beach (between calles 6 & 8).* ☎ *984/803-2022. www.playa-maya.com. 20 units. Doubles $112–$145. AE, MC, V.*

★ Jungla Caribe Hotel & Restaurant DOWNTOWN Smack dab on 5th Avenue, 1 block from the beach, La Jungla stands out with unique neoclassic tropical decor, comfortable rooms, and plenty of late-night activity. All but the eight single rooms are large, with gray-and-black marble floors, air-conditioning, and big bathrooms with bidets. Catwalks lead to the tower suites in the back (the quietest). A notable Mexican restaurant wraps around a terrace facing Calle 8, and the hotel's interior courtyard has an attractive *cenote*-style pool, surrounded by vegetation and shaded by a gigantic *ramón* tree. *Av. 5 (at Calle 8).* ☎ *984/873-0650. www.jungla-caribe.com. 25 units. Doubles $90, suites $120–$130. AE, MC, V.*

★ Treetops DOWNTOWN The rooms at Treetops encircle a patch of preserved jungle (and a small *cenote*) that shades the hotel and lends it the proper tropical feel. Longtime Playa travelers often choose this hidden hotel, a half-block from the beach, because it's a remnant of the Playa del Carmen that has all but disappeared amid breakneck development. Rooms are ample, with balconies or terraces that overlook the greenery. One of the upper suites has the feel of a tree house. The other two suites are large, with fully appointed kitchenettes. The owners are American. *Calle 8 (near the beach).* ☎ *984/873-0351. 18 units. Doubles $50–$85, suites $125–$150. MC, V.*

Where to Dine

★★★ Casa Mediterránea

DOWNTOWN *ITALIAN* Tucked away on a quiet patio off Avenida Quinta, this small restaurant with a welcoming, relaxed atmosphere serves delicious, well-cooked food. The menu is mostly Northern Italian with several dishes from other parts of Italy. Except for the penne and spaghetti, the pasta is homemade, and the selection of Italian wines is broad. Their salads are good. For an entree, try the fish and shrimp ravioli or penne alla Veneta. *Av. 5 (between calles 6 & 8).* ☎ *984/876-3926. Entrees: $8–$15. No credit cards. Open daily 1–11pm. Reservations recommended in high season.*

★ El Chino DOWNTOWN *MEXICAN*

No, it is not a Chinese restaurant. Unlike a better-known eatery with a more Maya name, El Chino is *the* place to have authentic Yucatecan/Mexican fare, without a faux ambience and pricey menu. This sidestreet, family-run restaurant seats diners next to broad arched windows under a tall *palapa* roof. The open kitchen prepares an extensive selection of Mexican and local Yucatecan specialties such as *poc chuc,* pork tenderized in sour orange, served with rice and beans and pickled onions. *Av. 4 (between calles 10 & 15). No phone. Entrees $6–$13. No credit cards. Open daily 7am–11pm.*

★★★ John Gray's Place DOWN-

TOWN *INTERNATIONAL* John Gray, a former executive chef with Ritz-Carlton worldwide hotels, pegged his culinary reputation on his own dinner-only restaurants along the Riviera Maya. After the success of his Puerto Morelos restaurant, he opened this one in Playa, off 5th Avenue, on shady Calle Corazon.

Fajitas at one of the many sidewalk cafes on Quinta Avenida in Playa del Carmen.

The breast of duck and rack of lamb are mouthwatering. *Calle Corazon (5th Av.).* ☎ *984/803-3689. Entrees $10–$36. No credit cards. Open Mon–Sat 6–11pm. Reservations recommended.*

★ La Tarraya Restaurant

DOWNTOWN *SEAFOOD* It's right on the beach and owned by a fishing family, so you know the fresh catch is superb. It's also one of the oldest places around; a sign reads, "The restaurant that was born with the town." The ambience here is definitely unpretentious; it's just a wood hut directly on the white beach. But that's what paradise is, isn't it? *Calle 2 (at the beach).* ☎ *984/873-2040. Entrees $4–$7, whole fried fish $8 per kilo. No credit cards. Open daily 7am–9pm.*

Valladolid

1. Main Plaza
2. Cathedral of San Gervacio
3. Municipal Palace
4. El Kabah Café
5. San Roque Museum
6. Church of Santa Ana
7. Cenote Zací
8. Municipal Mercado
9. Yalat
10. Mercado de Artesanías
11. Calle 41A
12. Church of San Bernardino of Siena & Ex-Convento of Sisal
13. Cenotes Xke'ken & Samula

WHERE TO STAY & DINE

Bazar **17**
El Mesón del Marquéz **14**
María de la Luz **15**
Plaza Maya **16**

This 16th-century colonial-era city is in the very heart of the Yucatán—close enough to Cancún and Mérida to enjoy it as a day trip from either city, but distant enough to offer an authentic experience of living history. Maya from the countryside still come to town dressed in traditional clothes, and the unhurried pace of life grants visitors the leisure to stumble upon unexpected pleasures. It's compact, so you can follow the sights listed below as a walking tour. START: **Cancún. Trip length: Valladolid is 120km (74 miles) west of Cancún, accessed from Mérida Libre, Highway 180, or from its own exit on the Cuota. First-class buses run from Cancún's downtown bus terminal to the ADO terminal on calles 39 and 46. From Playa del Carmen, return to Cancún on Highway 307 and take the Cuota (toll road); exit before the airport.**

1 **Main Plaza.** Spanish Conquistadors led by Francisco de Montejo founded Valladolid (Ba-ya-do-*leed*) in 1543. Local Maya temples reminded them of the Roman ruins in Valladolid, Spain, so they took them as inspiration for the town's name, then tore them down to build the colonial buildings surrounding the shady main plaza. It's a center of activity on Sundays, and every day Maya women line the north side to sell traditional dresses, called *huipils,* as well as Yucatecan

Calle 41-A in Valladolid.

hammocks. Prices are good, with room to negotiate. Inquire at the tourist office about the trolley tour that leaves from the plaza on Calle 41. At dusk, birds fill the plaza's trees, and their squawks fill the air. *Calles 39 & 40.*

2 Cathedral of San Gervacio. Catholic churches built on central squares almost always face east, but local legend has it that this cathedral, constructed in 1706 to replace an earlier one from 1545, faces south as punishment because thieves stole from the altar. Its thick stone walls failed to prevent the Maya from sacking it in the Caste War uprising of 1847, which began in Valladolid. It's still large enough to impress with a towering *retablo* behind the altar. ⏱ *15 min. Calles 41 & 42. No phone. Open daily.*

3 Municipal Palace. Halfway up the worn stone steps to the second floor, City Hall proudly displays a coat of arms that features a list of Conquistadors who founded the "Valiant City" in 1543, after defeating the native Maya who defended *Zací* (the Maya name for the city, meaning "white hawk"). The arches and open center courtyard style are typically period Spanish. On the second floor, large paintings depict Yucatán history. The upstairs

windows yield a good view of the square. On Sunday evenings, a small concert takes place under the arches. The city's small tourism office is there, and a bank and the post office are next door. ⏱ *15 min. Calles 40 & 41.*

The upstairs corner balcony at **4 El Kabah Café,** with a view of the park, is an inviting spot for a cup of good Chiapas coffee, cappuccino, or a cold ice cream. Enter this small coffee shop on Calle 41 and climb the old marble stairs. *Calle 41. No phone. No credit cards.*

5 San Roque Museum. This tiny city museum is in a former hospital, Name of Jesus. The best part is the quiet memorial park in its backyard, a great place to take a break under shade trees. ⏱ *30 min. Calle 41 & 38. No phone. Free admission.*

6 Church of Santa Ana. *La Iglesia de los Indios*—the little church in Barrio Santa Ana on Calle 41 at 34—was a chapel built exclusively for the Maya Indians. In 1847, it played an ignominious role in Yucatán's long and bloody Caste War. In January of that year, wealthy hacienda owners armed the local Maya to help them drive out the

A horse and buggy in Valladolid.

Mexican Army. But the Maya turned on their arms suppliers and sacked the city. After the Yucatán seceded, a local Indian named Antonio Ay was accused of plotting an Indian rebellion. To make him an example, Valladolid's authorities shot him against the side of the chapel. The Maya who had hidden their firearms began attacking, first remote haciendas in the countryside, then small towns, and finally Valladolid.

In less than a year, Valladolid's citizenry once again were slaughtered and survivors fled in panic to the fortified walled cities of Mérida and Campeche. About to drive the Yucatecans entirely out of the peninsula, the Maya nonetheless called a "time out" to attend to their farms at corn-planting time. The desperate Yucatecans agreed to rejoin the Mexican state in exchange for soldiers to fight the Maya insurrection. Heavily armed garrisons fought the disorganized Maya for years before Valladolid went back to the peaceful, provincial town it is today. *Calle 41 at 34. No phone. Free admission.*

7 kids Cenote Zací. With overhanging vines and dark depths, this *cenote* provided the ancient Maya with water in the original town of *Zací.* The heavy foliage and mature

trees give the look and feel of natural jungle. A local man cliff-dives in the murky green water for tips. Zací features a *palapa*-roof restaurant serving Mexican food, and a small, inconsequential zoo. ⏱ *2 hrs. Calles 37 & 36. Admission $2.*

8 Municipal Mercado. Especially on Sunday mornings, Maya *campesinos* come into town to shop and sell their wares at this regional marketplace—a routine part of life in Valladolid since its founding. Food and produce predominate, but only realists should venture into the meat-market section. Look for the home-harvested honey, sold in recycled plastic bottles. *Calles 37 & 32.*

9 Yalat. Perhaps the best gift shop in the Yucatán, Yalat is owned by a North American who sells unique folk art from all over Mexico but specializes in the Yucatán. Inside her corner shop, you'll find artist-created woven tapestries; ceramics; polychrome vases; shell, stone, and silver jewelry; black pottery; beadwork; and hand-embroidered *huipils. Calles 39 & 40. No phone.*

10 Mercado de Artesanías. This colonial building houses stalls around a courtyard that sell

The Convento de San Bernardino.

Cenote Zaci.

traditional and artisan gifts and souvenirs, including wood carvings, *huipil* dresses, embroidered blouses and *guayabera* shirts, *rebozo* shawls, onyx, hammocks, and leather goods. *Calles 39 & 44.*

11 Calle 41A. The *Calzada de los Frailes* (Walkway of the Friars) is the prettiest street in the Yucatán—running diagonally from the corner of calles 41 and 46 to Calle 49. A shortcut to San Bernardino, the cobblestone street is lined by single-story colonial homes, restored and painted in gold, rust, and other period colors. The best time to stroll here is just before sunset. *Calle 41A (at calles 41 & 46).*

12 Church of San Bernardino of Siena & Ex-Convento of Sisal. The fortress-like religious complex of San Bernardino Church and the former Convent of Sisal is at the end of Calle 41A, behind a charming little square of restored colonial buildings. Designed in 1552 by Juan de Mérida, the same architect who would later build the cathedral, these are the oldest major Spanish buildings in the Yucatán. Inside, original 16th- and 17th-century paintings survive on the walls above the side altars.

Ask for admission to the quiet monastery garden, highlighted by a stone-domed gazebo built over one of the Yucatán's deepest underground *cenotes,* which gave the neighborhood of Sisal its name—a corruption of the Maya words *Sis Ha,* meaning cold water. *Calles 49 & 41A.*

13 kids Cenotes Xke'ken & Samula. Two of the most breathtaking sights in the natural Yucatán are the twin *cenotes* of Xke'ken and Samula, a short distance out of town, on the way to Chichén Itzá. Climb down slippery stone steps into warm and very humid caverns with stunning underground lakes. They're well lit, under high ceilings. Both have small holes in the roof that allow a shaft of bright daylight to illuminate the clear blue water. You can swim like Indiana Jones (wash off any sunblock first) or just "ohh" and "ahh" at the phenomena. ⏱ *4 hrs. Dzitnup, 4km (2.5 miles) west of Valladolid, off Hwy. 180. Admission $2. Open 7am–7pm.*

Where to Stay & Dine

Bazar HISTORIC CENTER On a corner opposite the park is a series of inexpensive little eateries serving three meals a day. The menus run from eggs rancheros to sandwiches to *comida corrida*, a daily "blue-plate" dinner special. A local specialty is *mondongo*, made from beef intestine. Try it and tell me how you like it. One dish we do eat is *longaniza*, a spicy regional sausage. *Calle 39 (at calle 40). No phone. Entrees $3–$9. No credit cards. Open 6am–9pm.*

★ **El Meson del Marqués** HISTORIC CENTER Originally the family home of its owner, the Meson grew over the years into a full-fledged quality hotel with a romantic courtyard restaurant serving Mexican fare. The rooms in back are new, built up three stories with a pool and private parking. A fixture in Valladolid since 1966. *Calle 39 (facing the square).* ☎ *985/856-2073. www.mesondelmarques.com. 90 units. Doubles $45. AE. Reservations recommended.*

★★ **Maria de la Luz** HISTORIC CENTER On the corner opposite the square, the Maria is a three-story, remodeled hotel that surrounds a large pool in its courtyard. At its hugely popular street-front Mexican restaurant, I always order the *poc chuc* or chicken in *mole*. The hotel's medium-size rooms are a good value, and the hotel has off-street parking. *Calle 42 (at Calle 39).* ☎ *985/856-2071. www.mariadela luzhotel.com. 70 units. $35. MC, V.*

★ **Plaza Maya** HISTORIC CENTER Tourists typically miss this clean little restaurant that, since 1988, has offered Mexican and authentic Yucatecan regional fare. The back dining room is palapa-covered and the kitchen, visible through a large glass window, is immaculate. The delicious Valladolid platter features up to eight local specialties that include longaniza (pork sausage) and venado (venison). Valladolid's own Xtabentun, a "Maya" liqueur made from local honey and anise, is a great after-dinner drink. *Calle 41 (between 48 & 50). No phone. Entrees $5–$10. No credit cards.* ●

El Mesón del Marquéz, a private home-turned restaurant in Valladolid.

The Best of Cancún in One Day

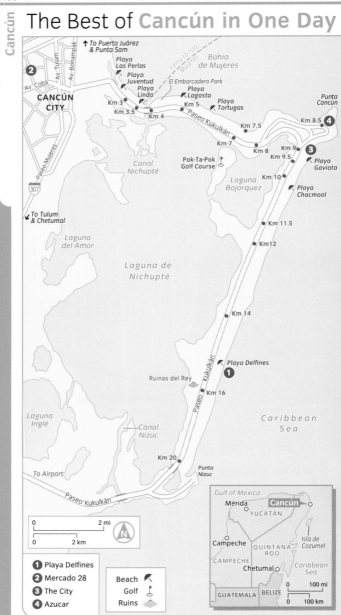

To Puerto Juárez & Punta Sam

2 CANCÚN CITY

Av. Coba
Av. Bonampak
Av. Tulum

Paseo Mujeres

307

To Tulum & Chetumal

Playa Las Perlas
Playa Juventud
Playa Linda
Km 3
Km 3.5
Km 4
Km 5
Km 7.5
Km 7
Km 8
Km 9
Km 9.5
Km 10
Km 11.5
Km12
Km 14
Km 16
Km 20

Bahía de Mujeres

Ferry to Isla Mujeres

El Embarcadero Park
Playa Lagosta
Playa Tortugas

Paseo Kukulkán

Punta Cancún

4

3
Playa Gaviota
Playa Chacmool

Pok-Ta-Pok Golf Course
Laguna Bojórquez

Canal Nichupté

Laguna del Amor

Laguna de Nichupté

Laguna Inglé

Canal Nizuc

Ruinas del Rey
Paseo Kukulkán
Playa Delfines
1

Caribbean Sea

To Airport

Paseo Kukulkán

Punta Nizuc

0   2 mi
0   2 km
N

1 Playa Delfines
2 Mercado 28
3 The City
4 Azucar

Beach 🏖
Golf ⛳
Ruins 🔺

Gulf of Mexico
Mérida
YUCATÁN
Campeche
QUINTANA ROO
CAMPECHE
Chetumal
GUATEMALA BELIZE

Cancún
Isla de Cozumel
Caribbean Sea

0   100 mi
0   100 km

Previous page: The beach at the Presidente InterContinental Cancún.

Can you Cancún in 1 day? Yes, you can. A morning swim, a good lunch, and some Mexican shopping, followed by dinner and an evening out, will make your Mexico experience something to write home about. But whatever you do, don't miss wandering down to the sea; paradisiacal beaches are why Cancún is Mexico's most visited tourist destination.

A stretch of the Cancún Hotel Zone.

1 Playa Delfines HOTEL
ZONE The best way to begin your day is to put on a bathing suit, slather on some sunscreen, and hit the beach. All beaches are free in Mexico, so if your hotel's sandbox isn't great, head to Playa Delfines, Km 18 on the boulevard. It's a public beach, which means no big hotel sits in front of it.

Your first glance is from the bluff above, from where the colors of the sparkling sea and brilliant sand are breathtaking. The bus stops in the parking lot, and from there you can descend faded wooden steps through greenery down to the white beach. It's our favorite place to hang out and swim, although the Caribbean waves can be strong.

For calmer waters, head to Playa Tortugas, facing Isla Mujeres, at Km 6.5. It's popular with tourists and

locals alike because of its gentle waves. A morning's swim in either place will get your juices flowing and keep you cool for the afternoon.

2 Mercado 28 DOWNTOWN
Despite the glut of shopping malls in the Hotel Zone, downtown Cancún offers the most Mexican goods and the most authentic gift and souvenir shopping experience in town—not to mention lower prices. Mercado 28 is the most popular, but several smaller flea markets line Avenida Tulum, the downtown's main drag.

Take any bus from the Hotel Zone with "Mercado 28" in the front window (usually the Ruta 2). For 75¢, it will drop you off at this block-square, covered market. During the heat of the afternoon, wander through the shaded aisles past vendor stalls plying a wide variety of

Poolside at the Westin Resort & Spa Cancún.

merchandise, from junk to gems. Clever shoppers can find silver jewelry at sterling prices—half of what you might pay in the United States—as well as T-shirts, embroidered blouses, leather goods such as hand-tooled belts and bags, and decorated pottery. Have a cold beer and a late lunch in any of several economical Mexican eateries located in the center garden of the market.

Directly next to the flea market is a charming village-style mall called **Plaza Bonita,** where you can pick up Maya copal incense in the herbalist's shop. Hamacas El Aguacate (www.hamacaselaguacate.com.mx) is a great place to find authentic Yucatecan hammocks. They have excellent prices and a huge selection of quality from nylon to cotton.

❸ The City HOTEL ZONE   Luckily, your 1 day in Cancún has an evening, because if there's one more thing Cancún is famous for, it's nightlife. The City is Cancún's biggest rock club. Critics sometimes compare it to a big barn, without intimate atmosphere, but the large open spaces fill with more than a thousand pulsating dancers, which make it Cancún's most popular nightspot. Next door in Forum by

the Sea, **Coco Bongo** packs in a slightly more diverse but almost as large a crowd for a fun night of clubbing. Go to either of these spots if you want to experience Spring Break all year round. See p 149.

❹ Azucar HOTEL ZONE   Salsa, meringue, and rumba are just some of the sizzling dance rhythms you'll hear at Azucar, the hottest of Latin nightclubs. A sophisticated, mixed audience comes to dance to the live Cuban and Latin American bands on stage, or to watch the scene from the bar. See p 148.

Like Azucar, **Glazz,** in La Isla Shopping Mall, also stands out among Cancún's many clubs for an urbane evening out. Its sleek lounge, fine restaurant, and dance floor that features live music and shows appeals to the over-30 crowd uninterested in Jello shots.

An oceanside Chac-Mool altar in Cancún.

Cancún Palmas de Oro Awards

Best Archaeological Tour
Chichén Itzá with Halach Winik Tours (☎ 998/892-8234)

Best Bottomless Cup of Joe
Sanborn's, Plaza Flamingo, Kukulcán Km 11.5 (☎ 998/885-1069)

Best Café con Leche
Los **Bisquets de Obregon,** Avenida Nader near the Radisson Hotel (☎ 998/887-6876)

Best Cuban Cigars
Smoker's Stylish, Plaza Bonita, next to Mercado 28 (☎ 998/884-0309)

Best Day Trip for Kids
Xcaret, Cancún departures, Kukulcán Km 9.5 (☎ 998/883-0470)

Best Fish & Beer Joint
Restaurante Rio Nizuc, near the bridge in the Hotel Zone (no phone)

Best Local Ruin
Yamil Lu'um (a handprint and a cat's bottom), Sheraton, Kukulcán Km 12.5

Best Nature Tour in Summer
Whale Sharks at Isla Holbox

Best Nature Tour Anytime
Sian Ka'an, with EcoColors, Calle Camarón (☎ 998/884-3667; www.ecotravelmexico.com)

Best Place for Betting
Yak, upstairs in Plaza Las Americas, Avenida Tulum

Best Prices on Silver
Any **downtown flea market,** with *mucho* negotiation

Best Tequila You've Never Heard Of
Oro Azul Reposado, aged 6 months in the highlands of Jalisco

Hotel Zone Hotels & Restaurants

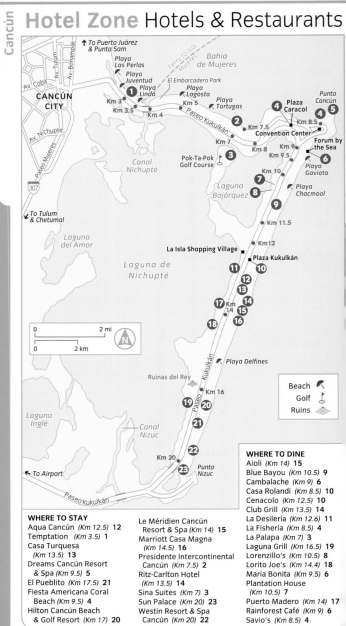

↑ To Puerto Juárez & Punta Sam

Playa Las Perlas
Playa Juventud
Playa Linda
❶
Playa Lagosta
El Embarcadero Park
Playa Tortugas
Playa Las Perlas

CANCÚN CITY

Av. Coba
Av. Tulum
Av.-Bonampak
Av. Nichupté
Paseo Mujeres
307
↙ To Tulum & Chetumal

Km 3
Km 3.5
Km 4
❷
Km 5
Paseo Kukulkán
Km 7.5
Km 7
Km 8
Km 8.5
Km 9
Km 9.5
Km 10
Km 11.5
Km12

Bahía de Mujeres

Plaza Caracol ❹
Punta Cancún
❹ Km 8.5 ❺
Convention Center
Forum by the Sea ❻
Playa Gaviota
Playa Chacmool
❼
❽
❾

Pok-Ta-Pok Golf Course ❸

Canal Nichupté
Laguna Bojórquez

Laguna del Amor

Laguna de Nichupté

La Isla Shopping Village ● Km12
Plaza Kukulkán
⓫ ❿
⓬
⓭
⓮
⓯
⓰
⓱ Km 14
⓲

Laguna Inglé

⚓ Playa Delfines

Ruinas del Rey
⓳ Km 16
⓴
㉑
㉒ Km 20
㉓ Punta Nizuc

Canal Nizuc

↙ To Airport
Paseo Kukulkán

0 —— 2 mi
0 —— 2 km
Ⓝ

Beach ⚓
Golf ⛳
Ruins ≋

Cancún City Hotels & Restaurants

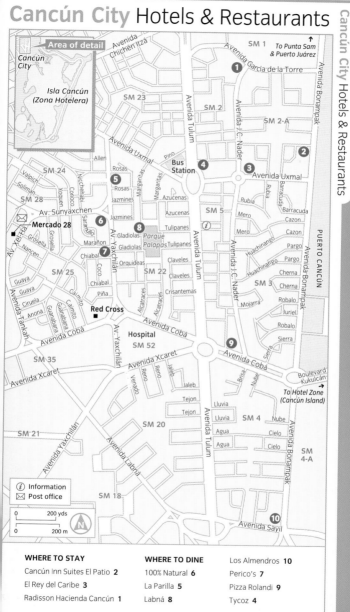

WHERE TO STAY

Cancún Inn Suites El Patio **2**

El Rey del Caribe **3**

Radisson Hacienda Cancún **1**

WHERE TO DINE

100% Natural **6**

La Parilla **5**

Labná **8**

Los Almendros **10**

Perico's **7**

Pizza Rolandi **9**

Tycoz **4**

Cancún Dining Best Bets

Best French Food
★★★ Aioli [$$–$$$] *Le Méridien Hotel, Kukulcán Km 14* (p 137)

Biggest Steaks
★★★ Cambalache [$$–$$$$] *Forum by the Sea, Kukulcán Km 9* (p 137)

Best Seafood Sampler
★★★ Casa Rolandi [$$–$$$] *Plaza Caracol Shopping Center, Kukulcán Km 8.5* (p 137)

Most Elegant Experience
★★★ Club Grill [$$–$$$$] *Ritz-Carlton Hotel, Kukulcán Km 13.5* (p 137)

Most Romantic Setting
★★ La Habichuela [$$–$$$] *Margaritas 25* (p 138)

Best-Kept Secret
★★ La Palapa [$–$$$] *Imperial Laguna Hotel, Calle Queztal, Kukulcán Km 7* (p 138)

Best Sunset View
★★ Laguna Grill [$$–$$$$] *Kukulcán Km 16.5* (p 138)

Best Live Lobster
★★★ Lorenzillo's [$$–$$$$$] *Kukulcán Km 10.5* (p 138)

Best Yucatecan Food
★ Los Almendros [$–$$] *Av. Tulum, 2 blocks north of the bus station* (p 138)

Most Fun
★ Perico's [$–$$$$] *Av. Yaxchilan 61* (p 139)

Best Brick-Oven Pizza
Pizza Rolandi [$] *Av. Cobá, between avs. Tulum & Nader* (p 139)

Best Baguette Sandwich
Ty-Coz [$] *Kukulcán Km 7.2* (p 139)

Most Fun for Kids
★★★ Rainforest Café [$] *Forum by the Sea, Kukulcán Km 9* (p 139)

Tropical bounty at the Fiesta Americana Coral Beach.

Cancún Restaurants A to Z

★★★ Aioli HOTEL ZONE *FRENCH*
For the quality and originality of the food, Aioli is exquisite. French and Mediterranean gourmet specialties in a warm, cozy bistro. *Le Méridien Hotel, Retorno del Rey, Kukulcán Km 14.* ☎ *998/881-2200. Entrees $15–$40. AE, DC, MC, V. Daily 6:30am–11pm.*

Blue Bayou HOTEL ZONE *CAJUN*
This hot supper club/cool jazz joint in the Caribe Hyatt received a "Distinguished Restaurant Award" for its Cajun-inspired cuisine. *Caribe Hyatt, Kukulcán Km 10.5.* ☎ *998/848-7800, ext. 53. Entrees $20 & up. AE, MC, V. Open daily 6–11pm.*

★★★ Cambalache HOTEL ZONE *STEAK* Enjoy your Argentine steak hand-carved, slow–charcoal grilled, and presented in a rich setting with superb service. *Forum by the Sea, Kukulcán Km 9.* ☎ *998/883-0902. Entrees $9–$45. AE, MC, V. Open daily 1pm–closing.*

★★ Casa Rolandi HOTEL ZONE *NORTHERN ITALIAN/SEAFOOD*
Under watchful Swiss-Italian eyes, Casa Rolandi proffers an extraordinary, intimate dining experience. The seafood platter is to die for. *Plaza Caracol Shopping Center, Kukulcán Km 8.5.* ☎ *998/883-2557. www.rolandi.com. Entrees $9–$30. AE, MC, V. Open daily 1–11:30pm.*

★★★ Cenacolo HOTEL ZONE *ITALIAN* Recipes here, from Tuscany and Romagna, are further authenticated by homemade pasta in this gorgeous Italian restaurant with tableside preparation, live piano music, and a large selection of wine. *Plaza Kukulcan, Kukulcán Km 13.* ☎ *998/885-3603. Entrees $12–$34. AE, MC, V. Open daily 1–11:30pm.*

Aioli, in the Hotel Zone.

★★★ Club Grill HOTEL ZONE *INTERNATIONAL* There's no place with a more elegant, stylish, or delicious menu. Gracious service in a candlelit dining room—while the band plays on. *Ritz-Carlton Hotel, Kukulcán Km 13.5.* ☎ *998/881-0808. Entrees $12–$40. AE, DC, MC, V. Tues–Sun 7–11pm.*

★★ La Destileria HOTEL ZONE *MEXICAN* Everything you ever wanted to know about tequila, plus tasty traditional Mexican fare. Try the *escamoles* (crisp fried ants). *Kukulcán Km 12.5.* ☎ *998/885-1086. www.cmr.ws. Entrees $8–$30. AE, MC, V. Open daily 1pm–midnight.*

★★★ La Dolce Vita HOTEL ZONE/ DOWNTOWN *ITALIAN/SEAFOOD* This romantic waterside restaurant is a Cancún favorite for homemade pasta dishes. We prefer their original location on Avenida Cobá, downtown near Avenida Nader, for its more Italian setting and lower prices. *Kukulcán Km 14.6.* ☎ *998/885-0150. www.cancunitalianrestaurant.com. Entrees $9–$29. AE, MC, V. Open daily noon–midnight.*

The restaurant at Dreams Cancún Resort & Spa.

★★ **La Fisheria** HOTEL ZONE SEA-FOOD   The tasty and expansive menu here features out-of-the-ordinary dishes such as shark fingers with jalapeño dip, and *Tikin-xic*, fresh fish filets spiced with Maya achiote. *Plaza Caracol, 2nd floor, Kukulcán Km 8.5.* ☎ *998/883-1395. Entrees $7–$21. AE, MC, V. Open daily 10am–midnight.*

★★ **La Habichuela** DOWNTOWN CARIBBEAN/MEXICAN   The garden setting and fine food make this a sweet place for romance. Their signature dish is *cocobichuela*—lobster and shrimp curry, served in a coconut shell. *Margaritas 25 (near Parque Palapa).* ☎ *998/884-3158. www.lahabichuela.com. Entrees $10–$35. AE, MC, V. Open daily noon–midnight.*

★★ **La Palapa** HOTEL ZONE INTER-NATIONAL   On a dock of the lagoon, this intimate restaurant boasts a talented Belgian chef/owner who prepares some of the zone's finest gourmet meals. *Imperial Laguna Hotel, Calle Queztal, Kukulcán Km 7.0.* ☎ *998/883-5454. Entrees $12–$27. MC, V. Open daily 7am–11pm; closed Sun.*

★ kids **La Parilla** DOWNTOWN MEXICAN   The super-popular, fun "Grill" offers patrons generous helpings, a cantina feel, and loud mariachis. Friday seafood buffet. *Av. Yaxchilan (near Rosas).* ☎ *998/884-5398. Entrees $5–$12. MC, V. Open daily noon–4am.*

★ **Labná** DOWNTOWN YUCATE-CAN   A showcase of Maya moods in a temple-like dining room, it's a good place to try cuisine from the Yucatán. *Margaritas 29, next to La Habichuela Restaurant & City Hall.* ☎ *998/892-3056. www.labna.com. Entrees $8–$18. AE, MC, V. Open daily noon–10pm.*

★★ **Laguna Grill** HOTEL ZONE FUSION   As magical as the tropical garden decor is, the real star of this eatery is the chef's fusion of Pacific-Rim and local flavors. Watch the sun set on the lagoon. *Kukulcán Km 16.5.* ☎ *998/885-0267. www.laguna grill.com.mx. Entrees $15–$45. AE, MC, V. Open daily 2pm–midnight.*

★★★ **Lorenzillo's** HOTEL ZONE LOBSTER/SEAFOOD   Under a giant *palapa*, this landmark spot offers air-conditioning and spectacular views from upstairs or the Sunset Pier. *Kukulcán Km 10.5.* ☎ *998/883-1254. www.lorenzillos.com.mx. Entrees $12–$50. AE, MC, V. Open daily noon–midnight.*

★★ **Lorito Joe's** HOTEL ZONE SEAFOOD   This informal eatery has a shrimp and lobster buffet, cold appetizers, stone crabs, and ceviche. Tamarind soft-shell crab and shrimp are specialties. *Kukulcán Km 14.5, across from the Marriott.* ☎ *998/885-1536. Entrees $9–$30. AE, MC, V. Open daily noon–11pm.*

★ **Los Almendros** DOWNTOWN YUCATECAN   This place is reputed for authentic Yucatecan cooking. The dining room is cool and hacienda-like. Enjoy local classics such as *poc-chuc. Tulum Av., 2 blocks north of the bus station.* ☎ *998/887-1332. Entrees $5–$14. AE, MC, V. Open daily 11am–9pm.*

★★ Mango Tango HOTEL ZONE
INTERNATIONAL/CARIBBEAN For a
fun night out in the Hotel Zone, try
the peel-your-own shrimp, big salads, Creole gumbo, or sizzling
meats here. Then stay for the sizzling floor show. *Kukulcán Km 14.5.*
☎ *998/885-0303. Entrees $12–$57.
AE, MC, V. Open daily 2pm–2am.*

★★ Maria Bonita HOTEL ZONE
NUEVO MEXICANO Mexico's varied
cuisine is amply represented by the
fixed-price dinners here. Try anything with *huitlacoche*—the exqui-
site-tasting fungus that grows on
corn. *Punta Cancún.* ☎ *998/848-
7000. Prix-fixe dinner $30–$45. AE,
DC, MC, V. Open daily 6:30–11:45pm.*

★ kids 100% Natural CANCUN
CITY *VEGETARIAN* Fresh fruits are
the staple here (try a *licuado*), but
100% also serves tasty light Mexican
fare with whole-grain breads and
veggie dishes. *Av. Sunyaxchen 63.*
☎ *998/884-0102. Main courses
$2.80–$13. MC, V. Daily 8am–11pm.*

★ kids Perico's DOWNTOWN *MEX-
ICAN* This bar/restaurant has a
booming and festive cantina setting
where diners might don sombreros
and form a conga line. *Av. Yaxchilan
61.* ☎ *998/884-3152. www.pericos.
com.mx. Entrees $9–$39. AE, MC, V.
Open daily noon–10pm.*

★ kids Pizza Rolandi DOWN-
TOWN *ITALIAN* Choose from two
dozen different wood-oven pizzas.
Selection of Italian staples includes
spaghetti and calzones. *Av. Cobá
(between avs. Tulum and Nader).*
☎ *998/884-4047. www.rolandi.com.
Entrees $4–$10. AE, MC, V. Open
daily noon–11pm.*

★ kids Plantation House HOTEL
ZONE *CARIBBEAN/FRENCH* This
clapboard lagoon-side restaurant
combines colonial charm with island
style. Crowded nightly. *Kukulcán
Km 10.5.* ☎ *998/883-1433. Entrees*

*$13–$35. AE, MC, V. Open daily
5pm–midnight.*

★★★ Puerto Madero HOTEL
ZONE *STEAK/LOBSTER* This cozy
lagoon-side restaurant serves some
of the zone's best charbroiled steak
and seafood platters in an evocative
Argentinean decor. *Marina Barra-
cuda, Kukulcán Km 14.* ☎ *998/
885-2827. www.puertomadero
cancun.com. Entrees $9–$39. AE,
MC, V. Open daily 1pm–1am.*

★★★ kids Rainforest Café
HOTEL ZONE *AMERICAN* Find
those American-style burgers and
fries the kids have been whining for.
Forum by the Sea, Kukulcán Km 9.
☎ *998/881-8130. Entrees $4–$14.
Open daily 11am–1am.*

★★ Savio's HOTEL ZONE *ITALIAN*
George Savio introduced good
Italian cooking to Cancún, but
what's best in this modern bistro
is the ravioli. *Plaza Caracol, Kukulcán Km 8.5.* ☎ *998/883-2085.
Entrees $9–$30. AE, MC, V. Open
daily 10am–midnight.*

★ Ty-Coz HOTEL ZONE/DOWN-
TOWN *SANDWICHES* When you just
want a cappuccino and a great sandwich on a fresh, crisp, hard roll, this
is the place. *Kukulcán Km 7.2 (opposite Presidente Hotel); Av. Tulum
(behind the Comercial Mexicana
Mega shopping center, opposite
the bus station).* ☎ *998/883-3564.
Baguettes $2–$3. No credit cards.
Mon–Fri 9am–11pm. Closed Sun.*

Cochinita Pibil banana leaf-wrapped pork.

Cancún Hotel Best Bets

Best Beach
★★★ Fiesta Americana Coral Beach [$$$$] *Kukulcán Km 9.5* (p 142)

Best Beds
★★ Westin Resort & Spa Cancún [$$] *Kukulcán Km 20* (p 145)

Best Sunday Buffet
★ Radisson Hacienda Cancún [$] *Av. Nader, SM2* (p 144)

Best Architecture
★★★ Aqua Cancún [$$$–$$$$] *Kukulcán Km 12.5* (p 141)

Best Spa
★★★ Le Méridien Cancún Resort & Spa [$$$–$$$$] *Returno del Rey, Kukulcán Km 14* (p 143)

Best Honeymoon Suite
★ Casa Turquesa [$$–$$$] *Kukulcán Km 13.5* (p 141)

Best for Spanish Lessons
Cancun Inn Suites El Patio [$] *Avs. Bonampak & Cereza* (p 141)

Most Mexican
★ El Pueblito [$$$] *Kukulcán Km 17.5* (p 141)

El Pueblito Hotel.

Most Ecological
El Rey del Caribe [$] *Avs. Uxmal & Nader* (p 142)

Best for Golf & Tennis
★ Hilton Cancún Beach & Golf Resort [$$$–$$$$] *Kukulcán Km 17* (p 142)

Quietest Location
Sina Suites [$] *Calle Quetzal, Kukulcán Km 7.5* (p 145)

Best Kids' Club
★★ Marriott Casa Magna [$$–$$$] *Kukulcán Km 14.5* (p 143)

Best In-Hotel Restaurant
★★★ Ritz-Carlton Hotel [$$$$] *Returno del Rey, Kukulcán Km 13.5* (p 144)

Most Helpful Staff
★ Presidente Inter-Continental Cancún [$$$] *Kukulcán Km 7.5* (p 143)

Best Location
★★ Dreams Cancun Resort & Spa [$$$] *Punta Cancún, Kukulcán* (p 141)

Cancún Hotels A to Z

★★★ Aqua Cancún HOTEL ZONE
The Aqua stands out as one of the best-looking buildings along the beach—a Maya-inspired winged hotel embracing white sands beside a turquoise sea. Better still are the superior facilities and simple, elegant decor. The Aqua boasts superb restaurants and a contemporary Mexican decor that inspires a sense of well-being. It's an exceptionally comfortable and relaxing environment. *Kukulcán Km 12.5. ☎ 800/343-7821. www.siente-aqua.com. 371 units. Doubles $200–$500. AE, DC, MC, V.*

Cancun Inn Suites El Patio
DOWNTOWN   Many guests at this European-style hotel stay long-term, drawn by the combination of excellent value and hospitality. You won't find bars, pools, or loud parties; but rather good service and impeccable accommodations. Each room has slightly different appointments and amenities, but all have white-tile floors and rustic-wood, Spanish-style furnishings. Some rooms have kitchenettes. The lounge has a large-screen TV, a library stocked with cultural books, and card and board games. All rooms except for the public areas are nonsmoking. *Avs. Bonampak & Cereza. ☎ 998/884-3500. www.cancun-suites.com. 12 units. Doubles $40–$56 per person. AE, MC, V.*

★ Casa Turquesa HOTEL ZONE
Romantic, tranquil, and elegant, Casa Turquesa is an oasis of relaxation in the midst of this playful island. If the Mediterranean-style design weren't appealing enough, the exceptional stretch of beach is sure to inspire. A boutique hotel catering to couples, it's noted for exceptional service. All suites feature king or queen beds and patios or balconies with private Jacuzzis.

Bathrooms are extra large. The beachfront pool is also attractive, with a swim-up bar. The hotel's Belle-Vue Restaurant serves international gourmet meals 24 hours a day, and the formal Celebrity Restaurant offers seafood and Angus beef from 6pm to midnight. *Kukulcán Km 13.5. ☎ 888/528-8300. www.casaturquesa.com. 33 suites. Doubles $205–$235. AE, DC, MC, V.*

★★ kids Dreams Cancun Resort & Spa HOTEL ZONE
Dreams Resort is among the island's most appealing places to stay, on 1.6 hectares (4 acres) of paradise at the tip of Punta Cancún. The setting is sophisticated, but the hotel is very welcoming to children. Rooms in the newer 18-story club section have extra services and amenities; rates here include full breakfast. Lower-priced rooms have lagoon views. Your room price includes gourmet meals, premium drinks, use of all resort amenities, watersports, airport transfers, and tips. *Punta Cancún, Kukulcán. ☎ 866/237-3267. www.dreamscancun.com. 381 suites. Doubles $174, club $320. AE, DC, MC, V.*

★ kids El Pueblito HOTEL ZONE
This hotel offers perhaps the top all-inclusive value in Cancún. Dwarfed by its ostentatious neighbors, El Pueblito resembles a sprawling Mexican hacienda. A meandering, free-form swimming pool with waterfalls runs between the buildings. Rooms are very large, with modern rattan furnishings, travertine marble floors, and large bathrooms. Each has either a small balcony or terrace. Minigolf and a water slide, plus a full program of kids' activities, make this ideal for families with children. Its more authentic atmosphere and garden grounds make it very appealing for

couples as an all-inclusive. *Kukulcán Km 17.5.* ☎ *998/885-0422. 293 units. Doubles $300. AE, MC, V.*

El Rey del Caribe DOWNTOWN In the center of the city a block off Avenida Tulum, this ecological hotel is an oasis where every detail seems to reflect a respect for the natural environment. You'll forget you're in the midst of the busy downtown in this tropical jungle setting, with blooming orchids and other flowering plants. They offer yoga and Tai Chi classes, and spa services, and are very active in local environmental issues. Rooms are sunny and pleasant and offer a choice of king or two full-size beds, a kitchenette, and a terrace. *Avs. Uxmal & Nader.* ☎ *998/884-2028. www.reycaribe. com. 24 units. Doubles $55–$100. MC, V.*

★★★ **Fiesta Americana Coral Beach** HOTEL ZONE This sophisticated hotel is in the heart of all things Cancún has to offer, with 300m (328 yd.) of prime beachfront. Everything is on a large scale; the oceanfront suites are oversize, and

the lobby is enormous. The rooms, with balconies facing the sea, were remodeled in 2004 with bathrooms that feature posh toiletries and top-of-the-line hair dryers. The excellent swimming beach is just steps from the pool. *Kukulcán Km 9.5.* ☎ *800/ 343-7821. www.fiestaamericana. com. 602 units. Doubles $200–$555. AE, DC, MC, V.*

★ **kids** **Hilton Cancún Beach & Golf Resort** HOTEL ZONE The Hilton is on 100 hectares (250 acres) of pristine beachfront property, a location that gives every room a sea view. Like the sprawling resort, rooms are grandly spacious and tastefully decorated in a minimalist style that came with a 2004 remodeling, with marble bathrooms and floors. The "kid-friendly" resort has one of the island's best children's programs—which allows mommy and daddy to get in a worry-free 18 holes of golf or a trip to the new Wellness Spa. *Kukulcán Km 17.* ☎ *800/228-3000. www.hilton cancun.com. 426 units. Doubles $98–$500. AE, DC, MC, V.*

Guestroom at the Cancún Hilton.

Le Méridien Cancún Resort & Spa.

★★★ Le Méridien Cancún Resort & Spa

HOTEL ZONE   Of the luxury properties in Cancún, Le Méridien is the most inviting, with a refined yet welcoming service. From the intimate lobby to the best concierge service in town, Le Méridien immediately makes guests feel pampered, more of an elegant boutique than an immense resort. The decor throughout is classy and comforting. Generous-size rooms have small balconies overlooking the pool with a view to the ocean. The hotel attracts many Europeans as well as younger, hipper travelers, and it's ideal for a romantic break. The Spa del Mar is one of Mexico's best. *Returno del Rey, Kukulcán Km 14.* ☎ *800/543-4300. www.lemeridien. com. 213 units. Doubles $195, suites $595. AE, DC, MC, V.*

★★ kids Marriott Casa Magna

HOTEL ZONE   This is quintessential Marriott, and those familiar with the chain's high standards will feel right at home with the attention to detail. With a half-circle of Roman columns, a domed foyer, and a lavishly marbled lobby, it's a bit like Las Vegas on the beach. Guest rooms have contemporary furnishings, tiled floors, and ceiling fans; most have balconies. Specially priced packages let up to two children stay free, and "Club Amigos" is a supervised children's program. Next door is its impressive sister hotel, the JW Marriott Cancún. *Kukulcán Km 14.5.* ☎ *800/228-9290. www.marriott. com. 452 units. Doubles $150–$250, suites $350. AE, MC, V.*

★ Presidente Inter-Continental Cancún

HOTEL ZONE   On one of the island's best beaches, facing the tranquil Bahía de Mujeres, the Presidente's location is reason enough to stay here, and it's just a 2-minute walk to Cancún's Pok-Ta-Pok Golf Club (see p 36). It's an excellent choice for a romantic getaway or for couples who indulge in golf, tennis, or shopping. The ideal location is close to the center of things, but on its own. Cool and spacious, the Presidente sports a postmodern design. All rooms have tastefully simple furniture, with two double beds or one king-size. Sixteen units on the first floor feature patios with

The pool at Le Méridien.

outdoor whirlpool tubs. There's a great free-form pool. *Kukulcán Km 7.5.* ☎ *800/327-0200. www.ichotels group.com. 299 units. Doubles $245–$300. AE, MC, V.*

★ Radisson Hacienda Cancún

DOWNTOWN   This is the nicest hotel in downtown Cancún, and a very good value. The Radisson offers all the expected comforts of a chain, yet in an atmosphere of Mexican hospitality. The hotel resembles a hacienda, and rooms are set off from a large rotunda-style lobby and a pleasant pool area. Accommodations feature cold air-conditioning, a balcony, and views of the garden, pool, or residential street. Stone-tile bathrooms have a combination shower and tub. The hotel attracts a large number of business travelers and offers very good service. Guests have access to a shuttle service to the beach or golf course. Downtown shops and restaurants are an easy walk. *Av. Nader, SM2.* ☎ *800/333-3333. www.radisson.com. 248 units. Doubles $100, jr. suites $140. AE, MC, V.*

★★★ Ritz-Carlton Hotel HOTEL
ZONE   For those who want to feel indulged in luxury on their vacation, this is the place. On 3 hectares (7½ acres) of superb white-sand beachfront property, the nine-story Ritz-Carlton continues to set the standard for elegance. The gorgeous beach here is long and wide, 370m (338 yd.), and all rooms overlook the ocean, pool, and tropical gardens. The style in both the public areas and guest rooms is sumptuous and formal. In all rooms, marble bathrooms have telephones, separate tubs and showers, and lighted makeup mirrors. Kayantá Spa offers an excellent selection of Maya and Mexican-inspired treatments. Damaged by Hurricane Katrina, the hotel was entirely remodeled in 2006. *Returno del Rey, Kukulcán Km 13.5.* ☎ *800/ 241-3333. www.ritzcarlton.com. 365 units. Doubles $409. AE, MC, V.*

★★ Temptation HOTEL ZONE
The adults-only Temptation resort is a spirited yet relaxed all-inclusive resort favored by younger adults. Surrounded by acres of tropical

gardens, it's at the northern end of the Hotel Zone, close to downtown, shopping, dining, and nightlife. It has a terrific beach with calm waters for swimming. The comfortable, modern rooms have views of the lagoon, garden, or ocean. The central building houses the lobby, restaurants, and Margaritas Bar. A variety of nightly entertainment takes place in the theater. Beaches here are clothing optional, which helps explain the younger clientele. *Kukulcán Km 3.5.* ☎ *800/211-1000. www.temptationcancun.com. 385 units. Doubles 2,016 pesos per person all-inclusive. AE, MC, V.*

Sina Suites HOTEL ZONE   The best deal in the Cancún Hotel Zone is this little all-suites hotel looking across the Bojórquez Lagoon (a part of the larger Nichupté, on the Caribbean side). It's not the beach, but it's a fabulous view anyway, especially in the evening when Cancún's hotels' lights reflect on the water. Each oversize suite features a basic kitchen, sitting room, and bedroom with a view. A large, appealing blue pool butts up against a sunken dining room, surrounded by tropical lawns and gardens. It's a few hundred meters south of Kukulcán on Calle Quetzal, next to the Pok-Ta-Pok Golf Course. *Calle Quetzal, Kukulcán Km 7.5.* ☎ *998/883-1017. www.cancun sinasuites.com.mx. 36 suites, 3 rooms. Jr. suite $120, master suite $160, doubles $60. AE, MC, V.*

★ **Sun Palace** HOTEL ZONE   For an all-inclusive resort on a great stretch of Caribbean beach, this member of the popular Palace Resorts chain is a prime pick—and the most elegant of the Palace properties in Cancún. Toward the southern end of the island, this all-suite resort is farther away from the action—which may be what you want, given all the goodies that go with a stay here. One of the best perks is the activities program,

which includes excursions to Tulum, Chichén Itzá, or Isla Mujeres. Suites feature modern Mexican decor, and all have marble floors and a combination bath and whirlpool tub. When you stay at a Palace resort, you have the option of playing at any of their other hotels, even on the Riviera Maya. *Kukulcán Km 20.* ☎ *800/346-8225. www.palaceresorts.com. 237 suites. Doubles $377–$450. AE, DC, MC, V.*

★★ **Westin Resort & Spa Cancún** HOTEL ZONE   Impressive with its elegant use of stone and marble, the strikingly austere architecture of this Westin is the signature of leading Latin American architect Ricardo Legorreta. The hotel consists of two sections, the main building and the more exclusive six-story tower. After suffering heavy damage from Hurricane Wilma, the resort completely remodeled and reopened late in 2006. Standard rooms are unusually large and beautifully furnished with cool, contemporary furniture. Rooms in the tower all have ocean or lagoon views, and terraces with lounge chairs. The Westin is a comfortable choice for people who want a little more seclusion. *Kukulcán Km 20.* ☎ *800/228-3000. www.westin.com. 293 units. Doubles $159–$450. AE, DC, MC, V.*

The beach at the Presidente InterContinental Cancún.

Cancún Nightlife & Shopping

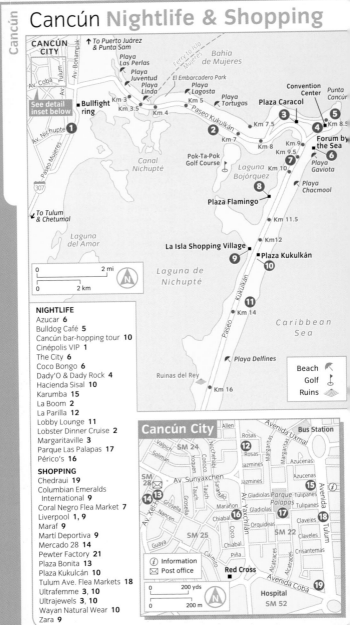

NIGHTLIFE
Azucar **6**
Bulldog Café **5**
Cancún bar-hopping tour **10**
Cinépolis VIP **1**
The City **6**
Coco Bongo **6**
Dady'O & Dady Rock **4**
Hacienda Sisal **10**
Karumba **15**
La Boom **2**
La Parilla **12**
Lobby Lounge **11**
Lobster Dinner Cruise **2**
Margaritaville **3**
Parque Las Palapas **17**
Périco's **16**

SHOPPING
Chedraui **19**
Columbian Emeralds
  International **9**
Coral Negro Flea Market **7**
Liverpool **1, 9**
Maraf **9**
Martí Deportiva **9**
Mercado 28 **14**
Pewter Factory **21**
Plaza Bonita **13**
Plaza Kukulcán **10**
Tulum Ave. Flea Markets **18**
Ultrafemme **3, 10**
Ultrajewels **3, 10**
Wayan Natural Wear **10**
Zara **9**

Cancún Nightlife Best Bets

Best Designated Drivers
★★★ Cancún Party Hopper Tour *Varied starting points* (p 148)

Hottest Nightclub
★★★ The City *Kukulcán Km 9.5* (p 149)

Best Crowd
★★ Coco Bongo *Forum by the Sea, Kukulcán Km 9.5* (p 149)

Wildest Rave
★ Dady'O *Kukulcán Km 9.5* (p 149)

Best Place to Be Out
★★ Karamba *Av. Tulum* (p 150)

Biggest Drinks
★★ Margaritaville *Flamingo Plaza, Kukulcán Km 11.5* (p 151)

Most Romantic
★★ Cancún Lovers Cruise *Royal Plaza & Marina, Kukulcán Km 6.2* (p 148)

Best Seat in the House
★★ Cinépolis VIP *Plaza Las Americas, Av. Tulum (at Av. Nichupté)* (p 149)

Hottest Latin Bands
★★★ Azucar *Punta Cancún, Kukulcán Km 9* (p 148)

Best Place to Meet Mexicans
★★★ Parque Las Palapas *Calles Alcatraces & Margaritas, SM 22* (p 151)

Most Relaxing Evening
★★ Lobby Lounge at the Ritz *Returno del Rey, Kukulcán Km 13.5* (p 151)

Most Mexican
★ La Parilla *Av. Yaxchilan* (p 150)

Sexiest Club
★★ Bulldog Café *Hotel Krystal, Kukulcán Km 9* (p 148)

After dark at the Westin Resort & Spa Cancún.

Cancún

Cancún Nightlife A to Z

Hacienda Sisal.

★★ Azucar HOTEL ZONE   This hip dance club features live music, with full bands imported from Cuba and other Latin American countries. It's hard to sit still when the horns blow and the rhythm takes over. It's the best Latin dance floor in Cancún, set in an intimate and sophisticated nightclub next to Dreams Resort on Punta Cancún. Sweet Azucar, which means "sugar," attracts a mixed crowd: both tourists and locals, younger and older, who just love to dance. If you don't but want to try, you're in luck; they offer free salsa lessons from 9:30 to 10:30pm every evening. *Punta Cancún, Kukulcán Km 9.* ☎ *998/848-7000. Cover $25. Open 9:30pm–4am.*

★★ Bulldog Café HOTEL ZONE Formerly the opulent dance club Christine, in the Hotel Krystal, Bulldog boasts enough space for more than 2,000 revelers for its signature laser-light shows. Infused oxygen, large video screens, and a titillating VIP Jacuzzi—filled with young, rich, and beautiful partiers—excite all the senses. The music ranges from hip-hop to Latin rock, with a heavy emphasis on infectious dance tunes. The cover charge is $12 per person or $25 for a domestic-drink-only open bar. *Hotel Krystal, Kukulcán Km 9.* ☎ *998/848-9850. www.bulldog cafe.com. Cover $25, open bar $45. 10pm until the party winds down.*

★★ Cancun Lovers Cruise HOTEL ZONE   Order up a 1-pound lobster or beef steak aboard a romantic cruise around the Nichupté lagoon on the *Columbus* galleon. The meal could be better, but the setting is unique. Afternoon and starlight cruises feature an open bar and live entertainment for dancing on the deck. *Marina Aquatours Pier, Kukulcán Km 6.2.* ☎ *998/849-4748. www.cancunloverscruise.com. $79. Departure 4:30pm.*

★★★ Cancun Party Hopper Tour HOTEL ZONE   As close to an official "Pub Crawl" as Cancún gets, a tour service guides participants from bar to club in the Hotel Zone. The price includes 2 hours and a complimentary drink in each of the four establishments. Inside you get semi-VIP treatment, avoiding any lines, and it usually ends at The City nightclub, by which time many of the crawlers are crawling. Designated English-speaking tour guides meet the group at Coco Bongo and spend the rest of the night making sure their VIP tables have plenty of drinks. *Varied starting points.* ☎ *998/881-9030. www.cancunparty hopper.com. $65. AE, MC, V. Lasts from 9pm–4am.*

★★ **Cinépolis VIP** DOWNTOWN You'll love to go to the movies here, upstairs in the Plaza Las Americas shopping center, on Avenida Tulum in front of the *Plaza de Toros* bull ring. Seats are wide and recline, with plenty of legroom in front. Current English-language Hollywood movies play here as soon as they subtitle them for Spanish viewers. Before the movie, the lounge has a full-service bar, and the snack areas serve Japanese food, sushi, and baguette sandwiches, as well as good old popcorn. *Plaza Las Americas, Av. Tulum (at Av. Nichupté).* ☎ *998/884-1410. Cover $6.*

★★★ **The City** HOTEL ZONE Cancún's hottest nightclub features progressive electronic music spun by some of the world's best DJs. The atmosphere and music sizzles with excitement. Its daytime incarnation is The City Beach Club, open at 8am, which boasts a wave pool for surfing and boogie-boarding, a waterslide, and food service. The Terrace Bar, overlooking Kukulcán, serves food and drinks all day, but the night comes alive after 10pm, when the 2,322 sq. m (25,000-sq.-ft.), multilevel club opens with stunning light shows, nine bars, a pulsating dance

floor, and VIP areas. A second City has opened in Playa del Carmen. *Kukulcán Km 9.5.* ☎ *998/848-8380. www.thecitycancun.com. Cover $20, w/open bar $40. Dance club closed Sun & Mon.*

★★ **Coco Bongo** HOTEL ZONE This is still one of the hottest spots in Cancún's club scene, despite some stiff competition from The City, next door. Coco Bongo is one huge pit, with no designated dance floor, so the 3,000 party-hardy patrons dance anywhere and everywhere—including on tabletops and on stage with the live band. The music is all over the board, including reggae, hip-hop, classic rock, and techno. It draws a mixed crowd, but the young dominate. Lots of whistle-blowing and yards of cheap tequila. *Forum by the Sea, Kukulcán Km 9.5.* ☎ *998/883-5061. www.cocobongo. com.mx. Cover $50; open bar. 11pm–dawn.*

★ **Dady'O & Dady Rock** HOTEL ZONE This two-headed nightclub, opposite the Forum by the Sea, is a super-popular place for young adults where the rock music rolls out onto the street. Actually, Dady'O is a mind-bending disco rave, with frequent long lines and a cover charge of $20. It opens at 10pm. Dady Rock is also a bar and grill is open 6pm until whenever, and combines live rock bands with

Coco Bongo in Cancún.

Light show at The City.

DJs, an open bar, full meals, a buffet, and dancing. *Kukulcán Km 9.5.* ☎ *998/883-3333. Cover $20, open bar $40.*

★ **Hacienda Sisal** HOTEL ZONE Next to the Royal Sands Hotel, the Hacienda Sisal is a standalone dinner nightclub, with a decor that evokes the romance of Old Mexico. It offers a Las Vegas–style buffet dinner show, complete with gorgeous costumes and plenty of leg, on Wednesday and Thursday. Mariachis play from 7 to 7:45pm; the show is from

Coco Bongo in the Hotel Zone.

8 to 9pm; and a dance band performs from 9pm to midnight. Only in Mexico would the dance band have Saturday night off. *Kukulcán Km 13.5.* ☎ *998/848-8220. Dinner show 495 pesos. Open 5pm–1am.*

★★ **Karamba** DOWNTOWN The seductive Karamba was recently remodeled and upgraded, and it's now drawing under-the-radar crowds of gay, transvestite, lesbian, and open-minded straight party people. It's a bit more edgy than your typical Spring-Breaky, frat-party disco clubs, and you won't find too many typical Cancún Hotel Zone tourists there. It's right in the middle of downtown, across the street from City Hall, so it's a relatively safe place. *Av. Tulum #9 (above Super Sandwich Shop).* ☎ *998/884-5398. www.karambabar.com. Cover $–$$. No credit cards. Opens at 11pm.*

★ **La Parilla** DOWNTOWN La Parilla grew from a small street-side grill into a local chain of Mexican restaurants, and there's no better place to have an authentic Mexican meal, sip a *cerveza,* and listen to the boisterous music of mariachis, the wandering minstrels of Mexico. Feel free to sing along if you know the tunes. *Av. Yaxchilan.* ☎ *998/884-5398. Open daily noon–4am.*

★★ **Lobby Lounge** HOTEL ZONE The ritzy Lobby Lounge, in the Ritz-Carlton Hotel, features live music to dance to and 120 premium tequilas for tasting or slow sipping. The lounge attracts a sophisticated, mature crowd—think well-heeled, in high heels. *Returno del Rey, Kukulcán Km 13.5.* ☎ *800/241-3333.*

★★ **Margaritaville** HOTEL ZONE Was Jimmy Buffett singing about Cancún when he described being "wasted away again in Margaritaville?" That's what they'd have you believe at this music-happy restaurant and bar that strives for a Parrothead concert vibe. Evenings feature live music mixed with Buffett concert videos and dancing. Naturally, they serve margaritas with a real bite at the bar, called "Fins." *Flamingo Plaza, Kukulcán Km 11.5.* ☎ *998/885-2375. No cover. Open 11am–1am.*

★★★ kids **Parque Las Palapas** DOWNTOWN This park, anchored by a giant *palapa*-covered stage, is the scene of frequent festivals, fiestas, and celebrations, depending on the holiday. But you can depend on live tropical music concerts and a fair for *Noches Caribeñas* (Caribbean Nights) every Sunday at 7:30pm. Often things happen here during the day and other weekend evenings. It's well worth a shot to show up. *Calles Alcatraces & Margaritas (between avs. Tulum & Yaxchilan). Free.*

★ **Périco's** DOWNTOWN This Cancún legend is a cantina-style bar and restaurant where the waiters wear bandoliers and wide sombreros, and the barstools are real leather saddles. Mariachis play on stage or at your table, and once in a while everyone gets up in a conga line. It's good clean fun. *Av. Yaxchilan 61.* ☎ *998/884-3152. Open 1pm–1am.*

The Cancún streets teem with revelers after dark.

Cancún Shopping A to Z

★ **Chedraui** DOWNTOWN The supermarket/department store of choice in downtown Cancún is this two-story building on the corner of avenidas Tulum and Cobá. Downstairs is a supermarket and bakery; upstairs it sells department store–type items such as clothes. Everything costs less than in the Hotel Zone, so buy your snorkel gear here. Another location is in Plaza Las Americas. *Avs. Tulum & Cobá.* ☎ *998/884-1913. MC, V. Open 6am–11pm.*

★★ **Columbian Emeralds International** HOTEL ZONE You may never have heard of them, but this precious-stone-jewelry business has enjoyed a reputation for quality and value for more than 30 years. Their duty-free store in Cancún belies the size of their online business. Their rings, necklaces, bracelets, and earrings are crafted of not only emeralds, but of diamonds, sapphires, tanzanite, rubies, gold, pearls, and semiprecious stones as well. Best of all, I could browse without pressure to buy. *La Isla Shopping Mall.* ☎ *998/883-1219. www. colombianemeralds.com. Daily 10am–10pm.*

Coral Negro Flea Market HOTEL ZONE Straddling the middle of Kukulcán Boulevard, where the island bends, the "Black Coral" is a series of small shops in a long white building. If you're not leaving the Hotel Zone, it's a good place to get souvenirs—and an introduction to the negotiation process (otherwise you'll pay too much). *Kukulcán Km 9.5.* ☎ *998/883-0758. Credit cards accepted in some locations. Open 7am–11pm.*

★ **Liverpool** HOTEL ZONE/DOWNTOWN In Mexico, Liverpool is a

Wares from Mercado 28 downtown.

luxury department-store chain with a wide selection of name-brand goods from top designers and manufacturers. Their new "Duty Free" outlet in La Isla Shopping Mall features upscale items including jewelry, pens, watches, cameras, and perfumes, with savings over U.S. prices. *La Isla Shopping Mall & Plaza Las Americas, downtown.* ☎ *998/ 848-7880. www.liverpool.com.mx.*

★★ **Maraf** HOTEL ZONE Maraf was established in 1981 by a Mexican family that opened a jewelry store in Cancun's first shopping center. They must have done it right, because they claim their new "jewelry boutique" in Plaza Kukulcan is the largest specialty jewelry shop in Mexico. They do a good job bridging the gap between traditional and avant-garde designs, with a wide mix of products that includes *atelier* custom-made jewelry, classic time-pieces, and leather fashion accessories. *La Isla Shopping Mall.* ☎ 998/883-1251. www.maraf.com.

★ kids Martí Deportiva DOWN-TOWN/HOTEL ZONE

It can be a blast for sports-minded tourists to shop in Mexico's largest chain of sports stores, chock full of tempting goods. Martí offers a full range of sports supplies, active gear, snorkel equipment, clothing, and team jerseys (especially *fútbol*). Ironically, baseball is more popular in Yucatán than soccer, and the Leones, the professional baseball team in Mérida, won the Mexican League Championship in 2006. They're located in Plaza Las Americas, downtown, with a soccer shop and Nike outlet in La Isla Shopping Mall as well. ☎ 998/887-6756. www.marti.com.mx.

Jewels from Columbian Emeralds.

★★★ kids Mercado 28 DOWN-TOWN

This shaded open-air market, *Mercado Veinte-ocho,* has usurped the other flea markets on Avenida Tulum—where hawkers

La Isla Shopping Village.

claim it's "cheaper than Kmart"—as the most popular place to shop. The wider aisles here alleviate some of the pressure when you're eyeballing the goods, but the prices are not necessarily lower. They have some pleasant eateries in the center for typical Mexican food. *Avs. Tankah & Sunyaxchen. No credit cards.*

★★★ Pewter Mexicano DOWN-TOWN

Many travelers make this a stop on their journey to find an authentic Mexican gift to take home. The dazzling pewter pieces here come in an array of designs and images. Mirrors, trays, napkin holders, service sets, wall decor, traditional religious icons, and novelty pieces all shine brightly in this amazing shop. Prices are excellent, and they ship all over the globe. *Plaza Bonita (next to Mercado 28), Av. Xel-Ha.* ☎ 984/884-9720.

★★★ Plaza Bonita DOWNTOWN

In a cute Mexican-village setting with multicolor buildings, Plaza Bonita is my favorite place to shop. The highlights include an herbal

Cancún's Major Malls

Besides a number of flea markets and a few shops downtown, most of the shopping options in Cancún are in malls, and most of those are in the Hotel Zone. Here's a roundup:

★★ kids **Forum by the Sea** HOTEL ZONE   This entertainment and restaurant-heavy shopping mall houses Harley-Davidson, Levi's, Swatch, Diesel, and Tommy Hilfiger. Restaurants include Cambalache, Rainforest Café, Caliente, and Hard Rock Café. *Kukulcán Km 9.* ☎ *998/883-4425. Open 10am–midnight; restaurants and bars open later.*

★★★ kids **La Isla Shopping Mall** HOTEL ZONE   La Isla is Cancún's largest, poshest mall. As in an open-air "village," shops line walkways crisscrossed by small canals. Its Luxury Avenue includes Ultrafemme, Bvlgari, Crabtree & Evelyn, and Liverpool. It has a boardwalk facing the lagoon, an interactive aquarium, movies, and restaurants. *Kukulcán Km 12.5.* ☎ *998/883-5025. www. laislacancun.com.mx. Open daily 10am–10pm.*

★★★ **Plaza Bonita** DOWNTOWN   Plaza Bonita is our favorite place to shop in a cute Mexican village setting with multicolor buildings. The highlights include an herbal shop that sells copal incense, Smoker's Stylish for the freshest Cuban cigars, and the must-visit Pewter Factory, which has the best price and selection for handcrafted pewter and pottery for the home. They ship to the U.S. *Next to Mercado 28 (behind the post office), Av. Xel-Ha.* ☎ *998/ 884-7105. www. plazabonita.com.mx. Open Mon–Sat 10am–8pm; Sunday 10am–6pm.*

★★★ **Plaza Caracol** HOTEL ZONE   Near the Convention Center and all the action, Plaza Caracol is a good mix of great restaurants and nearly 200 shops, including Cartier Jewelry, Waterford Crystal, Sybele Boutique, UltraJewels, Samsonite luggage, and Guess. If La Isla is just too big for you, this plaza is perfect. *Kukulcán Km 8.5.* ☎ *998/883-1038. www.caracolplaza.com. Open daily 10am–10pm.*

shop that sells copal incense, Smoker's Stylish for the freshest Cuban cigars, and the must-visit Pewter Factory, which has the best price and selection for handcrafted pewter and pottery for the home. They ship to the U.S. *Next to Mercado 28 (behind the post office). Av. Xel-Ha.*

★★★ kids **Plaza Kukulcan** HOTEL ZONE   As the largest American-style indoor mall, in one huge building,

Plaza Kukulcan is very popular with shoppers and diners alike. There's a Señor Frog's store, Gaitán Leather, Tikal (which sells Guatemalan textile clothing), several leather-goods stores, and a store specializing in silver from Taxco among its many offerings. Fashion Gallery features designer styles. An upstairs food court is home to 16 different fast-food outlets, and the plaza has an

★ **Plaza Flamingo** HOTEL ZONE This centrally located, air-conditioned mall has a popular scenic walking path along the lagoon behind it. Their small fast-food court is good for a cheap eat. Small shops feature clothes, jewelry, and sporting goods. *Kukulcán Km 11.* ☎ *998/883-2855. www.flamingo.com.mx. Open daily 9am–9pm.*

★★★ **kids** **Plaza Kukulcan** HOTEL ZONE As the largest American-style indoor mall, in one huge building, Plaza Kukulcan is very popular with shoppers and diners alike. There's a Señor Frog's store, Gaitán Leather, Tikal (which sells Guatemalan textile clothing), several leather-goods stores, and a store specializing in silver from Taxco among its many offerings. Fashion Gallery features designer fashions. An upstairs food court houses 16 different fast-food outlets, and it has an English-language first-run cinema. Restaurants include OK Maguey, Ruth's Chris, and a Houlihan's. *Kukulcán Km 13.* ☎ *998/885-2200. www.kukulcanplaza.com. Open daily 10am–10pm. Restaurants open later.*

★★ **Plaza Las Americas** DOWNTOWN A Sears store anchors one end of this middle-class mall, the upscale Mexican department store Liverpool is in the center, and a Chedraui is at the other end. Parking is available underground, and on the small second level there's the super-cool VIP Cinépolis movie house and Yax Sports Book. *Av. Tulum between avs. Sayil & Nichupté.* ☎ *998/887-5893. Open daily 10am–10pm.*

Plaza Maya Fair HOTEL ZONE Frequently called the "Mayfair," the Maya Fair is the oldest shopping center in the Hotel Zone. It has a lively center with restaurants such as Sanborn's and Outback Steak House, but other, newer malls have sapped its sales spirit. *Kukulcán Km 8.* ☎ *998/883-0862. Open daily 9am–9pm.*

English-language first-run cinema. Restaurants include OK Maguey, Ruth's Chris, and a Houlihan's. *Kukulcán Km 13.* ☎ *998/885-2200. Open 10am–11pm. Restaurants open later.*

★★ **kids** **Tulum Avenue Flea Markets** DOWNTOWN Avenida Tulum once boasted the best flea-market bargains and was a popular stop when tourists went downtown. They're still offering bargains, but it's to fewer people since Mercado 28 rose to fashion. Ki Huic is the oldest and largest of the three *mercados* (markets) downtown, with street-front stalls and an indoor labyrinth of stalls as well. At the far side, on Avenida Nader, are some good small restaurants. Plaza Mexico is a much smaller series of stalls near the middle of Tulum, and Plaza

Street vendors downtown.

Garibaldi, on the corner with Avenida Uxmal, is also a good place to haggle for what you want. All sell typical souvenirs, clothing, and gifts. *Av. Tulum, between avs. Cobá & Uxmal. Open 9am–10pm with a mid-afternoon siesta in some shops.*

★★★ **Ultrafemme** HOTEL ZONE/ DOWNTOWN This duty free–priced perfume and cosmetics shop is now open at 10 locations in the Riviera Maya, so they must be doing something right. They carry Lancôme, Estée Lauder, Clinique, Dior, Chanel, La Mer, La Prairie, Helena Rubenstein, Origins, Shiseido, and Mac, among others. Located in the Hotel Zone in Plaza Caracol, Plaza Flamingo, and La Isla's "Luxury Avenue," the prices seem a tad better in their downtown, Avenida Tulum store. *Also located in Plaza Las Americas, & in Playa del Carmen & Cozumel. Open 11am–10pm.*

★★ **UltraJewels** HOTEL ZONE/ DOWNTOWN UltraJewels is the "official" retailer of Rolex in the Riviera Maya and a major dealer in such select brands as Cartier, Chopard, Mont Blanc, Tiffany & Co., Roberto Coin, David Yurman, and other world-famous jewelers. Renowned designers such as Christofle, Lalique, Lladró, and Swarovski have created items in their exclusive gift lines. Locations are in the Hotel Zone in Plaza Caracol and on Luxury Avenue in La Isla Shopping Mall, and downtown in Plaza Las Americas. They have another store on Cozumel in Punta Langosta Plaza. *Kukulkán Km 8.5.* ☎ *998/883-1225. Open 11am–10pm.*

★ **Wayan Natural Wear** HOTEL ZONE This is a stylish store that focuses on "natural clothing" made from cottons, many of which are hand-dyed or left in their organic color, as well as pottery and handicrafts. Wayan, which roughly means "Here I Am" in Maya, features Mexican and African goods, with a touch of Indonesia thrown in, in styles that have a multilevel appeal. The shops are decorated like the interior of a big hut, with colors and designs that excite, so even just looking is fun. Very different. *Plaza Flamingo & Plaza Kukulcan.* ☎ *998/883-2855.*

Zara HOTEL ZONE Zara is a hip, American-style store selling fashionable women's clothing, shoes, and accessories in La Isla Shopping Mall. Its up-to-date designs of such pieces as nautical-themed baggy trousers, colorful tops and sports jumpers, ultramodern shoes, imaginative accessories—plus a small selection of children's clothes—draw a mostly young clientele. *La Isla Shopping Mall.* ☎ *998/883-5025. www.zara. com. Daily 9am–10pm.* ●

The
Savvy Traveler

Before You Go

Government Tourist Offices

The Mexican Government Tourist Board has offices in major North American cities, in addition to the main office in Mexico City (☎ **555/278-4200**).

UnitedStates:Chicago(☎**312/228-0517**); Houston (☎ **713/772-2581,** ext. 105, or 713/772-3819); Los Angeles (☎ **310/282-9112**); and New York (☎ **212/308-2110**). The Mexican Embassy is at 1911 Pennsylvania Ave. NW, Washington, DC 20005 (☎ **202/728-1750** or 202/728-1600). Canada: 2055 Rue Peel, Suite 1000, Montreal, QC H3A 1V4 (☎ **514/288-2502**); Commerce Court West, 199 Bay St., Suite 4440, Toronto, ON M5L 1E9 (☎ **416/925-0704**); 710 West Hastings St., Suite 1177, Vancouver, BC V6E 2K3 (☎ **604/684-1859**); Embassy office: 1500-45 O'Connor St., Ottawa, ON K1P 1A4 (☎ **613/233-8988;** fax 613/235-9123).

When to Go/Weather

High season in the Yucatán is December 20 through Easter. This is the best time for calm, warm weather; snorkeling, diving, and fishing (the calmer weather means clearer and more predictable seas); and for visiting the ruins that dot the interior of the peninsula. Book well in advance if you plan to be in Cancún around the holidays. Low season is the day after Easter through mid-December; during low season, prices may drop 20% to 50%. In Cancún and along the Riviera Maya, demand by European visitors is creating a summer high season, with hotel rates approaching those charged in the winter months.

Mexico's dry season runs from November to April, and the rainy season stretches from May to October. It isn't a problem if you're staying close to the beaches, but for those bent on road-tripping to Chichén Itzá, Uxmal, or other sites, temperatures and humidity in the interior can be downright stifling from May to July. Later in the rainy season, the frequency of tropical storms and hurricanes increases; such storms, of course, can put a crimp in your vacation. But they can lower temperatures, making climbing ruins a real joy, accompanied by cool air and a slight wind. November is especially ideal for Yucatán travels. Cancún, Cozumel, and Isla Mujeres also have a rainy season from November to January, when northern storms hit. This usually means diving visibility is diminished—and conditions may prevent boats from even going out.

Mexico has two main climate seasons: rainy (May to mid-Oct) and dry (mid-Oct to Apr). Hurricane season particularly affects the Yucatán Peninsula and the southern Pacific coast, especially June through October. However, if no hurricanes strike, the light, cooling winds, especially September through November, can make it a perfect time to tackle the pre-Hispanic ruins that dot the interior of the peninsula.

Norte (northern) season runs from late November to mid-January, when the jet stream dips far south and creates northerly winds and showers in many resort areas. These showers usually last for only a couple of days.

June, July, and August are unrelentingly hot on the Yucatán Peninsula and in most coastal areas, though temperatures rise only into the mid-80s to 90°F (mid-20s to 32°C). Most of coastal Mexico experiences temperatures in the 80s (20s°C) in the hottest months.

Festivals & Special Events

During national holidays, Mexican banks and governmental offices—including Immigration—are closed.

JAN. New Year's Day (Año Nuevo). National holiday. Perhaps the quietest day in all of Mexico; most people stay home or visit church. All businesses close. In traditional indigenous communities, new tribal leaders are inaugurated with colorful ceremonies rooted in the pre-Hispanic past. (January 1)

Three Kings Day (Día de Reyes). Nationwide. Commemorates the Three Kings bringing gifts to the Christ Child. On this day, children receive presents, much like the traditional gift-giving that accompanies Christmas in the United States. (January 6)

FEB. & MAR. Carnaval. This celebration takes place over the 3 days preceding Ash Wednesday and the beginning of Lent. It is celebrated with special gusto in Cozumel, where it resembles Mardi Gras in New Orleans, with a festive atmosphere and parades. Transportation and hotels are packed, so it's best to make reservations well in advance and arrive a couple of days before the celebrations begin.

Ash Wednesday. The start of Lent and a time of abstinence, this is a day of reverence nationwide, but some towns honor it with folk dancing and fairs.

Spring Equinox, Chichén Itzá. On the first day of spring, the Temple of Kukulkán—Chichén Itzá's main pyramid—aligns with the sun, and the shadow of the plumed serpent moves slowly from the top of the building down. When the shadow reaches the bottom, the body joins the carved stone snake's head at the base of the pyramid. According to ancient legend, at the moment that the serpent is whole, the earth is fertilized to ensure a bountiful growing season. Visitors come from around the world to marvel at this sight, so advance arrangements are advisable. The serpent view is at its peak on March 21, but the shadow can be seen from March 19 to 23. Elsewhere, the equinox is celebrated with festivals and celebrations to welcome spring in the custom of the ancient Mexicans, with dances and prayers to the elements and the four cardinal points, to renew their energy for the year. It's customary to wear white with a red ribbon.

APRIL Holy Week (Semana Santa). This celebrates the last week in the life of Christ from Palm Sunday to Easter Sunday with somber religious processions almost nightly, spoofing of Judas, and reenactments of specific biblical events, plus food and craft fairs. Businesses close during this traditional week of Mexican national vacations.

If you plan on traveling to or around Mexico during Holy Week, make your reservations early. Airline seats on flights into and out of the country will be reserved months in advance. Buses to almost anywhere in Mexico will be full, so try arriving on the Wednesday or Thursday before Good Friday. The week following Easter is also a traditional vacation period.

MAY Cinco de Mayo. National holiday. This holiday celebrates the defeat of the French at the Battle of Puebla. (May 5)

Cancún Jazz Festival. For dates and schedule information, check ☎ 800/44-MEXICO or www.cancun.info.

SEPT. Independence Day. This day of parades, picnics, and family reunions throughout the country celebrates Mexico's independence from Spain. At 11pm on September 15, the president of Mexico gives the famous independence *grito* (shout) from the National Palace in Mexico City, and local mayors do the same in every town and municipality all over Mexico. On September 16, every city and town conducts a parade in which both government and civilians display their pride in being Mexican. For these celebrations, all important government buildings are draped in the national colors—red, green, and white—and the towns blaze with lights. (September 15 and 16; September 16 is a national holiday)

Fall Equinox, Chichén Itzá. The same shadow play that occurs during the spring equinox repeats at the fall equinox. (September 21 to 22)

OCT. **"Ethnicity Day" or Columbus Day (Día de la Raza).** This commemorates the fusion of the Spanish and Mexican peoples. (October 12)

NOV. **Day of the Dead (Día de los Muertos).** The Day of the Dead is actually 2 days: All Saints' Day, honoring saints and deceased children; and All Souls' Day, honoring deceased adults. On the 2 nights, children dress in costumes and masks, often carrying mock coffins and pumpkin lanterns through the streets, into which they expect money will be dropped. (November 1 and 2; November 1 is a national holiday)

Revolution Day. National holiday. This commemorates the start of the Mexican Revolution in 1910 with parades, speeches, rodeos, and patriotic events. (November 20)

Sixth Annual Yucatán Bird Festival, Mérida, Yucatán. Bird-watching sessions, workshops, and exhibits are the highlights of this festival, designed to illustrate the special role birds play in our environment and in the Yucatán territory. *Call ☎ 800/44-MEXICO or check out www.yucatanbirds.org.mx for details. (Mid-November)*

DEC. **Feast of the Virgin of Guadalupe.** Throughout the country, religious processions, street fairs, dancing, fireworks, and Masses honor the patroness of Mexico. This is one of Mexico's most moving and beautiful displays of traditional culture. The Virgin of Guadalupe appeared to a young man, Juan Diego, in December 1531, on a hill near Mexico City. He convinced the bishop that he had seen the apparition by revealing his cloak, upon which the Virgin was emblazoned. Every village celebrates this day. (December 12)

Christmas. Mexicans extend this celebration and often leave their jobs beginning 2 weeks before Christmas all the way through New Year's Day. Many businesses close, and resorts and hotels fill up. Significant celebrations take place on December 24.

New Year's Eve. As in the rest of the world, New Year's Eve in Mexico is celebrated with parties, fireworks, and plenty of noise. (December 31)

Useful Websites

- **www.cancunmx.com**: This site is a good place to start planning. There's a database of answers to the most common questions, called "The Online Experts."

- **www.cancun.info**: The official site of the **Cancún Convention & Visitors Bureau** lists excellent information on events and attractions. Its hotel guide is one of the most complete available, and it has a great multimedia page.

- **www.intheroo.com**: Even if you visit this site for its quirky name alone, you'll also find it useful for its comprehensive listing of all things Playa del Carmen.

- **www.isla-mujeres.net**: The official site of the **Isla Mujeres Tourism Board** provides complete information on Isla, from getting there to where to stay.

- **www.myislamujeres.com**: Get a local's view of the island; especially notable are the active chat room and message boards.

- **www.cozumel.net**: While a bit cluttered, this site is chock full of useful info. Click on "About Cozumel" to find schedules for ferries and island-hop flights, and to check the latest news. There's also a comprehensive listing of B&Bs and vacation-home rentals, plus great info on diving, maps, and a chat room.

- **www.travelnotes.cc**: This site has 1,000 pages of information with photos of Cozumel—with an emphasis on ocean activities.

- **www.rivieramaya.com**: Good general info that's kept up-to-date. You'll find a comprehensive list of accommodations and service providers for this coast as well as special deals that some hotels occasionally offer through this website.

- **www.locogringo.com**: This is a good resource for travel information for the southern Riviera Maya—Akumal and Tulum.

- **www.mayayucatan.com**: Yucatán's Ministry of Tourism maintains this site. It has an update section and good general info on different destinations in the state.

- **www.mexonline.com/yucatan. htm**: A nice roundup of vacation rentals, tour operators, and information on the Maya sites. For more information on Mexico's indigenous history, see the links on the pre-Columbian page (www. mexonline.com/precolum.htm).

- **www.yucatantoday.com**: Clean, informative, and well-maintained, this site includes updated features as well as guides on everything from baseball to travel safety.

Getting **There**

By Plane

The Yucatán has two sizeable international airports: **Cancún International Airport** (Carretera Cancún-Chetumal Km 22; ☎ **998/ 848-7200** or 998/886-0322, both numbers in Spanish only; www. cancun-airport.com) offers the most extensive service. **Merida– Licenciado Manuel Crecencio Rejon Int´l Airport** (☎ **557/163- 96**) is smaller, located 13km (8 miles) from the city center on the southwestern outskirts of town, near the entrance to Highway 180.

The main airlines operating direct or nonstop flights from the United States to Mexico are Aeromexico (☎ **800/237-6639;** www. aeromexico.com), Air France (☎ **800/237-2747;** www.airfrance. com), Alaska Airlines (☎ **800/252- 7522;** www.alaskaair.com), American Airlines (☎ **800/223-5436;** www.aa.com), Continental (☎ **800/ 537-9222;** www.continental.com), Frontier Airlines (☎ **800/432-1359;** www.frontierairlines.com), Mexicana (☎ **800/531-7921;** www.mexicana. com), Northwest/KLM (☎ **800/ 225-2525;** www.nwa.com), Taca

(☎ **800/400-8222;** www.taca.com), United (☎ **800/538-2929;** www. united.com), and US Airways (☎ **800/428-4322;** www.usairways. com). Southwest Airlines (☎ **800/ 435-9792;** www.southwest.com) serves the U.S. border.

The main departure points in North America for international airlines are Atlanta, Chicago, Dallas/ Fort Worth, Denver, Houston, Los Angeles, Las Vegas, Miami, New York, Orlando, Philadelphia, Phoenix, Raleigh/Durham, San Antonio, San Francisco, Seattle, Toronto, and Washington, D.C.

By Car
See "Getting Around: By Car," below.

Getting **Around**

By Plane
Mexico has two large private national carriers: Mexicana (☎ **01-800/509-8960** toll-free in Mexico) and Aeromexico (☎ **01-800/021-4000** toll-free in Mexico), in addition to several up-and-coming regional carriers. Mexicana and Aeromexico offer extensive connections to the United States as well as within Mexico.

Several new regional carriers are operated by or can be booked through Mexicana or Aeromexico. Other regional carriers include Volaris (☎ **800/122-8000** toll-free in Mexico; www.volaris.com.mx) and Interjet (☎ **551/102-5555;** www.interjet.com.mx). For points inside the state of Oaxaca only—Oaxaca City, Puerto Escondido, and Huatulco—contact Zapotec Tours (☎ **800/44-OAXACA,** or 773/506-2444 in Illinois). The regional carriers are expensive, but they go to difficult-to-reach places. In each applicable section of this book, we've mentioned regional carriers with all pertinent telephone numbers.

Click Mexicana, a Mexicana affiliate (☎ **998/884-2000**), flies from Cozumel, Mexico City, Mérida, Chetumal, and other points within Mexico.

By Car
Most Mexican roads are not up to U.S. standards. Driving at night is dangerous—the roads are rarely lit; trucks, carts, pedestrians, and bicycles usually have no lights; and you can hit potholes, animals, rocks, dead ends, or uncrossable bridges without warning. The spirited style of Mexican driving sometimes requires super vision and reflexes.

Mexico charges some of the highest tolls in the world for its network of new toll roads; as a result, they are rarely used. Generally speaking, though, using toll roads cuts travel time. Older toll-free roads are generally in good condition, but travel times tend to be longer. And in general, the roads in the Yucatán are generally flat and free of unexpected twists and turns.

You'll get the best **car-rental** price if you reserve a car at least a week in advance in the United States. U.S. car-rental firms include Advantage (☎ **800/777-5500** in the U.S. and Canada; www.arac.com), Avis (☎ **800/331-1212** in the U.S., 800/TRY-AVIS in Canada; www.avis. com), Budget (☎ **800/527-0700** in the U.S. and Canada; www.budget. com), Hertz (☎ **800/654-3131** in the U.S. and Canada; www.hertz. com), National (☎ **800/CAR-RENT** in the U.S. and Canada; www.

nationalcar.com), and Thrifty (☎ **800/847-4389** in the U.S. and Canada; www.thrifty.com), which often offers discounts for rentals in Mexico. For European travelers, Kemwel Holiday Auto (☎ **800/678-0678;** www.kemwel.com) and Auto Europe (☎ **800/223-5555;** www.autoeurope.com) can arrange Mexican rentals, sometimes through other agencies. These and some local firms have offices in Mexico City and most other large Mexican cities. You'll find rental desks at airports, all major hotels, and many travel agencies.

Cars are easy to rent if you are 25 or over and have a major credit card, valid driver's license, and passport with you. Without a credit card, you must leave a cash deposit, usually a big one. One-way rentals are usually simple to arrange but more costly.

Car-rental costs are high in Mexico because cars are more expensive. The basic cost of the 1-day

rental of an economy vehicle (Ford Fiesta) at press time, with unlimited mileage (but before 15% tax and $15 daily insurance), was $35 in Cancún and $25 in Mérida. Renting by the week gives you a lower daily rate.

By Bus

Mexican buses run frequently, are readily accessible, and can get you almost anywhere you want to go. They're often the only way to get from large cities to other nearby cities and small villages.

By Taxi

Taxis are the preferred way to get around most of Mexico's resort areas. Fares for short trips within towns are generally preset by zone, and are quite reasonable compared with U.S. rates. For longer trips or excursions to nearby cities, taxis can generally be hired for around $15 to $20 per hour, or for a negotiated daily rate.

Fast **Facts**

ABBREVIATIONS Dept. (apartments); Apdo. (post office box); Av. (*avenida;* avenue); c/ (*calle;* street); Calz. (*calzada;* boulevard). "C" on faucets stands for *caliente* (hot), "F" for *fría* (cold). "PB" *(planta baja)* means ground floor; in most buildings the next floor up is the first floor (1).

ATMS/CASHPOINTS & BANKS Banks tend to be open weekdays 9am until 5pm, and some open for a half-day on Saturday. Most major cities and resort areas have plentiful ATMs. Universal bankcards (such as the Cirrus and PLUS systems) can be used. The exchange rate is generally more favorable than that at a currency house. Most machines offer Spanish/English menus and

dispense pesos, but some offer the option of withdrawing dollars.

BUSINESS HOURS In general, businesses in larger cities are open between 9am and 7pm; in smaller towns many close between 2 and 4pm. Most close on Sunday. In resort areas it is common to find stores open at least in the mornings on Sunday, and for shops to stay open late, often until 8 or even 10pm. Bank hours are Monday through Friday from 9 or 9:30am to anywhere between 3 and 7pm. Increasingly, banks open on Saturday for at least a half-day.

CAR RENTALS See "Getting Around," p. 162.

DRUG LAWS Mexican officials have no tolerance for drug users, and jail is their solution, with very little hope of getting out until the sentence (usually a long one) is completed or heavy fines or bribes are paid. Remember, in Mexico the legal system assumes you are guilty until proven innocent.

ELECTRICITY The electrical system in Mexico is 110 volts AC (60 cycles), as in the United States and Canada. In reality, however, it may cycle more slowly and overheat your appliances. To compensate, select a medium or low speed on hair dryers. Many older hotels still have electrical outlets for flat two-prong plugs; you'll need an adapter for any plug with an enlarged end on one prong or with three prongs.

EMBASSIES & CONSULATES The Embassy of the **United States** in Mexico City is at Paseo de la Reforma 305 (☎ **555/080-2000** or 555/511-9980). Visit www.usembassy-mexico.gov for addresses of the U.S. consulates inside Mexico. There are U.S. Consulates General in Cancún (☎ **998/883-0272**); Cozumel (☎ **987/872-4574**); and Mérida (☎ **999/925-5011**).

The Embassy of **Australia** in Mexico City is at Rubén Darío 55, Col. Polanco (☎ **525/511-012-200**). The Embassy of **Canada** in Mexico City is at Schiller 529, Col. Polanco (☎ **555/724-7900**). There is a Canadian consulate in Cancún (☎ **998/883-3360**) as well. The Embassy of the **United Kingdom** in Mexico City is at Río Lerma 71, Col. Cuauhtémoc (☎ **555/242-8500;** www.embajadabritanica.com.mx). The Embassy of **Ireland** in Mexico City is at Bulevar Cerrada, Avila Camacho 76, 3rd floor, Col. Lomas de Chapultepec (☎ **555/520-5803**).

EMERGENCIES In case of emergency, dial ☎ **065** from any phone within Mexico. For the **police**, dial ☎ **060.** The 24-hour **Tourist Help Line** in Mexico City is ☎ **01-800/987-8224** or 555/089-7500, or you can now simply dial **078.** The operators don't always speak English, but they are always willing to help. The tourist legal assistance office (Procuraduría del Turista) in Mexico City (☎ **555/625-8153** or 555/625-8154) always has an English speaker available. Though the phones are frequently busy, they operate 24 hours.

HOLIDAYS See "Festivals & Special Events," p 159.

INTERNET ACCESS In large cities and resort areas, most top hotels offer business centers with Internet access and wi-fi access in the rooms. You'll also find cybercafes in destinations that are popular with expats and business travelers. Even in remote spots, Internet access is common.

LANGUAGE Spanish is the official language in Mexico. English is spoken and understood to some degree in most tourist areas. Mexicans are very accommodating with foreigners who try to speak Spanish, even in broken sentences. You may also hear people speaking the indigenous Maya language. For basic vocabulary, refer to "Spanish Basics."

LEGAL AID International Legal Defense Counsel, 111 S. 15th St., 24th Floor, Packard Building, Philadelphia, PA 19102 (☎ **215/977-9982**), is a law firm specializing in the legal difficulties of Americans abroad.

LIQUOR LAWS The legal drinking age in Mexico is 18; however, asking for ID or denying purchase is extremely rare. Grocery stores sell everything from beer and wine to national and imported liquors. You can buy liquor 24 hours a day, but during major elections, dry laws often are enacted for as much as 72 hours in advance of the election—and they apply to tourists as well as local residents. It is illegal to drink in the street, but many tourists do so. Use your judgment—if you are getting drunk, you are more likely to get stopped by the police.

MAIL Postage for a postcard or letter is 1 peso; it may arrive anywhere from 1 to 6 weeks later. A registered letter costs 1.90 pesos. Sending a package can be quite expensive and unreliable; it takes 2 to 6 weeks, if it arrives at all. The recommended way to send a package or important mail is through FedEx, UPS, or another reputable international mail service.

NEWSPAPERS & MAGAZINES There currently is no national English-language newspaper; however, there is a monthly magazine called *Inside Mexico* that can be found at some bookstores and newsstands. Newspaper kiosks in larger cities carry a selection of English-language magazines.

POLICE Especially in the tourist areas, most police are very protective of international visitors. Several cities, including Cancún, have a special corps of English-speaking Tourist Police to assist with directions, guidance, and more. If you have an emergency, dial ☎ 060 for police assistance.

SMOKING Smoking is not permitted or accepted in many public places, including restaurants, bars, and hotel lobbies. However, you will still find the occasional smoker.

TAXES The 15% IVA (value-added) tax applies on goods and services in most of Mexico, and it's supposed to be included in the posted price. This tax is 10% in Cancún and Cozumel. There is a 5% tax on food and drinks consumed in restaurants that sell alcoholic beverages with an alcohol content of more than 10%; this tax applies whether you drink alcohol or not. Tequila is subject to a 25% tax. Mexico imposes an exit tax of around $24 on every foreigner leaving the country, as well as a tourism tax of $18.

TELEPHONE & FAX The **country code** for Mexico is **52. To call Mexico** from the United States, dial 011-52, then the two- or three-digit area code, and then the eight- or seven-digit number. **To make international calls:** To make international calls from Mexico, first dial 00, and then the country code (U.S. or Canada 1, U.K. 44, Ireland 353, Australia 61, New Zealand 64). Next, dial the area code and number. **For directory assistance:** Dial ☎ 040 if you're looking for a number inside Mexico. *Note:* Listings usually appear under the owner's name, not the name of the business, and your chances of finding an English-speaking operator are slim to none. **For operator assistance:** If you need operator assistance in making a call, dial **090** to make an international call, and **020** to call a number in Mexico. **Toll-free numbers:** Numbers beginning with 800 within Mexico are toll-free, but calling a U.S. toll-free number from Mexico costs the same as an overseas call.

TIME ZONE Central time prevails throughout the Yucatán. All of Mexico observes **daylight saving time.**

TIPPING Most service employees in Mexico count on tips for the majority of their income, and this is especially true for bellboys and waiters. Bellboys should receive the equivalent of 50¢ to $1 per bag; waiters generally receive 10% to 20%, depending on the level of service. It is not customary to tip taxi drivers, unless they are hired by the hour or provide touring or other special services.

TOILETS Public toilets are not common in Mexico, but an increasing number are available, especially at fast-food restaurants and Pemex gas stations. These facilities and restaurant and club restrooms commonly have attendants, who expect a small tip (about 50¢).

Yucatán **History**

10,000–1500 B.C. Archaic period: Hunting and gathering; later, the dawn of agriculture: domestication of chiles, corn, beans, avocado, amaranth, and pumpkin. Mortars and pestles in use. Stone bowls and jars, obsidian knives, and open-weave basketry developed.

1500 B.C.–A.D. 300 Pre-Classic period: Olmec culture develops large-scale settlements and irrigation methods. Cities spring up. Olmec influence spreads over other cultures in the Gulf Coast, central and southern Mexico, Central America, the lower Mexican Pacific coast, and the Yucatán. Several cities in central and southern Mexico begin the construction of large ceremonial centers and pyramids. The Maya develop several city-states in Chiapas and Central America.

1000–900 B.C. Olmec San Lorenzo center is destroyed; the Olmec begin anew at La Venta.

600 B.C. La Venta Olmec cultural zenith.

A.D. 300–900 Classic period: Broad influence of Teotihuacán culture and the establishment there of a truly cosmopolitan urbanism. Satellite settlements spring up across central Mexico and as far away as Guatemala. Trade and cultural interchange with the

Maya and the Zapotec flourish. The Maya perfect the calendar and improve astronomical calculations. They build grandiose cities at Palenque, Calakmul, and Cobá, and in Central America.

683 Maya King Pacal is buried in an elaborate tomb below the Palace of the Inscriptions at Palenque.

800 Bonampak murals are painted.

900 Post-Classic period begins: More emphasis is placed on warfare in central Mexico. The Toltec culture emerges at Tula and replaces Teotihuacán as the dominant city of central Mexico. Toltec influence spreads to the Yucatán, forming the culture of the Itzaés, who become the rulers of Chichén Itzá.

909 This is the date on a small monument at Toniná (near San Cristóbal de las Casas), the last Long Count date yet discovered, symbolizing the end of the Classic Maya era.

1156–1230 Tula, the Toltec capital, is abandoned.

1325–1470 Aztec capital Tenochtitlán is founded; Aztecs begin military campaigns in the Valley of Mexico and then thrust farther out, subjugating the civilizations of the Gulf Coast and southern Mexico.

1516 Gold found on Cozumel during aborted Spanish expedition of Yucatán Peninsula arouses interest of Spanish governor in Cuba, who sends Juan de Grijalva on an expedition, followed by another, led by Hernán Cortez.

1518 Spaniards first visit what is today Campeche.

1519 Conquest of Mexico begins: Hernán Cortez and troops make their way along the Mexican coast to present-day Veracruz.

1521 Conquest is complete after Aztec defeat at Tlatelolco.

1521–24 Cortez organizes Spanish empire in Mexico and begins building Mexico City on the ruins of Tenochtitlán.

1524–35 Cortez is removed from power, and royal council governs New Spain.

1526 King of Spain permits Francisco Montejo to colonize the Yucatán.

1535–1821 Viceregal period: 61 viceroys appointed by king of Spain govern Mexico. Control of much of the land ends up in the hands of the Church and the politically powerful. A governor who reports to the king rather than to viceroys leads the Yucatán.

1542 Mérida is established as capital of Yucatán Peninsula.

1546 The Maya rebel and take control of the peninsula.

1559 French and Spanish pirates attack Campeche.

1562 Friar Diego de Landa destroys 5,000 Maya religious stone figures and burns 27 hieroglyphic painted manuscripts at Maní, Yucatán. Those Maya believed to be secretly practicing pre-Hispanic beliefs endure torture and death.

1810–21 War of Independence: Miguel Hidalgo starts movement for Mexico's independence from Spain but is executed within a year; leadership and goals change during the war years, but Agustín de Iturbide outlines a compromise between monarchy and republic.

1822 First Empire: Iturbide ascends throne as emperor of Mexico, loses power after a year, and loses life in an attempt to reclaim throne.

1824–64 Early Republic period, characterized by almost perpetual civil war between federalists and centralists, conservatives and liberals, culminating in the victory of the liberals under Juárez.

1864–67 Second Empire: The French invade Mexico in the name of Maximilian of Austria, who is appointed emperor of Mexico. Juárez and liberal government retreat to the north and wage war with the French forces. The French finally abandon Mexico and leave Maximilian to be defeated and executed.

1847–66 War of the Castes in the Yucatán: Poverty and hunger cause the Maya to revolt and gain control of half of the peninsula before being defeated by the Mexican National Army. But lingering warfare lasts well into the 20th century in the most remote parts of the peninsula.

1872–76 Juárez dies, and political struggles ensue for the presidency.

1877–1911 Porfiriato: Porfirio Díaz, president/dictator of Mexico for 33 years, leads country to modernization by encouraging foreign investment in mines, oil, and railroads. Mexico witnesses the development of a modern economy and a growing disparity between rich and poor. Social conditions, especially in rural areas, become desperate.

1911–17 Mexican Revolution: Francisco Madero drafts revolutionary plan. Díaz resigns. Leaders jockey for power during period of great violence, national upheaval, and tremendous loss of life.

1917–40 Reconstruction: Present constitution of Mexico is signed; land and education reforms are initiated and labor unions strengthened; Mexico expropriates oil companies and railroads. Pancho Villa, Zapata, and presidents Obregón and Carranza are assassinated.

1940 Mexico enters period of political stability and makes steady economic progress. Quality of life improves, although problems of corruption, inflation, national health, and unresolved land and agricultural issues continue.

1974 Quintana Roo achieves statehood and Cancún opens to tourism.

1994–97 Mexico, Canada, and the United States sign the North American Free Trade Agreement (NAFTA). An Indian uprising in Chiapas sparks countrywide protests over government policies concerning land distribution, bank loans, health, education, and voting and human rights.

1999 The governor of Quintana Roo goes into hiding following accusations of corruption and ties to drug money. After many months in hiding, he turns himself in and is imprisoned.

2000 Mexico elects Vicente Fox of the PAN party president.

2002 The PAN party wins the governorship of the Yucatán.

2005 Two hurricanes, Emily and Wilma, inflict great damage on Cancún, Cozumel, and the Riviera Maya.

2006 Felipe Calderón, candidate for the PAN, wins an extremely close presidential election over Andrés Manuel López Obrador, candidate for the PRD. The PRI candidate, Roberto Madrazo, comes in a distant third.

2007 Chichén Itzá is named one of the "New 7 Wonders of the World," thus boosting popularity and status of the already-popular Maya historical site.

2009 The AH1N1 virus breaks out in Mexico and dramatically affects tourism in the region. Hotels and services fight back with huge discounts and promotions.

Yucatecan **Architecture**

Pre-Hispanic Forms

Mexico's pyramids were truncated platforms crowned with a temple. Many sites have circular buildings, such as El Caracol at Chichén Itzá, usually called the observatory and dedicated to the god of the wind. El Castillo at Chichén Itzá has 365 steps—one for every day of the year. The Temple of the Magicians at Uxmal has beautifully rounded and sloping sides. Evidence of building one pyramidal structure on top of another, a widely accepted practice, has been found throughout Mesoamerica.

Architects of many Toltec, Aztec, and Teotihuacán edifices alternated sloping panels (talud) with vertical panels (tablero). Elements of this style occasionally show up in the Yucatán. Dzibanché, a newly excavated site near Lago Bacalar in southern Quintana Roo state, has at least one temple with this characteristic. The true arch was unknown in Mesoamerica, but the Maya made use of the corbelled arch—a method of stacking stones that allows each successive stone to be cantilevered out a little farther than the one below it, until the two sides meet at the top, forming an inverted V.

The Olmec, considered the parent culture of Mesoamerica, built pyramids of earth. Unfortunately, little remains to tell us what their buildings looked like. The Olmec, however, left an enormous sculptural legacy, from small, intricately carved pieces of jade to 40-ton carved basalt rock heads.

Throughout Mexico, carved stone and mural art on pyramids served a religious and historical function rather than an ornamental one. Hieroglyphs, picture symbols etched on stone or painted on walls or pottery, functioned as the written language of the ancient peoples, particularly the Maya. By deciphering the glyphs, scholars allow the ancients to speak again, providing us with specific names to attach to rulers and their families, and demystifying the great dynastic histories of the Maya. For more on this, read A Forest of Kings (1990), by Linda Schele and David Freidel, and Blood of Kings (1986), by Linda Schele and Mary Ellen Miller. Good hieroglyphic examples appear in the site museum at Palenque.

Carving important historical figures on free-standing stone slabs, or stelae, was a common Maya commemorative device. Calakmul has the most, and good examples are on display in the Museum of Anthropology in Mexico City.

Pottery played an important role, and different indigenous groups are distinguished by their different use of color and style. The Maya painted pottery with scenes from daily and historical life.

Pre-Hispanic cultures left a number of fantastic painted murals, some of which are remarkably preserved, such as those at Bonampak and Cacaxtla. Amazing stone murals or mosaics, using thousands of pieces of fitted stone to form figures of warriors, snakes, or geometric designs, decorate the pyramid facades at Uxmal and Chichén Itzá.

Spanish Influence

With the arrival of the Spaniards, new forms of architecture came to Mexico. Many sites that were occupied by indigenous groups at the time of the conquest were razed, and in their place appeared Catholic churches, public buildings, and palaces for conquerors and the king's bureaucrats. In the Yucatán, churches at Izamal, Tecoh, Santa Elena, and Muná rest atop former pyramidal structures. Indian artisans, who formerly worked on pyramidal structures, were recruited to build the new buildings, often guided by drawings of European buildings. Frequently left on their own, the indigenous artisans implanted traditional symbolism in the new buildings: a plaster angel swaddled in feathers, reminiscent of the god Quetzalcoatl, and the face of an ancient god surrounded by corn leaves. They used pre-Hispanic calendar counts—the 13 steps to heaven or the nine levels of the underworld—to determine how many florets to carve around the church doorway.

To convert the native populations, New World Spanish priests and architects altered their normal ways of teaching and building. Often before the church was built, an open-air atrium was constructed to accommodate large numbers of parishioners for services. Posas (shelters) at the four corners of churchyards were another architectural technique unique to Mexico, again to accommodate crowds. Because of the language barrier between the Spanish and the natives, church adornment became more explicit. Biblical tales came to life in frescoes splashed across church walls. Christian symbolism in stone supplanted that of pre-Hispanic ideas as the natives tried to make sense of it all. Baroque became even more baroque in Mexico and was dubbed churrigueresque or ultrabaroque. Exuberant and complicated, it combines Gothic, baroque, and plateresque elements.

Almost every village in the Yucatán Peninsula has the remains of missions, monasteries, convents, and parish churches. Many were built in the 16th century following the early arrival of Franciscan friars. Examples include the Mission of San Bernardino de Sisal in Valladolid; the fine altarpiece at Teabo; the folk-art retablo (altarpiece) at Tecoh; the large church and convent at Mani with its retablos and limestone crucifix; the facade, altar, and central retablo of the church at Oxkutzcab; the 16-bell belfry at Ytholin; the baroque facade and altarpiece at Maxcanu; the cathedral at Mérida; the vast atrium and church at Izamal; and the baroque retablo and murals at Tabi.

When Porfirio Díaz became president in the late 19th century, the nation's art and architecture experienced another infusion of European sensibility. Díaz idolized Europe, and he commissioned a number of striking European-style public buildings, including many opera houses. He provided European scholarships to promising young artists who later returned to Mexico to produce Mexican subject paintings using techniques learned abroad.

Mexican Muralism

As the Mexican Revolution ripped the country apart between 1911 and 1917, a new social and cultural Mexico was born. In 1923, Minister of Education José Vasconcelos was charged with educating the illiterate masses. As one means of reaching people, he invited Diego Rivera and several other budding artists to paint Mexican history on the walls of the Ministry of Education building and the National Preparatory School in Mexico City. Thus began the tradition of painting murals in public buildings, which you will find in towns and cities throughout Mexico and the Yucatán.

Spanish Basics

Useful Phrases

ENGLISH	SPANISH	PRONUNCIATION
Good day	Buen día	Bwehn dee-ah
Good morning	Buenos días	Bweh-nohs dee-ahs
How are you?	¿Cómo está?	Koh-moh eh-stah
Very well	Muy bien	Mwee byehn
Thank you	Gracias	Grah-syahs
You're welcome	De nada	Deh nah-dah

ENGLISH	SPANISH	PRONUNCIATION
Goodbye	**Adiós**	Ah-*dyohs*
Please	**Por favor**	Pohr fah-*bohr*
Yes	**Sí**	See
No	**No**	Noh
Excuse me	**Perdóneme**	Pehr-*doh*-neh-meh
Give me	**Déme**	*Deh*-meh
Where is . . . ?	**¿Dónde está . . . ?**	*Dohn*-deh eh-*stah*
the station	**la estación**	lah eh-stah-*syohn*
a hotel	**un hotel**	oon oh-*tehl*
a gas station	**una gasolinera**	oo-nah gah-soh-lee-*neh*-rah
a restaurant	**un restaurante**	oon res-tow-*rahn*-teh
the toilet	**el baño**	el *bah*-nyoh
a good doctor	**un buen médico**	oon bwehn *meh*-dee-coh
the road to . . .	**el camino a/hacia . . .**	el cah-*mee*-noh ah/*ah*-syah
To the right	**A la derecha**	Ah lah deh-*reh*-chah
To the left	**A la izquierda**	Ah lah ees-*kyehr*-dah
Straight ahead	**Derecho**	Deh-*reh*-choh
I would like	**Quisiera**	Key-*syeh*-rah
I want	**Quiero**	*Kyeh*-roh
to eat	**comer**	koh-*mehr*
a room	**una habitación**	oo-nah ah-bee-tah-*syohn*
Do you have . . . ?	**¿Tiene usted . . . ?**	Tyeh-neh oo-*sted*
a book	**un libro**	oon *lee*-broh
a dictionary	**un diccionario**	oon deek-syoh-*nah*-ryoh
How much is it?	**¿Cuánto cuesta?**	*Kwahn*-toh *kweh*-stah
When?	**¿Cuándo?**	*Kwahn*-doh
What?	**¿Qué?**	Keh
There is (Is there . . . ?)	**(¿)Hay (. . . ?)**	Eye
What is there?	**¿Qué hay?**	Keh eye
Yesterday	**Ayer**	Ah-*yer*
Today	**Hoy**	Oy
Tomorrow	**Mañana**	Mah-*nyah*-nah
Good	**Bueno**	*Bweh*-noh
Bad	**Malo**	*Mah*-loh
Better (best)	**(Lo) Mejor**	(Loh) Meh-*hohr*
More	**Más**	Mahs
Less	**Menos**	*Meh*-nohs
No smoking	**Se prohibe fumar**	Seh proh-*ee*-beh foo-*mahr*
Postcard	**Tarjeta postal**	Tar-*heh*-tah poh-*stahl*
Insect repellent	**Repelente contra insectos**	Reh-peh-*lehn*-teh *cohn*-trah een-*sehk*-tohs

More Useful Phrases

ENGLISH	SPANISH	PRONUNCIATION
Do you speak English?	¿Habla usted inglés?	*Ah*-blah oo-*sted* een-*glehs*
Is there anyone here who speaks English?	¿Hay alguien aquí que hable inglés?	Eye *ahl*-gyehn ah-*kee* keh *ah*-bleh een-*glehs*
I speak a little Spanish.	Hablo un poco de español.	*Ah*-bloh oon *poh*-koh deh eh-spah-*nyohl*
I don't understand Spanish very well.	No (lo) entiendo muy bien el español.	Noh (loh) ehn-*tyehn*-doh mwee byehn el eh-spah-*nyohl*
The meal is good.	Me gusta la comida.	Meh *goo*-stah lah koh-*mee*-dah
What time is it?	¿Qué hora es?	Keh *oh*-rah ehs
May I see your menu?	¿Puedo ver el menú (la carta)?	*Pweh*-doh vehr el meh-*noo* (lah *car*-tah)
The check, please.	La cuenta, por favor.	Lah *kwehn*-tah pohr fa-*borh*
What do I owe you?	¿Cuánto le debo?	*Kwahn*-toh leh *deh*-boh
What did you say?	¿Mande? (formal) ¿Cómo? (informal)	*Mahn*-deh *Koh*-moh
I want (to see) . . .	Quiero (ver) . . .	*kyeh*-roh (vehr)
a room	un cuarto or una habitación	oon *kwar*-toh, *oo*-nah ah-bee-tah-*syohn*
for two persons	para dos personas	*pah*-rah dohs pehr-*soh*-nahs
with (without) bathroom	con (sin) baño	kohn (seen) *bah*-nyoh
We are staying here only . . .	Nos quedamos aquí solamente . . .	Nohs keh-*dah*-mohs ah-*kee* soh-lah-*mehn*-teh
one night	una noche	*oo*-nah *noh*-cheh
one week	una semana	*oo*-nah seh-*mah*-nah
We are leaving . . .	Partimos (Salimos) . . .	Pahr-*tee*-mohs (sah-*lee*-mohs)
tomorrow	mañana	mah-*nya*-nah
Do you accept . . . ? traveler's checks?	¿Acepta usted . . . ? cheques de viajero?	Ah-*sehp*-tah oo-*sted* *cheh*-kehs deh byah-*heh*-roh
Is there a laundromat . . . ? near here?	¿Hay una lavandería . . . ? cerca de aquí?	Eye *oo*-nah lah-*bahn*-deh-*ree*-ah *sehr*-kah deh ah-*kee*
Please send these clothes to the laundry.	Hágame el favor de mandar esta ropa a la lavandería.	*Ah*-gah-meh el fah-*bohr* deh mahn-*dahr* eh-stah *roh*-pah a lah lah-*bahn*-deh-*ree*-ah

Numbers

1	uno	*(ooh-noh)*
2	dos	*(dohs)*
3	tres	*(trehs)*
4	cuatro	*(kwah-troh)*
5	cinco	*(seen-koh)*
6	seis	*(sayes)*
7	siete	*(syeh-teh)*
8	ocho	*(oh-choh)*
9	nueve	*(nweh-beh)*
10	diez	*(dyehs)*
11	once	*(ohn-seh)*
12	doce	*(doh-seh)*
13	trece	*(treh-seh)*
14	catorce	*(kah-tohr-seh)*
15	quince	*(keen-seh)*
16	dieciseis	*(dyeh-see-sayes)*
17	diecisiete	*(dyeh-see-syeh-teh)*
18	dieciocho	*(dyeh-syoh-choh)*
19	diecinueve	*(dyeh-see-nweh-beh)*
20	veinte	*(bayn-teh)*
30	treinta	*(trayn-tah)*
40	cuarenta	*(kwah-ren-tah)*
50	cincuenta	*(seen-kwen-tah)*
60	sesenta	*(seh-sehn-tah)*
70	setenta	*(seh-tehn-tah)*
80	ochenta	*(oh-chehn-tah)*
90	noventa	*(noh-behn-tah)*
100	cien	*(syehn)*
200	doscientos	*(do-syehn-tohs)*
500	quinientos	*(kee-nyehn-tohs)*
1,000	mil	*(meel)*

Food Terms

Achiote   Small red seed of the annatto tree.

Achiote preparado   A Yucatecan-prepared paste made of ground achiote, wheat and corn flour, cumin, cinnamon, salt, onion, garlic, and oregano.

Agua fresca   Fruit-flavored water, usually watermelon, cantaloupe, chia seed with lemon, hibiscus flour, rice, or ground melon-seed mixture.

Antojito   Typical Mexican supper foods, usually made with masa or tortillas and having a filling or topping such as sausage, cheese, beans, and onions; includes such things as tacos, tostadas, sopes, and garnachas.

Atole   A thick, lightly sweet, hot drink made with finely ground corn and usually flavored with vanilla, pecan, strawberry, pineapple, or chocolate.

Botana   An appetizer.

Buñuelos   Round, thin, deep-fried crispy fritters dipped in sugar.

Carnitas   Pork deep-cooked (not fried) in lard, and then simmered and served with corn tortillas for tacos.

Ceviche   Fresh raw seafood marinated in fresh lime juice and garnished with chopped tomatoes, onions, chiles, and sometimes cilantro.

Chayote   A vegetable pear or mirliton, a type of spiny squash boiled and served as an accompaniment to meat dishes.

Chiles en nogada   Poblano peppers stuffed with a mixture of ground pork and beef, spices, fruits, raisins, and almonds. Can be served either warm—fried in a light batter—or cold, sans the batter. Either way it is then covered in walnut-and-cream sauce.

Chiles rellenos   Usually poblano peppers stuffed with cheese or spicy ground meat with raisins, rolled in a batter, and fried.

Churro   Tube-shaped, breadlike fritter, dipped in sugar and sometimes filled with cajeta (milk-based caramel) or chocolate.

Cochinita pibil   Pork wrapped in banana leaves, pit-baked in a pibil sauce of achiote, sour orange, and spices; common in the Yucatán.

Enchilada   A tortilla dipped in sauce, usually filled with chicken or white cheese, and sometimes topped with mole (enchiladas rojas or de mole); or with tomato sauce and sour cream (enchiladas suizas—Swiss enchiladas); or covered in a green sauce (enchiladas verdes); or topped with onions, sour cream, and guacamole (enchiladas potosinas).

Escabeche   A lightly pickled sauce used in Yucatecan chicken stew.

Frijoles refritos   Pinto beans mashed and cooked with lard.

Garnachas   A thickish small circle of fried masa with pinched sides, topped with pork or chicken, onions, and avocado, or sometimes chopped potatoes and tomatoes, typical as a botana in Veracruz and the Yucatán.

Gorditas   Thick, fried corn tortillas; slit and stuffed with a choice of cheese, beans, beef, chicken; with or without lettuce, tomato, and onion garnish.

Horchata   Refreshing drink made of ground rice or melon seeds, ground almonds, and cinnamon and lightly sweetened.

Huevos mexicanos   Scrambled eggs with chopped onions, hot green peppers, and tomatoes.

Huitlacoche   Sometimes spelled "cuitlacoche." A mushroom-flavored black fungus that appears on corn in the rainy season; considered a delicacy.

Manchamantel   Translated, means "tablecloth stainer." A stew of chicken or pork with chiles, tomatoes, pineapple, bananas, and jicama.

Masa   Ground corn soaked in lime; the basis for tamales, corn tortillas, and soups.

Mixiote   Rabbit, lamb, or chicken cooked in a mild chile sauce (usually chile ancho or pasilla) and then wrapped like a tamal and steamed. It is generally served with tortillas for tacos, with traditional garnishes of pickled onions, hot sauce, chopped cilantro, and lime wedges.

Pan de muerto   Sweet bread made around the Days of the Dead (Nov 1–2), in the form of mummies or dolls, or round with bone designs.

Pan dulce   Lightly sweetened bread in many configurations, usually served at breakfast or bought in any bakery.

Papadzules   Tortillas stuffed with hard-boiled eggs and seeds (pumpkin or sunflower) in a tomato sauce.

Pibil   Pit-baked pork or chicken in a sauce of tomato, onion, mild red pepper, cilantro, and vinegar.

Pipián   A sauce made with ground pumpkin seeds, nuts, and mild peppers.

Poc chuc   Slices of pork with onion marinated in a tangy sour orange sauce and charcoal-broiled; a Yucatecan specialty.

Pozole   A soup made with hominy in either chicken or pork broth.

Pulque   A drink made of fermented juice of the maguey plant; best in the state of Hidalgo and around Mexico City.

Quesadilla   Corn or flour tortillas stuffed with melted white cheese and lightly fried.

Queso relleno   "Stuffed cheese," a mild yellow cheese stuffed with minced meat and spices; a Yucatecan specialty.

Rompope   Delicious Mexican eggnog, invented in Puebla, made with eggs, vanilla, sugar, and rum.

Salsa verde   An uncooked sauce using the green tomatillo and puréed with spicy or mild hot peppers, onions, garlic, and cilantro; on tables countrywide.

Sopa de flor de calabaza   A soup made of chopped squash or pumpkin blossoms.

Sopa de lima   A tangy soup made with chicken broth and accented with fresh lime; popular in the Yucatán.

Sopa de tortilla   A traditional chicken broth–based soup, seasoned with chiles, tomatoes, onion, and garlic, served with crispy fried strips of corn tortillas.

Sopa tlalpeña (or caldo tlalpeño)   A hearty soup made with chunks of chicken, chopped carrots, zucchini, corn, onions, garlic, and cilantro.

Sopa tlaxcalteca   A hearty tomato-based soup filled with cooked nopal cactus, cheese, cream, and avocado, with crispy tortilla strips floating on top.

Sope   An antojito similar to a garnacha, except spread with refried beans and topped with crumbled cheese and onions.

Tacos al pastor   Thin slices of flavored pork roasted on a revolving cylinder dripping with onion slices and juice of fresh pineapple slices. Served in small corn tortillas, topped with chopped onion and cilantro.

Tamal   Incorrectly called a tamale (tamal singular, tamales plural). A meat or sweet filling rolled with fresh masa, wrapped in a corn husk or banana leaf, and steamed.

Tikin-xic   Also seen on menus as "tik-n-xic" and "tikik chick." Charbroiled fish brushed with achiote sauce.

Torta   A sandwich, usually on bolillo bread, typically with sliced avocado, onions, and tomatoes, with a choice of meat and often cheese.

Xtabentun   Pronounced "shtah-behn-toon." A Yucatecan liquor made of fermented honey and flavored with anise. It comes seco (dry) or crema (sweet).

Zacahuil   Pork leg tamal, packed in thick masa, wrapped in banana leaves, and pit-baked, sometimes pot-made with tomato and masa; a specialty of mid- to upper Veracruz.

Index

See also Accommodations and Restaurant indexes, below.

Photo **Credits**

Golf Resort ; p. 143: Courtesy Le Méridien Cancún Resort & Spa ; p. 144: Courtesy Le Méridien Cancún Resort & Spa ; p. 145: Courtesy Presidente InterContinental Cancun; p. 147: Courtesy Westin Resort & Spa Cancún ; p. 148: Courtesy Hacienda Sisal; p. 149: © Hisham Ibrahim/Photov.com/Alamy; p. 150, top: Courtesy The City; p. 150, bottom: Courtesy The City; p. 151: © PCL/Alamy; p. 152: © Grant Rooney/Alamy; p. 153, top: Courtesy Colombian Emeralds International; p. 153, bottom: © Walter Bibikow/AGE Fotostock; p. 156: © Jon Arnold/DanitaDelimont.com; p. 157: © Glow Images RF/PhotoLibrary.